THE STORY OF
AMERICAN TOYS

THE STORY OF
AMERICAN TOYS

FROM
THE PURITANS
TO THE PRESENT.

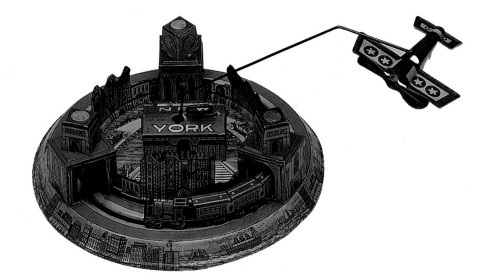

RICHARD O'BRIEN

ABBEVILLE PRESS ⚡ PUBLISHERS ⚡ NEW YORK

Editor: Alan Axelrod
Designer: Julie Rauer
Production manager: Dana Cole

First edition

Published in the United States of America by Abbeville Press, Inc.

Library of Congress Cataloging-in-Publication Data

O'Brien, Richard, 1934–
The story of American toys from the puritans to the present / by
Richard O'Brien.
p. cm.
ISBN 0-89659-921-3
1. Toy industry—United States—History. 2. Toys—Collectors and
collecting—United States. I. Title.
HD9993.T693U66   1990
338.4'768872'.0973—dc20   89-18295
                                                     CIP

JACKET FRONT: Dagwood's Solo Flight, by Marx, 1941 (Bizarre Bazaar, New York). JACKET SPINE: Mr. Potato Head, by Hasbro, 1952 (Hasbro). FRONT FLAP: Buck Rogers wind-up space ship, by Marx, 1935 (Don Hultzman). BACK FLAP: Louis Marx's Butter and Egg Man wind-up, ca. 1940 (Scott Smiles). JACKET BACK (CLOCKWISE FROM UPPER LEFT): A Transformer, by Hasbro, 1987 (Hasbro); Hubley taxis, mid to late 1940s (Bizarre Bazaar, New York); Charles M. Crandall's Pigs in Clover, 1889 (Wilkinson Collection, Detroit Antique Toy Museum); Toots and Casper comic-strip pull toy, ca. 1921 (Bizarre Bazaar, New York); Barbie, by Mattel, 1959 (Mattel Toys). HALF-TITLE PAGE: "Puritan" river boat, by James Fallows, ca. 1880 (Sotheby's, New York). FRONTISPIECE: Marx's Brightelite Filling Station and tin litho car with battery-operated lights, ca. 1930 (Bizarre Bazaar, New York). TITLE PAGE: A Marx tin wind-up, 1928 (Bizarre Bazaar, New York). DEDICATION PAGE: Cast-iron train set by Pratt & Letchworth, 1880s-1890s (Mapes Auctioneers, Vestal, New York).

TO MARY ANN

CONTENTS

PREFACE · 8

1
EARLY DAYS · 10

2
THE CIVIL WAR AND AFTER · 24

3
TURN-OF-THE-CENTURY FLOWERING · 52

4
TWENTIES BOOM TIME · 86

5
DEPRESSION PLAYTHINGS · 116

6
WORLD WAR II: MAKING DO · 154

7

POSTWAR AND THE FIFTIES · 164

8

THE SOARING SIXTIES · 186

9

THE TURBULENT SEVENTIES · 202

10

THE CORPORATE EIGHTIES · 214

EPILOGUE—OR PROLOGUE · 236

SOURCES · 242

INDEX AND PHOTO CREDITS · 244

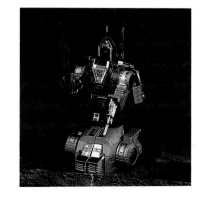

The reason for this book is simple. In the decades since the last of its sort was published a wealth of information has been uncovered. Most of it has emerged because of the boom in old American toys that began in the 1970s and because this country's toy collectors are interested in much more than the toys themselves. They want to learn everything they can about the companies and people who produced them. A number of men and women who innocently began by buying their first old toy or two soon found themselves feverishly searching copyright and patent records, poring over old newspapers and magazines, and busily seeking out former toy company workers, owners, and their descendants. Some have even gone as far as stopping people of the right age in towns and cities where toy factories once existed and pumping them for information. Frequently they were rewarded.

This, then, is a distillation of the discoveries of all of us in the field: the pioneers, my contemporaries, and myself. Within the bounds of its scope, the book is, I think, complete—till a few more years pass, and the next history is done.

Two emotions leap forward when doing a book like this. The first is humility. From the beginning the writer knows there's no way he could put such a work together without the help of others.

The second is gratitude. Whether it's that toy collectors are especially generous or that human nature has more going for it than it's usually given credit for, I don't know. I do know of the many people I approached for help, very, very few ignored me or turned me down. Thanks, sizeable thanks, go then to a host of good men and women.

Longtime friends Jim Harmon, Ed Poole, Norbert Schachter, and Bill Kaufman came through with photos. So did Ron Fink; Fairfield, Connecticut, auctioneer Lloyd W. Ralston; Orville C. Britton; Dick and Nancy Dice; Charles W. Best; Bob Black; the Forbes Magazine Collection, New York; Rodney A. Heesacker; Carol and Jerry Dinelli; Jack Matthews; Bill Nutting; Scott Smiles and his photographer Mike Adams; Brad Krewson; Edward W. Black; Gary Linden; Don Coviello; Arlan Coffman; Frank Ferrara; Ray Funk; R. F. Sapita; Superman fan extraordinaire Danny Fuchs; Barbara and Jonathan Newman of The Paper Soldier, Clifton Park, New York; and Charles D. Richards.

The author in the summer of 1937, with a brand-new wooden boat. OPPOSITE

That same boat more than a half-century later, still in the author's possession (though on loan for some years to his son). The hollow lead Barclay pirate came aboard in late 1937 or very early 1938. INSET

Not only coming through, but deluging me with photos, were Ed Hyers Antique Toys of Asheville, North Carolina; John and Nora Knight of New York's Bizarre Bazaar; aviation enthusiast Perry R. Eichor; Lawrence Scripps Wilkinson and Barbara Niman of the Detroit Toy Museum's Wilkinson Collection, and their photographers Harry Wolf and Kevin Sharp; Wayne Pratt and Company of Marlborough, Massachusetts and their photographer, John Courville; Heinz Mueller of Continental Hobby House, Sheboygan, Wisconsin; Richard A. Gray and Rex E. Gray of *Toy Collector News*; Gail (Mrs. Clint) Seeley; Don Hultzman; Richard Mac-Nary; David Mapes of Mapes Auctioneers and Appraisers, Vestal, New York; the ever-helpful Dana Hawkes of Sotheby's, New York; the equally generous Robert Frye and Henry Kurtz of Phillips, New York; and the staff of Christie's East.

Contributing both photos and very helpful information were the ever-generous Joe Freed; Lee Stokes; Peter Fritz, coauthor of the invaluable book *The Big Toy Box at Sears*; Nat Polk of New York's near-legendary Polk's Hobbies; Chic Gast; the John Wright Company, Wrightsville, Pennsylvania; and some legendary names in the toy business: Hasbro, Mattel, Ertl, Tootsietoy, Kenner, Ohio Art, and *Playthings* magazine.

A final note. I live in a very small town. The local library is proportioned accordingly: nothing more than a small-sized ranch house. Yet to my amazement, the cheerful librarians therein came up with every book—many of them obscure, some obtainable only from other states—on my very long list. So to all of you on the staff of the Washington Township Library, Morris County, New Jersey, thank you. A bedazzled, very grateful thank you.

Richard O'Brien

EARLY DAYS

Rocking horses are a perennial toy in America and elsewhere. This one was illustrated in a British children's book, ca. 1820.
INSET

here were toys in America from the beginning.

From the very beginning, that is. Eskimo boys were given small harpoons with which they could imitate their fathers. Indian boys had tiny bows for the same reason. They also had targets, and leather balls, which they used for games like lacrosse. Though the documentation here is less clear, it is generally agreed that Indian girls had dolls and miniature cooking and eating implements.

When the Europeans arrived in the New World, toys came with them. It was only natural. Toys had been a part of European life for centuries. Even ancient Egypt has yielded artifacts that may well have been toys. Certainly by the time of classical Greece, toys had become everyday items. Greek adults played with hoops and jacks, and children threw balls. Girls enjoyed dolls and skipped rope; boys played marbles and rocked back and forth on hobby horses.

In Germany, doll makers were around at least as early as 1413. By the 1500s, with the toy makers of Nuremburg leading the way, toys were well within the cultural mainstream. Often such toys were a province of the rich, and more often than not, of the rich *adult*. In those days of limited amusements, the toy was one of life's few pleasant distractions. There were cup-and-ball toys, ingeniously intricate mechanical toys, and games played with figures of mounted knights.

So it was inevitable that when the first Europeans reached our shores, the wealthier parents among them—those who had been sent to govern—would allow their children to bring along a toy or two. Toys were also brought over to ingratiate the new arrivals with the denizens of the New World.

In 1585, would-be colonists from England came ashore on North Carolina's Roanoke Island. They had gifts for the Indians, and dolls were among the bounty. John White, a member of the expedition, made a drawing at the time that shows a virtually naked Indian girl holding the Elizabethan doll she'd been given.

One of the oldest surviving toys from early America is a doll that was brought to Pennsylvania in 1699 by William Penn. Made of wood, like most early toys, it has an oval face and slanted eyes.

Benjamin Franklin recalled that in 1713, when he was seven years old, he had come upon a store in Boston that sold toys. Charmed by a whistle for sale there, he had offered up a handful of coins—and only later found out he'd paid four times what it should have cost him. So, thanks to a greedy

Diabolo, a game of skill in which a spool is tossed on a string suspended between two sticks, was popular into the early twentieth century. From an eighteenth-century engraving.

storekeeper, and Franklin's memory of the incident, we have what seems to be the first record of an American shop that sold toys.

Whether or not they were American-made toys we do not know, but the likelihood is that they weren't. In 1695, the Reverend John Higginson had some words of advice to his merchant brother in England: toys had a chance of selling in the new country if they were imported "in small quantity." In the 1740s and 1750s one William Prince advertised toys for sale, noting that they came from England and the Netherlands.

If mentions of toys and American toy making (if it even existed) are scanty from the early days, it has to be remembered that colonial America was a land of hard life and even harder

religion. In 1653, for instance, a "Sunday law" in Boston forbade visiting ships in port, traveling, cooking, taking walks, or even making beds and sweeping on the Sabbath.

Not just Sundays were devoted to religion. The earliest colonists were hell-bent, as it were, on sustaining their bodies and, with whatever time was left, their souls.

Children were not exempt from these heavy responsibilities. As soon as they could make themselves useful, they were put to work, and when they weren't working it was incumbent upon them to devote themselves to God. In the late 1600s it wasn't uncommon for children to have to learn their catechism and even to begin reading by the age of two. The onus placed on

more frivolous activity is reflected in the words of one early settler who reminisced: "I was a very naughty boy, much given to play." Fathers like Cotton Mather (1663–1728) may have at times publicly despaired about the waywardness of their children, but they never relaxed the firm hand that guided them in work and devotion.

But these conditions gradually changed as, in time, the colonies began to prosper. By the end of the 1600s some visitors from Europe were stunned to find a level of general comfort they'd not known back home. And as the physical demands of colonial life grew easier, all aspects of living began to loosen up. Religion was no longer the child's sole leisure-time activity. In the late 1700s, dancing lessons were added, and musical instruction. Dolls, hoops, stilts, balls, tops, whistles, and bull-roarers began to turn up in ever-increasing quantities. (A bull-roarer was a toy, made from wood or some other hard material, which had a leather thong attached to a hole in the middle. When it was manipulated, a noisy, whirring sound emerged.)

Generally speaking, children in the South had an easier life than their Northern counterparts. The climate was gentler, the Anglican religious tradition was less strict, and the children were considered by some to be "spoiled and indulged." Nevertheless, toys made their first American appearance in New England. With its harsh climate and long winter nights, New England was more conducive to sitting down with a knife and carving out a whistle or a doll or a top, or taking a corn husk and sewing small garments for it and drawing or painting on a doll face. The sunnier South presented less need for such indoor distraction.

As the colonies continued to grow and prosper, more people began to have enough money to indulge themselves and their children. The number of advertisements for toys increased significantly in the 1700s. Although many of the toys—probably the bulk of them—were imported, some are known to have been made here during this period. An American dollhouse survives from 1744—luckily, it bears the date of its manufacture. In 1755, Plunkett Fleeson of Philadelphia announced in the *Pennsylvania Gazette* that he made "Drums, toy drums and coverings." The toy drums, he went on, were made from "spare

wood, empty nail kegs, vatted skins and cord." In 1768, Henry William Stiegel, a glassmaker, was turning out glass toys in Mannheim, Pennsylvania. In 1785 a Pennsylvania cabinetmaker, William Long, "respectfully inform[ed] the ladies and gentlemen of this city that he makes rocking horses in the neatest and best manner to teach children to ride, and to give them a wholesome and pleasing exercise."

Despite such flurries, the American toy industry seems not to have begun in earnest until the 1830s, when the young country was truly on the move: Fulton had made the first practical

steamboat trip on the *Clermont* in 1807 (leaving New York and arriving in Albany—150 miles away—thirty-two hours later), the Erie Canal had opened in 1826, and the first regularly scheduled steam-powered passenger train service had been inaugurated on December 25, 1830, in Charleston, South Carolina. Such breakthroughs in transportation meant that manufacturers could now afford to produce in mass, because their goods could be distributed and sold over large areas. Virtually as soon as American toys were being mass-produced, the industry became a relatively important one.

Children had more time to play, and their clothing had become more comfortable, making play easier. Children's Sunday books, which in earlier days had been grimly austere, now provided at least a modicum of amusement. Children's magazines began to appear, which amused adults as well as children, shaping their attitudes toward their offspring and giving children new status.

Still another factor—and, to this day, an enormous one in the toy business—was the acceptance of Christmas as a holiday and a time for gift giving. In 1798 an Englishman had written of his trip to Germany and noted the Germans celebrating Christmas with "great boughs of yews . . . laden with little tapers." Two years later, Queen Charlotte, the wife of George III, brought Christmas to England with a yew tree that held various treats and toys. After everyone had admiringly inspected the tree, each of the children was given sweets and a toy. (It was during this period that the word *toy* for the first time came to denote a child's plaything.) By the end of the Revolution, Americans had begun taking Christmas Day off. In 1823 "A Visit From St. Nicholas" was published in the Troy (New York) *Sentinel*, and in 1837 it was reprinted in a book.

American scrimshaw acrobat toy, ca. 1850, made of whale ivory and 5½ inches high. Perhaps a sailor carved this for his child. (Whaling Museum, New Bedford, Massachusetts) OPPOSITE, LEFT

In some American cultures, toys served religious or magical purposes. This shaman's conjuring puppet is from the Ojibwa Indians of Wisconsin. Height, 17 inches. (Milwaukee Public Museum; Anthropology Collection) OPPOSITE, RIGHT

A ship on wheels from the early nineteenth century, made of painted wood. (New-York Historical Society, New York)

With all of these factors promoting toy sales, the U.S. census of 1850 listed forty-seven toy makers, and researchers have since found that there were even more. Among these toy makers it's the "tin men" who emerged as the true pioneers in American mass manufacture of toys.

Edward Patterson appears to have been the first of the tin men, though there's no hard evidence that he ever produced toys. Patterson was an Irishman who arrived in this country sometime between 1730 and 1740. A tinsmith, he settled in Berlin, Connecticut, about 1740, where he produced the first American-made tinware. Patterson (sometimes spelled Pattison or

Paterson) was one of the original Yankee peddlers, at first selling his goods door-to-door, then later from horse and wagon, traveling from town to town with his wares.

Connecticut was home to most early American tin-toy makers, but the first toy manufacturer of record set up shop in Philadelphia and was known by two names—Francis, Field & Francis, as well as the Philadelphia Tin Toy Manufactory. This business—and it was a large one—was established at least as early as 1838.

Tin toys were put together from parts blanked out under great pressure, shaped, and then soldered together or tabbed. The tin was actually thin sheet steel plated with tin. Once assembled, the earliest tin toys were decorated by coating them with paint and then painting in details freehand; later, stencils were used. The tin toy developed partially because tin plate was an intriguing new material and process for manufacturers. Though the tin-toy technology was certainly available in Europe, all available documentation suggests that the United States was where it began, and Francis, Field & Francis proudly claimed their japanned (lacquered) tin toys were "superior to any imported."

Among the toys known to have been made by the company is a soldier on horseback holding a guidon—the horse is mounted on a wheeled board—which appeared in an American wholesaler's catalog about 1847–50. Other toys during the early period include horse-drawn wagon trains (one of them named the "General Taylor," after the hero of the Mexican-American

The earliest known manufactured American toy. Experts agree this came from Francis, Field and Francis about 1840. (Ed Hyers Antique Toys, Asheville, North Carolina)

War who was elected president in 1848); horses, dogs, and cows on wheeled platforms; a wheeled boat; a boy with a flag seated on a dog; and a locomotive. Francis, Field & Francis also manufactured dollhouse furnishings, including chairs, chests of drawers, and clocks. Employed for a time as the manufactory's foreman was James Fallows, a young immigrant from England who would one day become one of the great names in the early history of American toys.

Other Pennsylvania toy makers of the era were Gideon Cox of Philadelphia, who in 1825 was producing hobby horses, and Attleborough's Benjamin T. Roney, who was turning out tin toy drums in 1848. Asa Crandall, of Covington, was making wooden toys sometime between 1820 and 1849; of his son, Charles M. Crandall, we shall hear more. A bit later, from 1847 to 1857, E. W. Bushnell of Philadelphia manufactured hobby horses and velocipedes.

In the meantime, about 1847, or perhaps even earlier, William Tower, a Hingham, Massachusetts, carpenter whom *Toys and Novelties* magazine called (with questionable accuracy) "the founder of the toy industry in America," began making wooden toys during his leisure hours. He discovered that he wasn't alone; friends and acquaintances were also turning out toys in their spare time. During a period when work was scarce, they made enough toys to ac-

Although this Noah's Ark was made in Germany about 1850, it was brought to the United States or purchased here. The ark has fifty-five pairs of animals (not all are illustrated), including a unicorn and his mate. All of the animals can be stored in the ark. (Essex Institute, Salem, Massachusetts)

cumulate a surplus. It was Tower's idea to form a cooperative guild, thereby assuring a steady and salable supply of toys.

One of the guild members was Joseph Jacob, the owner of an axe factory, who created toy tools, among other toys. A local boat builder turned his hand to toy ships, and cabinetmakers designed furniture for dollhouses. There were about twenty members of what became the Tower Guild, which seems to have operated informally, members providing toys more or less at their own discretion, until at least 1915. Other guild toys included pails, tubs, doll swings, tenpins, and furniture.

By the mid-nineteenth century, New England had become a hotbed of toy making. In 1849, the *New England Mercantile Directory* listed a dozen woodenware manufacturers turning out playthings, including sleds, rocking horses, and wagons. But it was tin that was setting the pace, and an early giant in that field was George W. Brown. Born in Bolton, Connecticut, in 1830, Brown was apprenticed to a Forestville, Connecticut, clock maker when he was fifteen. In 1856, still in Forestville, he and an associate named Chauncey Goodrich founded George W. Brown and Company, toy makers. Like so many American toy makers of the day, Brown was an innovator. It was he who introduced the American clockwork toy, making use of the knowledge he had gained during his eleven years in the clock-making business. He not only invented many of his toys' internal mechanisms but may have designed all or most of the toys themselves.

Brown worked in tin, but like many early toy makers, didn't produce all the parts himself. The Union Manufacturing Company of Clinton, Connecticut (not to be confused with Brooklyn's Union Manufacturing Company of the 1870s), is known to have produced a number of "large

and small horses, in parts, men in parts and ladies in parts" for Brown between 1856 and 1861.

Because of the inherent difficulties in working with tin, Brown's toys were necessarily simple in line, but any lack of detail was made up for by the toys' brilliance of painted color, complemented by fine hand-stenciled decoration. In the course of more than twenty years of toy making, Brown's work spanned a wide range, in-

Horse pull toy, ca. 1840, made of carved wood, painted gray with a green saddle blanket, 20 x 16½ inches. (Essex Institute, Salem, Massachusetts)

Also keeping Connecticut prominent in the field of toy making was the Merriam Manufacturing Company, of Durham. Founded in the same year as George W. Brown and Company, Merriam also specialized in tin toys and, like Brown, made many nontoy items as well, such as tubs, pots, pans, and candlesticks. From the start, it spewed out a wide array of toys, including clockwork items. There were tin animals, express wagons, carriages, swords, wheelbarrows, hoop toys, swing toys, gigs, and dump carts. The clockwork toys included a fire pumper, a walking doll pushing a carriage, a locomotive, and a velocipede rider.

There was good reason for all the activity. Starting in the 1840s, virtually every town in America had a toy store; in New York City in 1844 there were eighty-eight of them.

It was during this period that the Crandalls turned up. There were actually two sets of them, most likely related. Benjamin Potter Crandall set up shop in Westerly, Rhode Island, sometime before 1841, making and selling baby carriages and a few toys. The local paper reported that Crandall's carriage (not a toy), a simple two-wheeler that sold for $1.50, was "the first baby carriage manufactured in America."

In 1841, Crandall moved to New York, taking with him all four of his sons: Benjamin, Jr., Charles Thompson (not to be confused with Charles M.), William Edwin, and Jesse Armour. Jesse was something of a prodigy, inventing an ingenious tool when he was eleven. (Virtually all the Crandalls were prodigious, with several hundred toy patents among them.) Jesse had been a whittler since the age of five, and when he began helping in his father's shop in 1845, he had the job of boring ten holes in a hub so that the spokes of the Crandall baby carriage wheels could be fitted in. Jesse noticed that all ten holes

The White Horse or Bell and Hammer Game was published in London by E. Wallis early in the nineteenth century, but enjoyed popularity on both sides of the Atlantic. (Museum of the City of New York; Gift of Ms. Frances G. Smith)

cluding all sorts of animal-drawn conveyances, animals, tops, rattles, whistles, flutes, wagons, buckets, swords, platform toys, fire engines, ships, trains, and hand cars (in 1856 Brown produced the first known clockwork train). Partly because of their simplicity, but probably also because Brown was a pioneer drawing on the traditions of the past, his toys have a one-of-a-kind look that suggests the work of folk artists.

had to be spaced the same distance apart, and needed to be made the same size and depth. So the eleven-year-old came up with a device that included a brace, gears, and ten bits that allowed him to drill ten perfectly aligned holes in a tenth of the time needed by the adult who had preceded him in the job. By age seventeen, Jesse was listed in a New York business directory.

In the 1840s, steel—not just tinned sheet steel—started turning up in Connecticut as a material for sled runners and children's jackknives. By 1850 cast iron also began to make its appearance. Iron toys begin as patterns that are placed in a special casting sand to form a mold. Molten iron is then poured into the molds, which have a brief life and have to be made over and over. The nature of iron and the sand as a molding medium dictate minimal detailing and give the toys a somewhat crude, heavy appearance.

Apparently, the first firm to cast toys in iron was J. & E. Stevens of Cromwell, Connecticut,

founded in 1843 by John and Elisha Stevens as a cast-iron hardware maker. By 1850 the Stevenses edged into the toy field as well, with a number of simple playthings—sad irons, garden tools, and, a bit later, pistols—as well as a huge volume of cast-iron wheels, which were sold to various toy makers. In the 1850s the company was producing a half-ton of iron toy wheels a week. (It's this dispersal of wheels that helps make identifying the makers of early toys so difficult, as few of those toys were marked—and they also had other parts from other manufacturers as well). The firm soon graduated into the ranks of the leading American toy companies, remaining among them for nearly a century.

Another material that caught the fancy of mid-century toy makers and purchasers was rubber. In 1839 Charles Goodyear had hit upon the idea of "vulcanizing" rubber, using chemicals to give it strength, elasticity, and stability. It was an innovation that earned him medals in London (1851) and Paris (1855) and the cross of the Legion of Honor (though, ironically, difficulties enforcing his patents denied him the fortune others reaped from his invention). By 1850, rubber toys were all the rage. "India Rubber Toys," an ad from that year boasted, "The most durable and economic of all, consisting of Air Balls, Ball Rattles, Rattle Boxes, Doll Heads, Dogs, Lions and Fish, etc."

The first of the toy enterprises specializing in the exciting new material (and employing the Goodyear patents) was the New York Rubber Co., of Beacon, New York, owned by Benjamin F. Lee, whose most popular product may have been rubber squeak toys, which, when squeezed, blew air out through a whistle, making a squealing sound. In 1851, Lee produced the first all-rubber doll, again using Goodyear's vulcanization patent.

Another material widely used during this era was paper. The first paper doll known to have been printed in the United States can be traced to 1854, in a book called *Fanny Gray*, published in Boston by Crosby, Nichols and Company, with art by John Greene Chandler. No more than three years later, McLoughlin Brothers, one of the major names in American toy history, came out with its first paper dolls and what may have been the first American paper soldiers. Later, in 1859, *Godey's Lady's Book* became the first magazine to feature paper dolls.

There were a number of companies that began in the pre–Civil War period that may not have turned out toys during their early days, but eventually did become toy makers of some prominence. A number of them started out manufacturing everyday articles in wood, and when they turned to toys, wood remained their primary material. Among these were Asa Greenwood, who built a wood-turning shop in Marlborough, New Hampshire, to make clothespins and bobbins. Sometime before 1852, Leonard Snow bought the company and began producing wooden toys. In 1852 Luther Hemenway became the new owner and continued wooden toy production for another fifty years.

In Pennsylvania, the Hawes Mfg. Co. of Towanda was in business by the 1830s. George Hawes eventually moved to New York, to Newark, New Jersey, and back to Pennsylvania (Monroeton), somewhere along the line getting into wooden toys and remaining in business at least until the turn of the century, issuing hundreds of thousands of toys.

In Massachusetts sometime before the Civil War, wooden toys of various sorts clattered their way out of the shops of Heywood Brothers, G. S. Greenwood, and W. L. Woodcock. Also in Massachusetts, in 1854, Noble & Cooley began producing skin-head toy drums, and did so for over a hundred years.

In Williamsburg, New York, S. L. Hill took out an 1858 patent on spelling blocks, wooden blocks featuring letters and numbers on their sides decorated with glued-on, brightly colored pictures. In New York City, a company began in 1848 that, as Peter F. Pia, made a variety of

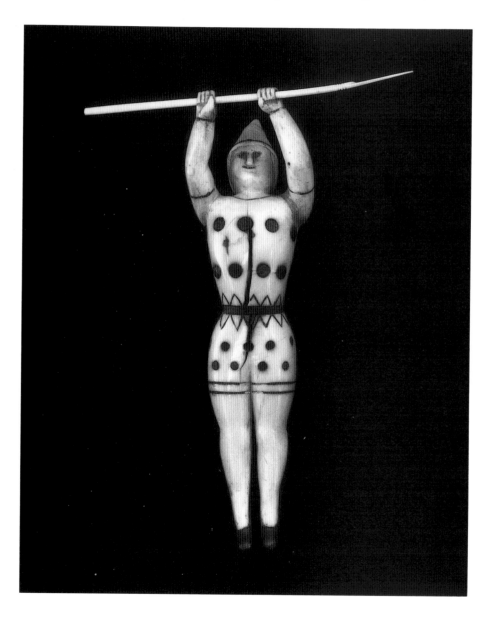

This Jumping Jack Clown, ca. 1800, has a carved wooden head, arms, and legs hung on wooden pegs. (New-York Historical Society, New York)

pewter toys well into the 1900s, including doll-house furniture, candelabra, trains, miniature replicas of George Washington's inaugural coach, "George Washington" hatchets, tea sets, bird whistles, and water pistols with rubber bulbs.

Just before the outbreak of the Civil War, the Maynard Tape Primer was invented. Developed to detonate muzzle-loading arms, the tape resembled what we now know as paper caps, and in fact led to them. By 1859, J. & E. Stevens's catalog offered Fire Cracker Pistols and several different cannon, all of which shot caps. However, while toy pistols were being patented in the late 1850s, cap guns did not appear until after the Civil War. Before the war, patents confined themselves to peashooters and cork poppers, most of which were made primarily of wood with metal working parts and trim.

On the eve of Civil War, toy makers were not interested only in guns. The first patent for a doll was issued in the United States in 1858 (the U.S. Patent Office itself had opened in 1836), and Jesse Crandall, on May 17, 1859, had received a patent for the "shoofly," a safe version of the hobby horse. Kids had a tendency to fall off hobby horses, so Jesse conceived a rocking toy that had two flat outlines of a horse, with a seat between them, and rockers below. It was a simple idea—so simple that many manufacturers tried to copy it, only to be gunned down by Jesse in court. A toy that exists in one form or another to this day, it meant big money to Crandall, who spent more than ten thousand dollars defending his patent.

An early nineteenth-century Jack in the Box, with a papier-mâché mask painted black with colored markings and a blue cloth night cap. (New-York Historical Society, New York)

"**P**rogress," a painted and stenciled tin locomotive from Stevens & Brown, ca. 1885. (Wayne Pratt and Company, Marlboro, Massachusetts) OPPOSITE

The Hula Hoop of its day— Charles M. Crandall's Pigs in Clover, from 1889. The last line of the boxtop instructions illustrates a very different America: "Any one who has ever attempted to drive pigs will appreciate this toy." (Wilkinson Collection, Detroit Antique Toy Museum) INSET

At first, the Civil War was a bane to the American toy industry; later, it proved to have been a boon. From 1861 to 1865, materials that would have gone into toy production were consumed in the war effort, and young men who might have worked in toy factories served in the army instead. The toy makers themselves frequently switched from manufacturing playthings to producing the goods of war.

That was the bad news. The positive side was that once the war was over, all the new industries that had sprung up to serve the cause of battle suddenly found themselves needing new outlets. Some became toy makers. Others became suppliers to the toy makers, providing a far greater range of materials and artisans than had previously been available. Still others took on the distribution of toys.

The patent records during the war years and the five years after offer the best indication of the shifts that were taking place. From 1861 to 1865, 17 patents for toys were taken out, nearly half of them for guns. In the five years that immediately followed, 166 were issued. Many of these were for toys that moved, propelled by mechanical works or by steam. They were a reflection—as toys almost always are—of what was happening in the country. The railroads had taken over, charging the whole country with a sense of movement. On May 10, 1869, the transcontinental railroad was completed, with a golden spike at Promontory, Utah, not only marking the junction of the Central Pacific and the Union Pacific, but, more importantly, linking the eastern and western regions of the country, and making possible the rapid distribution of goods on a national scale.

In 1878 the first commercial telephone exchange opened in New Haven, Connecticut, and in that same year four American toy manufacturers exhibited their wares at the Paris Exposition Universelle. A year later, on February 22, F. W. Woolworth opened his first five-and-ten in Utica, New York.

Meanwhile, in the years immediately following the war, the two most prominent of the toy-making Crandalls expanded on earlier successes. Charles M. Crandall, who had taken over his late father's business at age sixteen, was one of the few early toy makers who took care to place his name on his toys. He also believed in toys that invited participation, rather than passive pleasure, as one of his great toys of this period attests: Crandall's Building Blocks. As has happened on occasion in the history of toy making, it was the craftsman's own children who inspired the invention.

Crandall was making croquet sets at the time, as croquet enjoyed a huge vogue in 1865. Charles M. had invented a way of joining the wood used in the sets by means of a tongue-and-groove arrangement. When his two children became ill, he brought home some of the grooved wood for them to play with as they convalesced. The grooves made it easy to arrange the pieces of wood into various structures, and the children were soon hooked. When they were well, they continued to use the blocks, often with their friends, who enjoyed them too. Finally, parents began to ask Crandall to provide some for their offspring. A light bulb went on, and Crandall applied for a patent, issued February 5, 1867.

Sales were brisk—the blocks could make forts, houses, barns, stables, and churches—and then the enterprising Crandall sent them to the nation's master showman, P. T. Barnum, who put them on view at his museum, where they promptly created a sensation. As Crandall advertised, "The only limit of what can be made with my blocks is in the imagination of the user."

American Agriculturist, a popular magazine of the day, reviewed the blocks, hailing them as an exciting new children's sensation. Then another light bulb went on—this time over the heads of the magazine's publishers, whose company was called Orange Judd.

They wrote to Crandall, suggesting a contract as the toy maker's wholesale selling agents. He agreed, and a long and profitable association resulted. Sales of the building blocks, which were made of unpainted, undecorated wood, climbed over the ten thousand mark in the first year, tripled the following year, and remained an important part of Crandall's line for many years.

Crandall's next huge hit was in 1874, when he came up with the Acrobats, which used the same tongue-and-groove idea as the blocks and

Captain Kidd's Castle, lithographed paper on wood, patented 1884. Charles M. Crandall produced it in Montrose, Pennsylvania. (Arlan Coffman) OPPOSITE

McLoughlin Brothers' Cob House Blocks came out in the 1870s. Sold as a combination of "picture, alphabet, spelling, game, puzzle and building blocks," they were lithographed paper on wood. (Arlan Coffman) RIGHT

The famous Crandall's Building Blocks, from Charles M. Crandall, patented 1867. By the end of the nineteenth century, the magazine *Inventive Age* reported that Crandall's blocks could be found in the nurseries of almost every civilized nation. Sir Henry Morton Stanley ("Dr. Livingstone, I presume.") brought them to the Congo as gifts. (Arlan Coffman) OPPOSITE

was covered under the same patent. Each of the Acrobats was a six-piece affair with two arms, two legs, a body, and a head. Unlike the austere-looking blocks, the Acrobats were gaily painted, had intricately designed costumes, and wore huge smiles. They could be arranged in different positions, and their parts were interchangeable. That year, Crandall advertised that approximately fifteen hundred boxes of one of his toys —quite likely the Acrobats—were being shipped every day to meet the huge demand.

In 1875, he quickly followed up with a variation on the Acrobats called the Menagerie, a group of tongue-and-groove animals, each with seven to ten parts.

In 1876, Crandall came out with two new types of blocks. His Masquerade blocks were witty, imaginative, even ingenious: by turning the blocks, the expressions of a depicted face could be changed. Oddly, the other type, called Expression blocks, didn't have any means of changing expressions. There's some belief that the man depicted on these blocks is Crandall himself, as the lower section of the blocks reads "Compliments of the Inventor." Crandall—if Crandall it is—is shown as a kind of Gulliver,

featured tongue-and-groove arrangements with moveable arms, desks and seats for the children and teacher, and printing on the wooden books that could actually be read (all of them on different grade levels). The whole effect was artistic, in the way of folk art, and there was an additional note of realism: none of the toothy grins of the Acrobats was echoed here. This, after all, was school.

Although it was more properly a game than a toy, the most famous of Charles M. Crandall's inventions was his Pigs in Clover. This consisted of two circles within a circle, each of the two featuring an opening through which marbles could be rolled. The trick was to get three marbles from the outer circle to the inner circle by

with tiny figures below him building structures from his blocks, while others, equally small but bolder, climb onto his face, the less lucky of them falling off. Another odd aspect of the Expression blocks is that when they were arranged to show the Gulliver-like scene, their reverse side showed the alphabet—but read from right to left.

In 1877, Crandall came up with one of his more charming sets, Crandall's District School. According to a flier for the toy, it contained Good Scholars, Roguish Boys, Sober Teacher, Bad Dunce, Nice Books, and even, for Mary's sake apparently, a Happy Lamb. Again, the set

jiggling the game. It looked easy and was, in fact, nearly impossible. The game took the country by storm, catching up adults as well as children. Members of Congress were reported to be frantically absorbed in trying to master the damned thing, inspiring a rash of newspaper ed-

E.I. Horsman's Obelisk Alphabet Blocks, patented in 1882. These were sold to commemorate Cleopatra's Needle, which was transported from Egypt to New York in 1879 and unveiled in the city's Central Park on January 22, 1881. (Arlan Coffman)

Hill's Spelling Blocks, patent date 1858. Hill was the first manufacturer in America to produce blocks in great quantity. (Arlan Coffman)

itorials. Also making the papers was the story of the man who, driven to distraction by the game, threw it out a train window and then acted as if he were going to do the same thing to himself.

In all, Charles M. Crandall produced scores of different toys and games right up to the turn of the century, all of them wood, and all of them, from what evidence remains—and a number of his toys have survived—of great charm. Crandall, who had factories at one time or another in Pennsylvania (Covington and Montrose) and New York (Waverly, where the firm was known as the Waverly Toy Works), died in Waverly on June 30, 1905.

In the meantime, Jesse Crandall was busy, too—so busy that he came to be known as "The

Charles M. Crandall's District School was an important early toy, all wood, and first sold in 1877. (Wilkinson Collection, Detroit Antique Toy Museum)

Crandall's John Gilpin wood toy, 1870, complete with box. (Ed Hyers Antique Toys, Asheville, North Carolina)

Child's Benefactor." Located in New York and Brooklyn, and already the inventor of the shoofly, Jesse Crandall had another idea that has remained attractive to children to this day: the concept of nested blocks. One side of the block was open, to receive the next smaller one, the remaining sides (in Crandall's version) attracting the eye (and the buyer) with brightly colored pictures. Like Charles M., Jesse Crandall was a prodigious inventor. Among his toy innovations were velocipedes (beginning in 1868), trains that hooked together, sand molds (for beach play), tops, guns, noisemakers, an ice sleigh, a patented spring rocking horse, a folding sled, a blackboard, and jointed dolls. In 1876, he won a gold medal at the Philadelphia Exhibition.

Not that it was all glory. In 1913, the toy maker gave an interview shortly after celebrating his eightieth birthday. Standing in an aisle between tin soldiers and rocking horses he recalled, "I surely was not gifted with the business brain. I've had money once in a while, a few days or so, and then lost it all." But, he admitted, "I was happy in the gaining and happy in the losing. It was such a fine shade of difference that you could not easily grasp the sensation."

Obviously, some of the money went to lawyers. "No patent is a patent till it has been fought for," he stated flatly. "You get a piece of paper, but you don't get protection till you have spent a lot of money in court to keep up the dignity of that same patent."

Crandall went on to remember that he had been carving "animals and figures since I was five, when I first nearly cut my finger off, right up to now, and I expect to go right on till I die. My first patent was taken out in 1859. It was a spring horse. The Prince of Wales rode one when he was a child, and you see what a horseman he has developed into now!"

Many of his ideas, he explained, came to him while he slept: "the alarm of the future rings me up, and I'm on the carpet in a second with my pad on my knee."

Other Crandalls involved in toy making were Jesse's brothers Charles T., William Edwin,

and Benjamin, plus Charles T.'s son, Charles T. Crandall, Jr. On Charles M.'s side, there was his son, Fred W. Crandall, who started his own toy firm in Elkland, Pennsylvania. In 1907, his line of toys included pianos, chairs, bureaus, and tables.

Another important name established in the business shortly before the Civil War was Joel Ellis. He began in 1859 in Springfield, Vermont, producing his toys under three firm names: Ellis, Britton and Eaton; Vermont Novelty Works; and the Cooperative Manufacturing Company. Ellis was a force into the 1890s, making riding toys, a few wooden dolls, hoops, carriages, nine-inch toy fence rails, and, in 1862, a forerunner of

Ellis, Britton & Eaton of Springfield, Vermont, made this Joel Ellis-designed wooden spindle doll carriage with stenciling about 1870. (Wilkinson Collection, Detroit Antique Toy Museum)

An early doll, 20 inches high, by Izannah Walker of Central Falls, Rhode Island. The paper label shows a patent date of November 4, 1873. (Wilkinson Collection, Detroit Antique Toy Museum)

Folding Kites.

A kite 54 inches high and 46 inches wide will instantly fold like an umbrella, to a roll only three feet long and 2 inches diameter, not as large as an ordinary umbrella. The UMBRELLA and FOLDING HIGH FLYER are constructed as above, while the HIGH FLYER and DIAMOND are made and shipped "Knocked Down," but so arranged that they may be readily put together by the boys without the use of any tools whatever.

Kites are among the oldest toys. This folding version was sold by Milton Bradley in 1870 and probably furnished a few nightmares. (Milton Bradley)

Lincoln Logs. During the Civil War he produced a cannon that shot marbles a distance of forty to sixty *feet*.

Also beginning just before the war was a man who became one of the giants of the toys and games industry. His name was Milton Bradley, and the company he founded is still very much in business. A quintessential New England Yankee, Bradley could boast a family that had landed in America in 1635 at Salem, Massachusetts. Indian raids were a part of his heritage; some of his ancestors survived (one twice captured by Indians) and some did not. Bradley himself was born in Vienna, Maine, on November 8, 1836. In 1847 his family moved to Lowell, Massachusetts, and in 1856 to Hartford, Connecticut.

Milton Bradley had been putting himself through the Lawrence Scientific School and was in the middle of his second year when his parents moved to Hartford. Unable to support himself while going to school, he was forced to drop out and move with his parents. When he could not find a job in Hartford, he sought work in Springfield, Massachusetts. The year was 1856, and Springfield was a growing city—proudly claiming its population had soared all the way past fourteen thousand, making it the fastest-growing city in New England.

Bradley, who kept a diary through much of his life, noted the following conversation he had had with a foreman at the Wason Car-Manufacturing Company (which manufactured railroad engines and cars):

Bradley: "Have you a draftsman?"
Foreman: "No."
Bradley: "Do you want one?"
Foreman, rubbing his jaw: "Ye-es."
Bradley: "Well, I'm the man for the job."
Foreman, to the unimpressive-looking youth: "*You* are a draftsman?"
"I am."
"Can you draw a locomotive?"

The closest Bradley had been to a train was his ride to Springfield that day. After a little hesitation, he replied, "I never have, but I think I could."

The upshot was that Bradley got the job (although the foreman told another worker, "He's a damn green-looking cuss"), and worked for the firm a while. Later, he was hired back to design a special railroad car for the Pasha of

Egypt. Bradley did so well on the project that he was rewarded with a colored lithograph of the finished car. It was that lithograph that led him toward his vocation.

Lithography had been invented in 1796 by a Bavarian who had discovered that a drawing done with a certain type of crayon on limestone would, when the stone was moistened, hold a greasy ink. Paper pressed tightly against the stone would then pick up the ink. Later, zinc substituted for limestone, but Bradley began and ended with stone.

Bradley went into the lithography business, where he had his ups and downs. One day, in the late summer of 1860, he was suffering one of his downs, and a longtime friend suggested they play a game. The game had been manufactured in England, and as he played Bradley found himself enjoying it more and more. As a child, Bradley had derived great pleasure from playing games like chess and checkers with his father,

and those early seeds combined with his feelings of that evening: Bradley became persuaded that he should come up with a game that would employ eye-catching lithography.

It took him a week to design one. A few months later he made his first trip to New York, with several hundred packages of what he'd chosen to call The Checkered Game of Life. To Bradley's astonishment, at his first stop—a Manhattan stationery store—he found the owner buying everything he was carrying. By the second day, he was sold out.

In the winter of 1860–61 Bradley sold forty thousand copies of his game. But by spring the war had begun, and Bradley, like so many others in the toys and games field, turned to war production. However, during the war, Bradley came up with a kit called Games for Soldiers, which he gave away to the troops he'd seen staring emptily into campfires, with nothing to occupy them during their free hours.

The Patent Soap Bubble Toy.

Good for all seasons. The children may amuse themselves without danger of injury to the carpet. With a bit of rubber tube applied to an ordinary gas burner, gas bubbles may be made which can be exploded to the great delight of the juveniles.

An elemental—if not entirely safe—Milton Bradley toy from 1870. (Milton Bradley)

Milton Bradley's illusion-of-motion toy, "The Popular Zoetrope." (Milton Bradley)

The initial response was so good he began selling the kits, which got him back into the games business. Shortly after, he came out with his first toy, a lithographed Contraband Gymnast. The gymnast was black and got his name because during the hostilities slaves were considered "contraband of war."

Bradley's first big toy after the war came in 1866, when he devised the Myrioptican, which, turned by a crank and illuminated from behind by a lamp, unfolded scenes of the Civil War, with a narrative text accompaniment.

His next visual toy was a version of the celebrated Zoetrope, or wheel of life, which worked on the principle of the persistence of vision. A strip of drawings that showed figures in the process of an action was placed inside a drum. As the drum was spun, an observer, watching through slits on the outside of the drum, would see the figures seemingly in motion. The device, which had originated in Europe in 1834, came with several different strips and sold for $2.50. It was such a sensation that a friend wryly informed Bradley that the toyman had perfected perpetual motion—because of all the people perpetually spinning his Zoetrope. The toy sold well all the way into the early 1900s and was, in fact, a precursor of motion pictures.

Although primarily a games manufacturer, Bradley continued to make such toys as a wheeled representation of an aquarium, a lawn mower, a folding kite, various forms of toy villages and farms, castles, and, during World War I, the first toy machine gun, which shot thirty-six wooden bullets at one loading (Bradley also furnished lithographed soldiers for the bullets to knock over).

Bradley would have been a major manufacturer in any case, but his publication in the fall of 1869 of *Paradise of Childhood: A Practical Guide to Kindergartners*, by Edward Wiebe, was his catapult to greatness in the field. Wiebe was a German immigrant and neighbor of Bradley's who had pressed him for some time to publish his manuscript, which was dedicated to the ideas of Friedrich Froebel, a German who had conceived the idea of kindergarten. At Wiebe's urging, Bradley attended a lecture by Elizabeth Peabody, who had opened a kindergarten in Boston in 1860. Her brilliant speech not only persuaded Bradley to publish Wiebe's book (Bradley's father had used Froebel-style methods in Milton's education), but also to produce toys that could be used in kindergartens, ones that would teach while they were being played with. Bradley turned out tops and geometric blocks, spheres, cubes, and cylinders, as well as various games and the first quality watercolors for children. Although the kindergarten line dripped red ink for a long time to come, Bradley never abandoned it—and it finally paid off handsomely. Even today, kindergarten toys and games are part of the Bradley line, among them the Sesame Street My First Games series. (The Game of Life, updated, is still sold, too.)

Another company that made great use of the lithograph was Bliss, likewise a New England toy enterprise. Its founder, Rufus Bliss, was born in Rehoboth, Massachusetts, in 1802. About 1832, after an apprenticeship with a carpenter and several woodworking firms, he set up the R. Bliss Manufacturing Company in Pawtucket, Rhode Island. It's not known precisely when the Bliss Company began making toys; that may

even have happpened after Rufus Bliss's retirement in 1863. But by 1871 its toys were being advertised. Generally made of wood, they encompassed a wide range: dollhouses, dollhouse furniture, animal-drawn conveyances, circus wagons, trolleys, Santa Claus in his sleigh, Noah's arks, trains, and ships. In 1883 Bliss came out with what might have been the first toy telephone set.

It was the color lithography that made Bliss's toys stand out, with their brilliant colors and considerable detail. Bliss ships, partly because of their attractiveness and partly because so few American firms made toy ships in any quantity, are particularly attractive to toy collectors, as are the firm's beautifully designed dollhouses.

The W. S. Reed Toy Company of Leominster, Massachusetts, was formed in 1875 and

This delicate-looking tin clockwork omnibus was made by George W. Brown about 1874. The stenciling, an important feature of many tin toys, provided detailing that couldn't be worked into the tin itself. (Sotheby's, New York)

produced wooden toys similar to those of Bliss; in fact, collectors' catalogs often identify ships and other toys as the work of "Bliss or Reed." In addition to ships, the company made construction and pull toys, trains, blocks, and mechanical circus toys. As with Bliss's toys, many Reed playthings were lithographed. In 1898, W. S. Reed was renamed the Whitney Reed Chair Company, but still produced toys.

The postwar period was a time of change. Embossed blocks were introduced in 1869, and the same year saw the introduction of celluloid, which soon became a toy-making material. Magnetic toys became popular on a small scale, the most popular being a tin fish, which could be caught by magnet instead of hook. Toy watches became such a rage after the war that one company, the American Toy Watch Company of Providence, Rhode Island, made nothing but. Clockwork toys also came to the fore. Although George W. Brown seems to have produced the earliest clockwork toy, the first patent for one appears to have gone to Enoch Rice Morrison in 1862, for a walking doll that was manufactured by New York's Martin and Runyan. The name of the toy alone gives it a place in history. It was a mouthful: "Hey, Mary, wanna play with my Autoperipatetikos?"

It was during this period that one of the fabled companies in the history of American toys emerged. Riley Ives was born in Connecticut in 1808, and his son Edward in 1839. By the late 1850s, Riley had established his own metal-stamping shop and during the Civil War turned out uniform buttons. About 1865 the firm found itself making tin whistles for use in New York Rubber's squeak toys. Ives's first true toys appear to have been hot-air items, which debuted in 1868. They were made of tin, had multiple, jointed parts, and were suspended over anything

that gave off heat—generally, a stove, but lamps, gas burners, and hot-air registers could also be used. When the rising column of hot air reached the toy, the parts moved. In the case of an Ives tin windmill, for instance, the windmill's sails revolved.

Edward Ives joined his father in the business about 1860. The factory building in which the hot-air toys were made was located on the property of one Cornelius Blakeslee, who appears to have become an associate early in the game. In 1870 the company moved to Bridgeport, Connecticut, for the purpose of manufacturing quality clockwork toys.

Quality, from that point at least, became the constant watchword at Ives. The first of Ives's handsomely turned-out clockwork toys were its No. 1 Boy on Velocipede, which measured nine

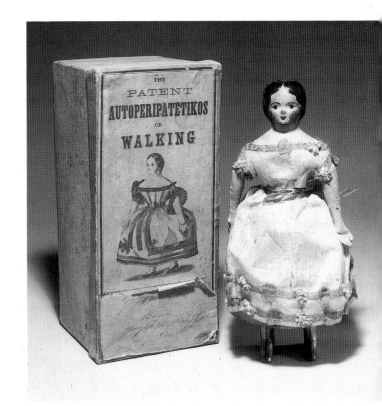

"The Patent Autoperipatetikos or Walking Doll," patented in 1862 by Enoch Rich Morrison, a breakthrough clockwork toy.

inches in height, and its No. 2 Single Oarsman, a man rowing a boat. The latter remained popular for more than a decade, and Ives was still turning out variations on the velocipede toy in the 1890s.

Like all the toys of the period, Ives's early toys bore a resemblance to folk art, but they were also superior to other clockwork toys being produced in this country. Within a few short years, Ives had a line of twenty or so clockwork playthings, most of them made of tin, gaily colored and decorated, with the Ives-designed clockwork made by the New Haven Clock Co. The mechanism was exceptionally strong, so that the toys could, when fully wound, run for as long as half an hour, and sometimes more. In a very short time, Ives became the most important name in the business, producing such items as a boy on a swing, swinging, as boys so often do, standing up; his body was made of wood, his arms and legs of tin, his shirt and pants of wool, and his hat of tin; an overhead mechanism provided the swinging action. Seated boys and girls were also made. Clockwork black dancers were popular, their dancing done atop a large, tongue-and-groove wooden box that concealed the mechanism. Ives's General Benjamin Franklin Butler was a walking toy, again a combination of materials, standing nine and a half inches high. (The real-life Butler was a Northern major gen-

A three-wheeled walking-horse toy from Ives, 1870s. (Ed Hyers Antique Toys, Asheville, North Carolina)

eral in charge of volunteers during the Civil War.) This toy was patented by Arthur Hotchkiss of Connecticut; many of Ives's toys were invented by his workers or others—though Ives himself also did a fair amount of brainstorming.

Another popular Ives clockwork toy was a

An Ives tinplate mechanical rowing toy, patented 1869. The oars and one hand are missing from this 11-inch-long toy. (Phillips, New York)

At left, an impressive early Ives toy: General Grant smoking a cigar (the toy actually did that), ca. 1876 and 14 inches high. At top, E.R. Morrison's "Walking Zouave," ca. 1862. At bottom, another Ives toy—like Grant, clockwork—the Preacher at the Pulpit. At right is a James Fallows toy of painted tin from the late nineteenth century. The pull toy is a foot long. (Sotheby's, New York)

Mechanical Bear that looked more like a nightmarish cartoon, despite the drawing on the side of the wooden box it came in, which was suitably bearlike. There was also a Mechanical Elephant, and even a Mechanical Suffragette!

Ives was Ives, Blakeslee & Company until about 1876 when another name was added, that of Jerome B. Secor. A sewing machine manufacturer in Chicago, Secor had been wiped out by the Great Fire of 1871 and moved in that year to Bridgeport, by chance becoming Ives's next-door neighbor. Secor had always been intrigued by mechanical toys, and when he opened up his new sewing machine company in Bridgeport, he found time as well to manufacture toy caged birds, which "sang" by means of a music box in the base. In 1873, when Secor displayed his sewing machines at the Vienna World International Exhibition, he sent along several of the birds, which were displayed atop the machines.

Secor's sewing machine company fell on hard times in 1875 and folded the next year.

Secor cast about for a new idea. Not surprisingly, toys sprang to mind, and he soon began manufacturing them, first in the attic and kitchen of his home, and later in a portion of the Ives, Blakeslee building. He worked mainly in two areas, producing rather large, high-quality clockwork toys—among them a woman piano player and a banjo player—and blank-cartridge and cap pistols. During his first year in the toy business, his clockwork singing birds won a medal at Philadelphia's Centennial Exhibition. Toward the end of the 1870s, Secor gave up distributing the toys himself and allowed them to be sold as part of the Ives line.

Secor appears to have manufactured the first cast-iron vehicle, a locomotive, which he brought out in 1880 or possibly as early as 1879. His patented American Songster whistling bird became a classic and was manufactured, in one form or another into the 1950s, perhaps even later.

By 1874, Edward Ives had invented a tin clockwork locomotive that whistled. By 1876, Ives's clockwork toys were the company's principle line, though its hot-air toys were still big sellers. The hot-air toys were also fitted onto Ives's stationary toy steam engines.

In the early 1880s, Ives was not only a prime manufacturer in the United States, he was one of the most important toy makers in the world, exporting to Europe and South America. When sales for a single toy reached 100,000, the figures were gratifying for Ives, but by this time no longer eyebrow-raising. An Ives catalog of the early 1880s—the firm issued two a season—ran to nearly two hundred pages. Ives was absorbing other companies and handling distribution for yet others, always making sure that what emerged under the company name bespoke quality. We'll return to Ives in later chapters.

century, and William Barton was the reason. He had come up with a technique for casting bells in one piece (European imports had been cast in two parts and then soldered together), which produced a stronger, less expensive bell. Barton moved from New York to East Hampton in 1808 and began production. His outfit became the East Hampton Bell Company in 1837, and in 1866 the firm's name was changed to the Gong Bell Company, far better known to fanciers of American-made toys.

Ives manufactured the cast-iron Polar Ice wagon shown above in the 1880s. The Gong Bell Company Trick Pony at right was also produced in the 1880s. The Liberty bell toy below is from Kyser and Rex, ca. 1885. (Ed Hyers Antique Toys, Asheville, North Carolina).

It was during the 1870s that cast iron came into its own. A peculiarly American material, cast iron was rarely used elsewhere for toys. Extremely popular was the bell toy, first patented in 1874 as a simple arrangement of two cast-iron wheels enclosing a two-tone chime, which rang when the wheels were pulled or pushed. Bell toys were almost wholly an American phenomenon; the few that were made in Europe tended to be exported to the United States.

East Hampton, Connecticut, was the hub of the bell-toy industry through the turn of the

Gong Bell may have made the first bell toy during the late 1860s or early 1870s. A revolving chime on two wheels, it was one of the first toys made simply to entertain. Soon the firm came out with tin animals hauling a chime. Sales were good, and more bell toys followed, among them an eagle with a bell in its beak riding a four-wheeled conveyance, a girl on a sleigh, and a bear on a cart with clappers attached to its feet; suspended between two large bells, the bear swiveled as he was pulled, and the clappers struck the bells. Gong Bell toy No. 51 consisted of two cast-iron goats, which butted a bell as the wheeled toy was pulled along. Gong Bell's toys can be identified by their fancy wheel designs;

Ives produced this painted clockwork tinplate Whistler locomotive about 1885. The wheels are cast iron, and the length 11 inches. (Sotheby's, New York) OPPOSITE

Two Ives clockwork bears from the 1870s. The drummer is 14 inches high. (Sotheby's, New York) OPPOSITE

many of the firm's patterns were made by Stevens, which also put out its own bell toys. Gong Bell was still manufacturing bell toys in the 1950s, though by then cast iron had given way to steel.

Barton's original success inspired imitators, seven of them springing up in the same vicinity. Among these was N. N. Hill, which made a small number of bell toys while spending most of its time casting bells, as did Gong Bell.

Watrous Manufacturing Co., which later merged with N. N. Hill, was another of the East Hampton bell toy makers, being established in 1884 by D. W. Watrous. Watrous and Hill were related by marriage and shared the same factory. Often the companies did work for each other, presumably when one was busy and the other less so. Watrous's bell toys were also cast iron.

James Fallows was another of the firms making bell toys, though Fallows also turned out many other varieties of toys. Fallows, who had worked as a foreman at Francis, Field & Francis, formed James Fallows & Company in Philadelphia in 1874. His toys were often marked "IXL," which probably was meant to mean "I excel." Certainly, Fallows did excel and is regarded as

one of the foremost names in early American toy making.

As might be expected from his Francis, Field & Francis background, Fallows worked mainly in tin (adding cast-iron wheels on his bell toys), and clockwork propelled some of his playthings. His line comprised more than two hundred different toys, with papier-mâché another frequent material. Fallows also made horse-drawn toys and riverboats with bells. The firm, which may have received initial backing from Ives, remained in business at least until the 1890s.

The "philosophic toy" was an important item in the 1870s, particularly to parents. In an age of

Mary and Lamb, an early tin pull toy from James Fallows of Philadelphia, 6½ inches long. (Wilkinson Collection, Detroit Antique Toy Museum)

A frog pull toy from James Fallows. Made of painted tin and cast iron in the late nineteenth century, this item features two frogs who kick each other when the toy is pulled. (Sotheby's, New York)

The magic lantern was one of the wonders of its day. It had been around in one form or another since the 1840s, coming into particular vogue after the Civil War. (The first patent had been taken out in 1863.) The magic lantern consisted of a box containing a lamp, a reflector that concentrated the light, a sequence of glass transparencies with pictures on them, and lenses that reduced or expanded the projected image. As time went on, slides were designed so that, when pushed through quickly, the drawings on them gave the illusion of movement. A variation on the magic lantern, the Polyopticon, which originated in the United States, didn't need glass slides at all; it could project drawings, photos, and engravings directly.

There were other optical toys as well. In addition to Milton Bradley's Zoetrope and Myrioptican, there were such items as the Chromatrope, the Praxinoscope, and the Kaleidoscope. The Chromatrope confined itself to colorful geometric forms, which could be revolved to produce various abstract images. The Praxinoscope, which dates from 1877, was similar to the Zoetrope, but employed mirrors. The Kaleidoscope had been patented in England in 1817, but had probably originated in the Orient some time before that. C. Bush, of Providence, Rhode Island, was manufacturing them here as early as 1874, employing wood, brass, cardboard, paper, and glass. Later, when manufacturers began making cheaper versions, philosophic toys lost their cachet and also their original outlets—having been abandoned by jewelers and opticians and embraced by toy and department stores.

By virtually any measure, the stand-out toy between the Civil War and the turn of the century was the mechanical bank. Reflecting Yankee thrift and the mechanical ingenuity that so

Kaleidoscopes were popular optical toys in the nineteenth century—and remain so today. This appeared in an 1869 magazine. (Culver Pictures)

invention, science was much on the public mind, and it seemed important to inculcate in children all the new theories. Consequently, companies sprang up with the sole purpose of producing toys that replicated scientific instruments or demonstrated scientific principles. Many of them —like toy microscopes and toy magic lanterns —were sold exclusively in jewelry stores and optical shops.

Cast-iron mechanical banks of the late 1800s. Top, left to right: William Tell, by Stevens, ca. 1896; Punch and Judy, by Shepard, 1884; and Speaking Dog, by Shepard, ca. 1884. Bottom, front: Bad Accident, by Stevens, ca. 1887. (Wayne Pratt and Company, Marlboro, Massachusetts)

marked the emergence of the new nation, it was a toy that easily persuaded children to save their pennies. The banks employed the preferred toy-making material of the day, cast iron, and often used humor—sometimes irreverently. Aside from dolls, the mechanical bank was the first toy to breed collectors.

It all began on December 21, 1869, when John Hall of Watertown, Massachusetts, was granted a patent for a mechanical bank. Once in production, the toy was called Hall's Excelsior Bank, and all evidence points to its being the first patented, commercially produced mechanical bank. It was a simple device, compared to some of the banks that followed it. When a glass knob at the front was pulled, a wooden monkey cashier, seated behind a desk, emerged from the top, his head swinging back and forth several times. When a coin was placed on the desk, the weight of it caused the cupola in which the money was enclosed to shut. J. & E. Stevens of Cromwell,

Connecticut, who produced it, also issued the three other Hall banks known to have been manufactured (though he patented many more): the Race Course Bank, the Tammany Bank, and the Lilliput Bank.

J. & E. Stevens was probably the busiest of the mechanical bank makers, with Shepard of Buffalo, New York; Kingsbury; Hubley; and Kyser and Rex (of Frankford, Pennsylvania) other important names. Altogether, over three hundred mechanical banks were invented, with more than thirty patents granted in the single year of 1880. The banks sold well through the 1920s, were revived in the 1950s, and have enjoyed a second revival in recent years, being manufactured (often crudely) in the Far East, and, in this country, by the John Wright Company of Wrightsville, Pennsylvania, which has been reproducing them in limited editions.

Many banks were patented by individuals (patents can be assigned only to individuals) and then sold (sometimes for such royalties as one dollar per dozen banks) or turned over to manufacturing companies. Connecticut's Charles A. Bailey was the most prolific inventor, with about thirty-two manufactured designs. After him came Philadelphia's James H. Bowen, with sixteen. Most of Bailey's designs were manufactured by J. & E. Stevens, and all of Bowen's were. Bailey, who manufactured some of his ideas for mechanical banks himself in a lead alloy, was eventually hired by Stevens to be its head designer. He worked for the firm exclusively from about 1890 to 1916.

The principle of the mechanical bank was simple. Sometimes a coin itself would initiate the action; often a lever had to be manipulated. The subsequent action, whatever it was, would result in the coin's being deposited in the bank.

The period in which the banks emerged was a time of open racial and national prejudice, and a number of them reflected this. There was the Reclining Chinaman bank, invented by

Stevens's Paddy and the Pig cast-iron mechanical bank, from 1882. (Sotheby's, New York)

The Picture Gallery Bank, cast iron, from Shepard, ca. 1885. (Ed Hyers Antique Toys, Asheville, North Carolina)

Bowen and manufactured by Stevens, which reflected the prejudice of the time against the immigrant Chinese. A reclining Chinese figure holds cards in one hand. When a penny is placed in his tunic, and a lever at the far end of the log he's lying on is pressed, one hand goes to his mouth as if covering a smile, while, as a gray rat pops out of the log, his other hand displays four aces. At the time, prejudices about the Chinese included stories and jokes about their gambling, shrewdness, sleeping on logs, and eating rodents.

Another group of immigrants making "native" Americans uneasy was the Irish, who were caricatured in a Paddy and the Pig bank. Bowen and Stevens again teamed up on this one. A jug of whiskey juts out of Paddy's pocket as he holds a pig between his legs. A penny on the pig's nose, a pull on the lever in Paddy's back, and the pig's left leg kicks the coin toward Paddy's mouth. The mouth opens, a long pink tongue shoots out and catches the coin, as Paddy's eyes roll upward.

By far the most toys in this gang depicted blacks. Some are out-and-out caricature, such as the Stump Speaker, which depicted a black politican of the era. This time Charles G. Shepard and Peter Adams of Buffalo, New York, were the inventors, with the Shepard Hardware Company, also of Buffalo, producing it. In this toy, the coin drops into the politician's carpet bag, while his jaw wiggles in gratitude.

Other banks of this type included Boys Stealing Watermelons (inventor and manufacturer unknown), the Jolly Nigger (Shepard, and later J. & E. Stevens), and I Always Did 'Spise A Mule by Bowen and Stevens, who teamed up again on still another bank with blacks—though (apart from its title) this one seems to show no particular prejudice. The Darktown Battery bank consists of three ballplayers—pitcher, batter, catcher—none pictured offensively. The pitcher's right hand has a spring mechanism. When a coin is placed between its thumb and palm and the arm drawn back, then released, the arm

The Bad Accident cast-iron mechanical bank, from 1887. (Sotheby's, New York)

shoots out, releasing the coin as the head snaps back; the batter lifts his bat, and, as he takes a strike, his head turns toward the catcher, whose head moves forward and hand moves to one side as the penny shoots into his chest. This toy, patented in 1888, had its name changed to Hometown Battery when it was reproduced by the *Book of Knowledge* in the 1950s; the ballplayers were painted as whites in that revived version.

Bowen and Stevens's Calamity Bank featured white football players. Right and left tackles are placed in position, a coin is dropped in the slot in front of the ball carrier, and a lever is pressed. Presto—calamity!—as the three players clang together.

Many banks featured circus motifs. There was Shepard's Humpty Dumpty bank, a puzzler (not a hint of hen fruit here) to anyone who

didn't know that back in the 1880s Humpty Dumpty was a famous American circus clown portrayed by George L. Fox. A simple toy, but obviously popular—as many exist today. The action merely consisted of the coin's shooting from Humpty's hand into his mouth as his eyes rolled upward. Other circus-oriented banks include Shepard's Trick Dog bank, which featured a dog and a clown with a hoop; Shepard's Circus Bank (a clown riding in a tiny pony cart); The Acrobats, Boy on Trapeze, Clown on Globe, and Tin Clown on Bar.

There were also organ-grinder banks, with a monkey tipping his hat as he receives a coin—four of them by Kyser and Rex. They also produced a fifth, organ-grinder bank, with a performing bear instead of a monkey.

The span of ideas was enormous: Jonah and the Whale (two types), Mama Katzenjammer and the Kids, Dentist, Punch and Judy, Santa Claus at the Chimney, Tank and Cannon, William Tell, Teddy [Roosevelt] and the Bear. One of the favorites was Hall and Stevens's Tammany bank, in which a fat politician slyly slipped a coin into his pocket.

Another type of movement toy also burst into view during this period. Steam was the exciting source of power in those days, and it was only a matter of time before the first steam toys were produced. The earliest emerged in the 1860s. According to *Knight's Dictionary of Mechanics* (1881), the dollar steam engine was an American invention, with six different patents for steam toys (some with whistles) issued between 1869 and 1872. The pioneer steam playthings were precision-made and sold through optical instrument shops, as were the other philosophical toys.

Steam toys must have given parents more pause than any of the others, particularly when placed in the hands of a child known to be unreliable. Parts had to be lubricated, potentially a messy operation, and more significantly, boilers had to be filled with water, a burner stoked with alcohol, and a match touched to it. Such announcements in ads as "harmless," "perfectly safe," and even, "The engine has a perfect-working Safety-Valve, which makes it impossible for the boiler to explode," could only have fueled a parent's apprehension all the more, particularly in an age of commonplace news reports about real steamboats and locomotives exploding. Despite this, steam toys had their vogue, with a handful of companies turning out a huge array of steam-powered playthings. The three biggest names—as far as we know—were Weeden, Buckman (which later became the Union Manufacturing Company and then Kraft and Huffington), and Eugene Beggs.

Weeden was the latest starter of the three, but endured the longest. Yet another New Englander, William N. Weeden was born in 1839. In 1882, having learned watch and jewelry making in his early days, he moved to New Bedford, Massachusetts, to set up his own business. He invented his first toy steam engine in 1884, which he marketed through the *Youth's Companion* magazine as a premium. In 1885, he patented an upright engine, which was particularly successful, and from 1889 on, steam toys and their accessories were the firm's specialty.

For the most part, Weeden concentrated on stationary engines. Like Charles M. Crandall, he saw worth in having a well-known brand name and seems never to have sold his toys anonymously. In the late 1930s, the Weeden Company was able to boast that one of their stationary steam-engine models had been in continuous production for over fifty years. Other Weeden steam toys included trains, an automobile, steamboats, and a fire pumper that actually pumped water. In 1887, a 13½-inch-high tin-and-cloth merry-go-round was specifically made —not necessarily by Weeden—to be powered by a Weeden upright steam engine.

A. Buckman, of Brooklyn, patented a toy steam engine in 1871, and during the 1870s was famous for his Young America engines. He and E. Buckman also patented several other steam toys, among them a steamboat, a fire engine, and a second steam engine. Buckman made stationary steam engines, steam-driven tools, fire engines, and steamboats. Some of them, under the Union Mfg. label, sold for as much as fifty dollars, though the usual price was in the one-dollar range.

As might be expected, the most popular of the steam toys was the steam locomotive. This was the particular province of Eugene Beggs, of Paterson, New Jersey. Beggs had been a foreman on the Marietta and Cincinnati Railroad in Ohio, and had also labored in the locomotive factory of Danforth and Cooke. In 1871 he patented a steam-powered toy locomotive and began turning them out. At times he sold them on his own, but at other times allowed other firms to distribute them: Ives (in which case they were manufactured exclusively for Ives and sold as Ives

Brooklyn's Buckman Manufacturing Co. produced this early steam-powered toy, a tin Twin Paddle Wheel Steamboat, about 1872. (Wilkinson Collection, Detroit Antique Toy Museum)

products), James McNair, and the National Toy Company. Beggs was another toy maker who believed in keeping his name up front; in jobbers' catalogs and premium magazines, where most of the other toys are anonymous, his train sets are specifically labeled "Beggs"—except those from the periods of his association with Ives.

Other makers of steam toys included Stevens, which sold a steam engine as early as 1872 (patented by R. Frisbie of that firm in 1871), and J. A. Pierce, who was making "Toy Steam Engines, Steamboats, Locomotives, Mechanical Toys, Working Models, etc." in Chicago in 1873.

A popular toy of this time, though it somehow seems to belong to an earlier age, was the bellows toy, which was generally manufactured in Pennsylvania. A figure, usually made of wood, plaster, or papier-mâché, was attached to a wooden platform. Beneath the platform was a bellows. When the toy was pressed, the bellows squeaked, producing a sound that passingly resembled what was supposed to issue from the "real-life" figure. In addition to cats and birds, there were dogs, cows, lions, monkeys—even bellows heads of children and adults that purportedly made both laughing and crying sounds.

Noah's Arks were another successful toy of the period, coming in all materials and sizes. They were particularly popular in homes where Sunday was strictly observed, as they were considered "Sunday toys," sufficiently related to the Bible to make them appropriate for play on an otherwise restricted day.

Jumping jacks enjoyed favor, and the Toy Manufacturing Company of East Weare, New Hampshire, specialized in them, beginning in 1872. The firm beat out all domestic competition. But the company's melancholy end will be noted later.

Animal toys were also popular. A rather grotesque conception today, animal pull toys covered with real hide, wool, or fur were much in demand in the late nineteenth century. Dexter, a famous racehorse of those days, was a popular model for toys during the 1870s and 1880s, with a number of makers distributing facsimiles not necessarily in real hide, but in tin and wood. Horse-drawn toys, of course, had long enjoyed a vogue, since the horse was the most important animal in the early days of this country. The Leo Schlesinger Company of New York City manufactured 180,000 "Dexters" between 1875 and 1880. But that was a drop in the bucket for Schlesinger. Nearly six million tin horses left the Schlesinger plant every year during the same period. Schlesinger, who founded his toy company in 1872, after years of experience in the toy business, was known for tin toys at low prices, many of them mechanical. In 1876, his putty blower (similar to a peashooter) was grabbed up by 2,880,000 children. Not a great twelve months, one would assume, for teachers who turned their backs on their classes. Tin beach toys were another of Schlesinger's specialties, millions of them being sold at ten cents each.

From 1860 to about 1879 George W. Brown and J. & E. Stevens combined forces, selling both tin and cast-iron toys. Their New York distribution firm, owned by them, was the American Toy Company.

Merriam was still in business, making toys for itself but also a huge number of long-tail, single-ear horses to "pull" Ives's clockwork carts (there was much subcontracting among manufacturers during this period). Another of Merriam's better-known products from this time was a hoop toy—a girl encircled by two vertical hoops, holding a child—that is frequently (and erroneously) thought to be a product of Althof, Berg-

Stevens's Big 6 cast-iron train set, ca. 1885. Length, 18 inches. (Mapes Auctioneers, Vestal, New York)

mann. Althof, Bergmann got its start when L. Althof teamed up with the Bergmann Brothers in 1867, as a jobbing firm. In 1874 the company secured two patents, one of them a bell toy with three soldiers. From then on, they were in business as manufacturers, though much of their manufacturing—perhaps even all of it—was farmed out. They had a large line of toys; thirty-five clockwork toys in 1874, dollhouse furniture, kitchen stoves, banks, and hoop toys. Their clockwork toys included a locomotive, a walking doll, a boy on a bicycle, and a carousel. Since they were jobbers as well as manufacturers, it is not certain how many of their toys were their own or even American-made.

Another busy manufacturer was E. Bassingdale Garton, whose Garton Toy Company was established at least as early as 1877 in Sheboygan, Wisconsin. As might be expected from its locale, the firm made sleds, but it also pushed out doll cradles, toy carts, horse-drawn bicycles, toy ironing boards, and, in later days, pedal cars. The firm lasted through at least four generations.

Not a toy maker, but a highly significant name in the history of American toys, was George Borgfeldt. Apparently a German immigrant, Borgfeldt had been a partner in the leading toy firm of Strasburg, Pfeiffer & Co. He conceived the idea of a sample house, where single versions of a toy would be on display for buyers who would place their orders there, thus saving delivery costs, as the toys were shipped to them straight from the factory. By the turn of

Stevens and Brown produced this tin kitchen during the 1880s. (Ed Hyers Antique Toys, Asheville, North Carolina)

Worn, but still attractive: Top left is an Althof Bergmann pull toy, the "Niagara," ca. 1880. Bottom, James Fallows's "Puritan" riverboat, ca. 1880. Top right, George W. Brown's "Monitor" pull toy, ca. 1870. All are painted tin, with stenciling. (Sotheby's, New York)

An Althof-Bergmann tin clockwork carousel from the 1870s. The doll cranking the handle of the mechanism has a bisque head. Diameter, 20 inches. (Sotheby's, New York)

A Cabriolet by Kenton, about 1885. Kenton offered later versions with different horses in 1911 and 1950. (Ed Hyers Antique Toys, Asheville, North Carolina)

The first toy made by Welker & Crosby, ca., 1880, and the only oversized piece made by them. (Ed Hyers Antique Toys, Asheville, North Carolina)

the century, Borgfeldt represented over 250 manufacturers, with more than eight thousand samples on view in his showroom. He died in 1903, but the firm he founded was a force into the middle of the century, closing in 1962.

Another long-lived firm (1844–1925) was Carpenter (Francis W. Carpenter, proprietor) of Harrison, New York, which received several pat-ents for toys made of malleable iron. Malleable iron differs from the usual iron in that it has a slight amount of give, making it less brittle. Many of Carpenter's toys were horse-drawn, with the parts manufactured by the Malleable Iron Works. Carpenter also made trains, and traded on the slogan, "Made of Malleable Iron to insure their durability."

The origin of Hull and Stafford of Clinton, Connecticut, is shrouded in some mystery. It may have evolved from Hull & Wright, which had been in business since 1866, or sprung from the loins of the Union Manufacturing Company, also of Clinton, which registered customers from 1854 to 1899. In any case, Hull and Stafford was a prominent toy maker of the day, producing mechanical tin toys, all of them manufactured in two equal halves and fastened by tabs.

Another major name was Pratt & Letchworth, a Buffalo, New York, company that also marketed its toys under the name Buffalo Toy Works. Pratt & Letchworth, which produced toys in both iron and steel from about 1880 into the 1890s, was best known for its horse-drawn vehicles, including a thirty-four-inch-long artillery caisson with four horses and four riders, a tallyho, a dray, a sulky, a hay cart, and a hose reel.

In 1875, Macy's had become the first department store to establish a toy section. Two years later, Montgomery Ward, after offering no toys in its first five years of mail-order catalogs, began selling them. In 1890, Ward's rival, Sears, Roebuck and Co. did the same.

Now fully established, the toy industry in America was about to burgeon.

TURN-OF-THE-CENTURY FLOWERING

By the 1890s, the whole country was in motion, charged with energy and powered by a new wealth that had evolved with the developing nation. The increasing prosperity in this era of Diamond Jim Brady and Lillian Russell was reflected in greater numbers of toys created for the pleasure of children. Toy catalogs, in turn, grew in size and came to look like the ones we know today. In 1877, a Butler Brothers catalog that went to store owners had featured few toys—some toy stoves and kitchen sets, dolls, rattles, noisemaking balloons, musical instruments, toy soldiers, kaleidoscopes, animals, "ingenious tumbler clowns," and a few others. *All* were imported. But by 1898, the Baltimore Bargain House offered more than thirty pages of toys, about 10 percent of its catalog. There were eight and a half pages of dolls and three and a half of musical toys; there were soldier and fireman outfits, jumping jacks, cap guns, popguns, swords, pewter soldiers, toy watches, clapping toys, bellows toys, shaking-head animals, stable toys, tea sets, Noah's Arks, doll accessories, a page of rubber toys and rubber dolls, steam toys, mechanical toys, trains, ships, bell toys, sad irons, mechanical banks, ranges, a large variety of iron animal-drawn toys, tin trains, animals, carts, kitchens and stoves, wooden laundry sets, blackboards, horse-drawn vehicles, doll cabs, doll carriages, express wagons, intricately lithographed steamboats and warships, steel wagons, and shooflies.

Behind such extensive inventories stood a burgeoning industry. The 1880 U.S. census had listed 173 manufacturers of toys and related products. Twenty years later, the number had jumped to 500, employing four thousand workers. A sign of the industry's progress was the emergence of what was the first trade magazine of the American toy industry, a monthly publication called *Playthings*, its first issue dated January 1903, with a subscription price of fifty cents a year. The premiere issue ran just twenty pages, including covers. Of its nine advertisers, the only one whose name still resonates is Germany's Hohner, of harmonica fame. The rest were now-defunct jobbers and importers. By the next issue, the American Soldier Company and Schoenhut ran ads, as well as Hohner and Germany's Steiff. As early as April, the important American companies advertising included American Soldier, Schoenhut, Gibbs, Ideal, and Toledo Metal Wheel. The final issue of the year had increased to thirty-six pages, including covers. Then, in 1909, a second toy trade magazine popped up. As *Toys and Novelties* magazine (later, *Toys and Bicycles*), it remained an industry force for decades. *Playthings* is still published.

The colorful tin trucks are from New Jersey's Chein (pronounced "chain"), ca. 1918. The intriguing-looking policeman is from New York's Bradford Company and was issued about 1914. (Bizarre Bazaar, New York) OPPOSITE

An A. C. Gilbert Stutz Racer, ca. 1914. (Bizarre Bazaar, New York) INSET

It was a new era, and inevitably gave birth to a small army of new toy manufacturers, many of them offering types of playthings that hadn't previously been seen. What helped this expansion was the growing number of jobbers in the 1880s and 1890s, the mail-order houses, and the spread of department stores, most of which now set up separate toy departments during the Christmas season. Another boost came from a U.S. customs law passed in 1891, which appealed to the consumer's patriotism by requiring that all imported goods be marked as such with their country of origin.

A dramatic new development in toys was electricity. Philadelphia's Novelty Electric Company may have been the first to enter the field, with electric trains as early as 1883. However, Carlisle & Finch was the firm that popularized them, beginning in 1896. Their first try, a brass streetcar, was a simple affair, with a small, rudimentary motor powered by a battery. The circle of track that came with it ran just three feet in circumference. Five hundred streetcars were produced initially; then an ad was placed in an 1897 issue of *Scientific American* and the company found itself deluged with orders. Locomotives soon followed.

Another new toy was the air rifle. As a non-toy, the gun went all the way back to the fifteenth century, and is first known to have been employed in America (with limited success) during the 1804–6 Lewis and Clark expedition. In 1885, the Markham Air Rifle Company of Plymouth, Michigan, introduced two toy air rifles, the Challenger and the Chicago. They were made almost wholly of wood and had surprising accuracy and power. Charles J. Hamilton, a watch and clock repairman who had invented a self-controlled windmill, saw the toys and hied himself to his workshop. When he was finished,

Toys from 1898, including a large assortment of the era's extremely popular bell toys.

An early flying whatsit, as advertised in the May 1909 *Playthings*. Actual airplanes of the day were often even less likely looking. (*Playthings*)

he persuaded the board of directors of the Plymouth Iron Windmill Company (which was marketing his early invention) to look over his handmade *metal* model of an air rifle. The company's vice-president/general manager looked it over and, employing a compliment of the day, exuberantly exclaimed, "Boy, that's a daisy!" So was born the Daisy BB gun.

In 1888, the first full year of production, eighty-six thousand guns were sold, and the next year business doubled. By 1895 the toy was doing so well that the firm changed its name from Plymouth Iron Windmill to the Daisy Manufacturing Company. By 1929, Daisy, in terms of advertising one of the most astute toy companies, had no U.S. competition.

American manufacturers were slow to turn out toy versions of the automobile, which had been around in this country since at least 1892–93, when the Duryea brothers had brought out the first horseless carriage. No doubt the main reason for the paucity of toy cars was the scarcity of the real thing on the American scene. In 1900, there were just eight thousand cars in this country and fewer than 150 miles of paved roads.

Just who finally made the first American toy car isn't known. Research suggests it could have been Hafner in 1901, although there is some speculation that Converse, Fallows, and Ives produced toy autos as early as 1895.

Hafner, of Chicago, began in 1900 as the Toy Auto Company, possibly not turning out its first model until the following year; by 1907 the firm had produced at least seven different clock-

work motor vehicles. By 1904, its name was changed to the W. F. Hafner Company, and the firm eventually evolved into the American Flyer toy trains company. Hafner himself set off on his own in 1914. His son joined the firm, called Hafner Manufacturing Company, in 1918, and the company turned out windup trains until it was bought by Wyandotte in 1950. Hafner's first cars were early enough to have tillers instead of steering wheels. They also came with plush seats and lead wheels coated with red lacquer.

A Fallows car is known with an 1887 patent date, but the clue is misleading, as it applies to the process Fallows used for pressing designs into his toys, rather than specifically to a toy car actually produced. As for Ives, owner Harry Ives (Edward's son) wasn't interested in cars—in fact, he actively disliked them. There is no evidence of a pre-1900 auto from that firm.

If Morton G. Converse and Company did turn out a toy auto in 1895, the theory is that it was inspired by the cars driven about at the Columbian World's Exposition in Chicago, where Converse had a large display. Converse's first toys had been wooden Noah's Arks, but its early automobiles were made of lightweight steel, which was pressed into shape. Converse had begun in 1877, and like several toy makers in Winchendon, Massachusetts, where it was located, turned out wooden toys, drums, hobby horses, doll furniture, carts, tool chests, dollhouses, boats, blocks, and pianos. By 1929 it employed three hundred workers and annually sold one hundred thousand toy drums alone.

Acme, of Chicago, produced a toy version of the 1903 curved-dash Oldsmobile roadster. It was a tin clockwork plaything, like Acme's other known vehicle, a delivery truck with a pressed-steel canopied roof. Jacob Lauth, Acme's owner, turned in 1905 to production of the real thing, under the name Lauth-Juergens Co.

An early and extensive line of toy cars was offered by D. P. Clark of Dayton, Ohio. Clark turned out friction toys of wood and metal, using the name Hill Climber. The company had been in business since 1898, manufacturing toys designed by Edith and Israel Boyer, and was one of the first manufacturers to use friction motors (moving the toy by hand against a surface and then releasing it activates the motor—no other source of power is used). In the early 1900s William Schieble became a partner, and when Clark left in 1909, the company was renamed Schieble Toy and Novelty. After splitting with Schieble, Clark formed the Dayton Friction Works and continued using Schieble's patents as well as the Hill Climber name, which Schieble felt was now his exclusive property. Protracted lawsuits followed, in addition to a continuing confusion as to who actually manufactured certain Hill Climber toys (in those free-wheeling early days, it is possible that other manufacturers used the name, too).

Simple but eye-catching is
this A. C. Gilbert delivery
truck from about 1915.
(Bizarre Bazaar, New York)

A C. Gilbert's U.S. Mail
tin wind-up, ca. 1915.
(Bizarre Bazaar, New York)

U.S. MAIL.

PARCEL POST.

A page from a 1908
catalog, showing D. P.
Clark toys.

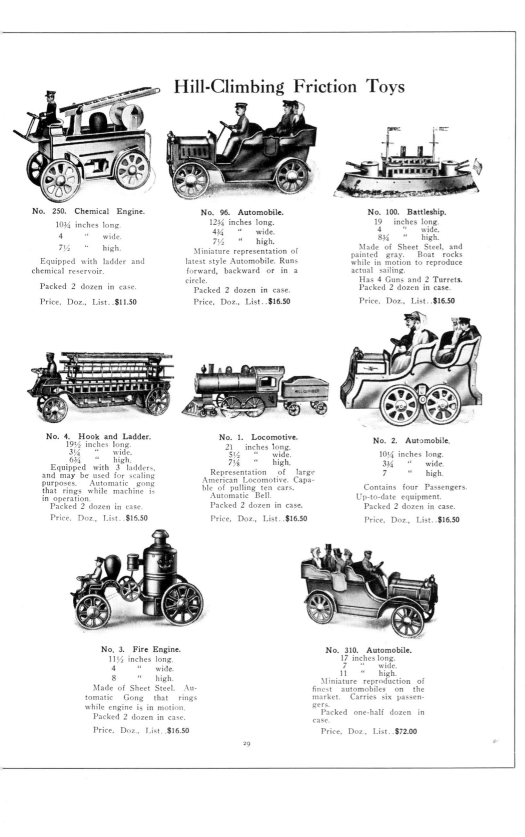

Hill-Climbing Friction Toys

No. 250. Chemical Engine.

10¾ inches long.
4 " wide.
7½ " high.

Equipped with ladder and chemical reservoir.

Packed 2 dozen in case.

Price, Doz., List..**$11.50**

No. 96. Automobile.

12¾ inches long.
4¾ " wide.
7½ " high.

Miniature representation of latest style Automobile. Runs forward, backward or in a circle.

Packed 2 dozen in case.

Price, Doz., List..**$16.50**

No. 100. Battleship.

19 inches long.
4 " wide.
8¾ " high.

Made of Sheet Steel, and painted gray. Boat rocks while in motion to reproduce actual sailing.

Has 4 Guns and 2 Turrets.
Packed 2 dozen in case.

Price, Doz., List..**$16.50**

No. 4. Hook and Ladder.

19½ inches long.
3¼ " wide.
6¾ " high.

Equipped with 3 ladders, and may be used for scaling purposes. Automatic gong that rings while machine is in operation.

Packed 2 dozen in case.

Price, Doz., List..**$16.50**

No. 1. Locomotive.

21 inches long.
5½ " wide.
7⅛ " high.

Representation of large American Locomotive. Capable of pulling ten cars. Automatic Bell.

Packed 2 dozen in case.

Price, Doz., List..**$16.50**

No. 2. Automobile.

10¼ inches long.
3¾ " wide.
7 " high.

Contains four Passengers. Up-to-date equipment.

Packed 2 dozen in case.

Price, Doz., List..**$16.50**

No. 3. Fire Engine.

11½ inches long.
4 " wide.
8 " high.

Made of Sheet Steel. Automatic Gong that rings while engine is in motion.

Packed 2 dozen in case.

Price, Doz., List..**$16.50**

No. 310. Automobile.

17 inches long.
7 " wide.
11 " high.

Miniature reproduction of finest automobiles on the market. Carries six passengers.

Packed one-half dozen in case.

Price, Doz., List..**$72.00**

29

An apparent offshoot of the toy car (for all anyone knows, it may have actually preceded it) was the pedal car. The bicycle was now a major force in the United States—there were four million on the road as early as 1896)—and it was only natural that sooner or later a toy maker would get the idea of putting out toy cars that a child could pedal more or less the way he did a bike. The curved-dash Olds was the first mass-produced car, debuting in 1901. As early as 1903, the Hermann-Vaughan Mfg. Co. of Indianapolis advertised its No. 6 Automobile in the May issue of *Playthings*. Other early companies— Gendron, Kirk-Latty, Sideway National, Garten, Toledo Metal Wheel, American National, and Pedalmobile—were reaching the market with their pedal versions of the automobiles of the day. By 1912, pedal cars featured side doors that opened and closed, windshields that could be raised or lowered, cranks that made noise when they were turned, rubber tires, and a vast array of such accessories as lamps, toolboxes, spare tires, and so on.

Another new item emerging during the turn of the century was the comic-strip toy. The comic strip began in this country with Richard Felton Outcault's "The Yellow Kid," who first appeared in a New York *Sunday World* strip called *Hogan's Alley* in 1895 and was clothed in his famous yellow nightgown in 1896. Although the Yellow Kid looked Chinese and bore the nickname he did, he was actually an Irish slum kid named Mickey Dugan. He caught on quickly and it was only a matter of time till he was spotted by enterprising capitalists as a figure who could help them tote up customers. There were various Yellow Kid products, toys among them. Thus, the first American comic-strip character became the first American comic-strip toy.

The Kenton (Ohio) Hardware Company

Three papier-mâché roly-polys from the early 1900s. At left is Uncle Sam. The next two are comic-strip toys: Foxy Grandpa and, at right, Happy Hooligan. The Uncle Sam is 12 inches high. (Phillips, New York)

was one of the first to climb aboard the Yellow Kid bandwagon, plopping him into cast-iron carts pulled by, in one case, a mule, and in another, a goat. He was a cap bomb by both Grey Iron and Ives, a squeeze toy, a squeak toy, a wood-and-tin pull toy, a whirligig, a sand pail, a bowling game, the star of a toy theater, and was also turned out in papier-mâché and wood by a new company called Schoenhut, which we'll discuss presently.

Outcault dropped "The Yellow Kid" in 1901 —which should make it easy to establish a relative time frame for Yellow Kid toys, but then there's the 1904 Grey Iron catalog showing the Yellow Kid cap bomb. In 1902 Outcault came up with his third comic strip—a second, "Poor Lil' Mose," had made lil' stir. It was called "Buster Brown."

Buster was a mischievous boy with a talking bulldog, Tige (who, like Buster himself, had made his first appearance in "The Yellow Kid"). Buster reflected his time; he was shrewd and had a keen feeling for business—as did his creator. Very shortly, forty-five different companies were licensed to put out Buster Brown products, showering Outcault with royalties. There were Buster Brown bisque-and-cloth dolls, paper masks, yo-yos, clickers, horns, rings, paper dolls, and a cast-iron cart pulled by Tige. (There was also a Buster Brown shoe company, of course, still very much with us today.) Meanwhile, Rudolph Dirks's "The Katzenjammer Kids" had slipped anchor in 1897, and cast-iron replicas of the kids, Mama, and the Captain were being turned out by Kenton. Among them were a mechanical bank, at least three bell toys, and, in 1912, a

Seeing New York bus that included Mama and several other cartoon characters.

Winsor McCay's "Little Nemo in Slumberland" was a beautifully drawn fantasy strip that began in 1905. Eight years later, New York's Strobel & Wilken Co. celebrated that creation's eminence with dolls of Nemo, Flip, Imp, Primus, and Dr. Pill.

The sluice gates were opened, and comic-strip luminaries flooded the newspapers and streamed into toy stores, a process that has yet to end.

Another popular toy from this era—one that once seemed an enduring staple of childhood, but which has largely disappeared in recent years—is marbles. In the late 1880s, the Samuel C. Dyke Company of South Akron, Ohio, became one of the nation's first manufacturers of marbles, turned out in clay, as many as thirty thousand in a day. By the 1890s, Ohio was a veritable hotbed of marble making, home of the Navarre Glass Marble Company in Navarre and M. B. Mishler in Ravenna. Soon another Ohio outfit, Albright and Lightcap of Lima,

which took over Mishler, was spewing out a million marbles a *day*.

The toy soldier is an item that has been issued in a multitude of forms over many eras. Until the great surge of organized collector interest that began with the 1976 publication of the *Old Toy Soldier Newsletter*, very little was known about American toy soldiers. Since then, much has been unearthed, though the early days of toy soldiers in this country are still cloudy. It *is* known that toy soldiers, probably imported, were sold here as early as December 27, 1777, when New York's *Tory Royal Gazette* advertised: "*Toys.* Christmas presents for the Young Folks who have an affection for the Art Military, consisting of Horse, Foot and Dragoons. Cast in metal, in beautiful uniforms. 18 S. a dozen."

Although there is some indication of other metal soldiers popping up in early America, the first sizeable U.S. market in military miniatures seems to have been created by paper soldiers. McLoughlin Brothers, a games and books company located in New York, is the first big name in the field, having produced paper soldiers as early as 1857. For eighty or more years it continued to print them and maintained first place in that category, which includes cardboard and paper mounted on wood. In the early days, McLoughlin printed its soldiers in strips of ten infantry or five cavalry. Like most toys, they were designed to catch the eye, and in their detail and brilliant coloring, they certainly did. The drawings were done by talented artists, and the subjects were varied—among them colonial soldiers, U.S. zouaves, sailors, cavalry, and foreign troops. When sold in sets, the cardboard McLoughlins had such accessories as cardboard tents and wood cannon and shells.

Around the turn of the century Parker Brothers and Milton Bradley joined in. One of

This imaginative set of lithographed blocks came from New York's Jasper H. Singer during the 1880s or 1890s. They could be used as soldiers, three-block figural puzzles, and alphabet blocks. (Bill Nutting)

the great names in American illustration, Maxfield Parrish, provided some of the art for Parker Brothers. Paper soldiers retained some popularity through World War II. Production since then has been minimal, though an occasional set has surfaced as recently as the 1960s and 1970s.

It was not until the turn of the century that American-made metal soldiers appear to have gained a foothold. (Since English children don't seem to have clutched the lead soldier to their breasts until 1868, it's almost certain the toy took longer to establish itself in the former colonies.)

Probably the first important lead soldier maker was American Soldier Company of Brooklyn, New York, which in its early days—before 1904—also operated under the name Eureka American Soldiers. American Soldier was founded in 1898 by C. W. Beiser, who devised

a tray that allowed both dealer and purchaser to raise lying soldiers to a standing position while still in the tray. The soldiers were hollow-cast for the most part, and in general seem to have

been copies of figures by Britains, an English manufacturer. Ads can't be taken for gospel, of course, but Beiser's claim in a February 1903 ad that its tray "created an American industry" suggests that Beiser can be credited as a pioneer.

Beiser's soldiers were usually painted the standard way, but in some cases, according to the ads, they were produced "in gold," and in black and gold. American Soldier lasted till about 1928, disappearing shortly before the Crash. In September 1930, Selchow & Righter advertised that it had bought all the rights, patents, trademarks, machinery, and stock of American Soldier Company's American Hero cowboy-and-Indian sets.

The second concern known to have produced metal soldiers during this period is William Feix. Like American Soldier Company, Feix

was located in Brooklyn, and in a 1900–1901 directory, a Wilhelm Fiex of the same address was listed as a "pinmfr." Presumably, *Fiex* was a typo and *Wilhelm* either wrong, too, or William's father or another relative. By 1903, however, Feix was advertising his toy soldiers in *Playthings*, and continued to advertise them at least as late as 1909. He was still in the toy business until 1926 or 1927, quite possibly making his living on soldiers (which were listed in the toy trades as late as 1925). The drawing in his ads shows soldiers that look exactly like those long attributed to McLoughlin. Whether the attribution has been wrong, or the illustration is simply misleading, or Feix produced for McLoughlin, or both firms simply pirated each other's work isn't known. Feix's longevity, however, suggests at the least that much of McLoughlin's "product" originated with Feix.

Until recently, McLoughlin Brothers was thought to be the earliest of these companies, based on the uniforms—early 1890s—and solid lead castings. However, recent research suggests that McLoughlin's metal soldiers didn't emerge until about 1910 (the earliest-known catalog that

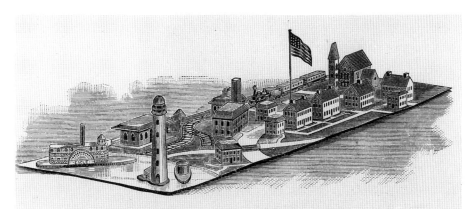

THE AMERICAN TOY VILLAGE.

The only Toy Village ever made in this country, and superior in design, finish, variety and construction to any ever offered in the market. A large map or plan of a village, with streets, canals, river, harbor, etc., lithographed in colors, accompanies each set. The pieces consist of Church, Blocks, single Houses, Passenger Station, Freight Depot, Coal Sheds, Railroad Train, Canal Boats, Monitor, Passenger Steamer; Lighthouse, etc., etc., and in addition to the plan designated on the map, may be arranged in various other ways. With a box of sand real hills, streets, etc., may be formed, and the buildings, etc., set in place, thus rendering it a Summer as well as Winter toy. The whole is packed in a strong, finely finished wooden box, with a large, elegant chromolithographed label covering the top.

features them is dated 1911, and other manufacturers were selling soldiers in those same uniforms right into World War I). In any case, there are strong indications that McLoughlin didn't actually manufacture lead soldiers, but simply functioned as a distributor who took total credit by emblazoning the McLoughlin logo on its boxed sets. Many are copies of Germanic figures (even the helmets and style of equipment are Germanic, not accurate representations of the U.S. soldier's regalia of the day). The early McLoughlins are nicely boxed, with attractive box-top art. In 1911 the sets ran in size from eleven pieces (sold for sixty cents) to thirty-seven ($2.50).

Riley Ives died in 1896. Harry Ives joined his father, Edward, in the business in 1890. Despite some setbacks—a national financial panic in 1893 and a short period of receivership in 1897

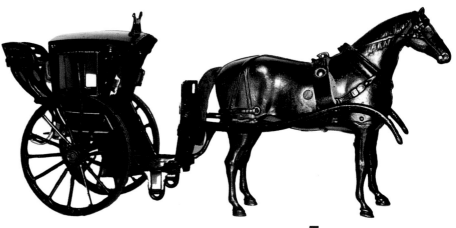

—the firm continued to turn out a staggering array of quality toys.

In the 1880s Ives had about forty employees. By the turn of the century there were one hundred Ives workers during the busy season, with a great deal of the primary work being done at outside factories. Their bright red locomotives

The Ives horse that pulled this hansom cab actually "walked" as it was pushed or pulled (Ed Hyers Antique Toys, Asheville, North Carolina). The Iron Bandwagon below, 32 inches long, is also by Ives. (Sotheby's, New York). Both toys date from the 1890s.

the form of a clockwork-powered trackless iron locomotive. By the 1890s, after Ives and other manufacturers had mastered the intricacies of cast iron, thousands of nicely modeled cast-iron trains, fire engines, horse-drawn wagons, cannon, cap pistols, and cap bombs flowed from the Ives factory straight to the distributors in New York. (The cannon were abandoned in the early 1900s, when one exploded in Harry Ives's face; it didn't injure him, but it definitely made him thoughtful.)

Ives's cap pistols consisted of both the usual sort—put a cap in the pistol, cock the hammer,

were a symbol of Ives's flash at the time, but the color was less symbolic a gesture than a present-day reader might think; many steam locomotives of the day actually sported brilliant colors rather than the black we are familiar with.

Ives's Bridgeport factory was looked on as something of a paradise in those early days. Edward Ives was benignly paternal to his workers, looking after them when they were ill or troubled, and Harry followed in his father's footsteps. Although production of Ives's famous clockwork toys continued, the turn of the century brought a change in the company's focus. Cast iron had come into its own, with iron pull toys appearing in the Ives line as early as 1879 in

pull the trigger, and bang!—and a second kind that was peculiar to its time. The animated cap pistol, a cast-iron gun that, when fired, performed an action, was made by Ives in at least nine types. There was the Butting Match version, which consisted of two boys on their hands and knees. When the pistol was fired, the rear boy would slide forward, butting heads with the other boy and firing the cap in the hat of the first boy at the same time. The Chinese Must Go version, a less than friendly pistol, had a Chinese man, complete with pigtail, who, when the trigger was pulled, closed his mouth: this fired off a

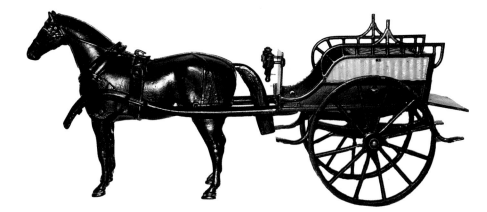

cap, while at the same time the Oriental victim was kicked in the seat of the pants by a derbied Occidental. The Punch and Judy version worked if you placed a cap on Judy's back. All you had to do then was pull the trigger and watch Punch, behind Judy, bend forward and strike her (as well as the cap) with his nose. Others in the series consisted of Clown on Barrel, Alligator, Clown (kicked by a mule), Duck, Sambo, and perhaps the most intriguing of all of them, the Just Out. This consisted of the head of a chicken placed behind an egg. When the head (which was the gun's hammer) struck the egg, it exploded both a cap and the egg itself, with a large chick popping out of the egg's front.

Ives also issued a few cast-iron cap bombs. These, when dropped to the ground, would make a cap explode. Many of them were in the shape of a head. At the top of the head was a ring to which a child could tie a string, for retrieval. Generally, when the cap bomb hit the ground, the mouth would close, exploding the cap. Ives's cap bombs included such heads as the Yellow Kid, Admiral Dewey, and a Chinese. Production on the entire cap pistol line was so huge that a dozen or more men had the sole task of riveting the weapons together.

A fire in December 1900 destroyed most of the factory, including almost all of Ives's tools and dies. The catastrophe prompted Harry Ives to retool for a new line of toys, clockwork trains that would run on tracks. In part, this was to meet competition. The Germans had been exporting train sets since the early 1890s, and the

There were a lot of original concepts in mechanical banks. This is Boy Robbing Bird's Nest from J & E Stevens, ca. 1906. (Ed Hyers Antique Toys, Asheville, North Carolina)

An Ives toy of great charm: Old Woman in Shoe from 1890. The shoe and wheels are iron, and the dolls bisque. Ives was generally regarded as the greatest toymaker of the era. (Wilkinson Collection, Detroit Antique Toy Museum)

The Artillery Bank from J & E Stevens, ca. 1900. (Ed Hyers Antique Toys, Asheville, North Carolina)

Lion Hunter mechanical bank by J & E Stevens, ca. 1907. (Ed Hyers Antique Toys, Asheville, North Carolina)

addition of tracks to theirs had quickly made trackless trains seem just a little too toylike to the children of America. Ives made the first clockwork track trains in this country.

In 1901, Ives brought out its line of O-gauge clockwork track trains, but it was late in 1901, and the company managed to sell just twenty-six hundred dollars' worth. There was no question about the trains' appeal, though, and sales took off in 1902. Eventually, more than two million were sold.

Ives soon expanded its line, making a trademark of the term "Toy Railroads" in 1907, since it was offering more than just trains: there were tunnels, stations, and a variety of accessories as well.

From 1907 on, Ives's principal product was

Two Hubley cast-iron brakes, one two-seated, the other three-seated, both from the early 1900s. The two-seater is 16 inches long. (Sotheby's, New York)

A Pratt & Letchworth four-seated brake, cast iron, from the early 1900s, 28 inches long. (Sotheby's, New York)

the toy train, although the company continued to produce a number of other toys as well. In 1908 it revived a large line of horse-drawn conveyances, and debuted stationary "steam" engines operated by clockwork.

Ives wasn't the only one making money on toy trains. In addition to Beggs's steam-powered jobs, there were competing cast-iron trains by such companies as Kenton, Dent, Stevens, Grey Iron, and Hubley, whose overhead railroad—a train mounted on an elevated track—was particularly attractive. There were also the popular pressed-steel and wood friction Hill Climber trains of Dayton-Schieble.

Beginning in 1902, there was a new rival, one who would overtake Ives and all the others, and become one of the most famous names in the history of toys. On March 13, 1902, the Lionel Manufacturing Company was incorporated.

Joshua Lionel Cowen was born in New York on August 25, 1877. When he was in his teens he took a job with the Acme Electric Lamp Company in Manhattan, where he assembled battery lamps. Cowen enjoyed experimenting in his spare time. While at Acme, he later claimed, he invented a dry-cell battery. There were several other inventions, each of them using battery-powered electricity. In 1901 he produced an "Electric Express" to be used as a showpiece in a shop window. It was powered by dry-cell batteries, which were wired not to the car, but the track. The Electric Express looked like an open freight car and quickly disappeared from the window when an intrigued customer purchased it. Cowen eventually had to make another dozen (at about four dollars each) for the shop owner.

Other orders quickly began arriving from competing stores, and Cowen and a partner found themselves very much in business. Soon the company was getting orders from as far away as Rhode Island (for twenty-five cars). In 1902 Cowen added a second toy, an electrically powered trolley. Streetcars crisscrossed the nation at the turn of the century and also had a charm that made them ideal as toys.

Lionel's trolley was carefully made, wrought entirely from metal. There were six reversible benches, gold pinstriping, and destination signs reading "City Hall Park" and "Union Depot." Lionel didn't manufacture the trolley itself. Morton E. Converse of Massachusetts had that honor, casually turning out a rival to its own windup toy streetcars. (Oddly, in his catalog, Cowen disparaged the trolley as he extolled his earlier toy. He claimed that the Electric Express gondola "will afford the user greater pleasure than the trolley car as it may be loaded and un-

A Hubley Single Track Elevated Railway with Clock Movement. This appears to be the No. 3 Clock Movement toy that was patented April 11, 1893, and shown in Hubley's "Second Edition" catalog, but with variations in the motor and the trim on the supports. The track circumference is the same as that of the Standard No. 3 toy, 8 feet, 4 inches. (Sotheby's, New York)

loaded. Six miniature barrels are supplied with each outfit." The barrels were a new addition.)

Obviously, Cowen didn't yet know what he had. In fact, in his first catalog, the cover advertised "Miniature Electric Cars with full accessories for Window, Display and Holiday Gifts." Cowen was still seeing his electric train first as a display item, and only second as something that could be given as a present. But his early instincts were correct in another area. He had quickly perceived that additional sales could be made (and the line strengthened) by adding accessories. The first, 1902 catalog showed not just that original Electric Express (which looked like a cigar box on wheels) and the streetcar, but a ten-inch-high, two-foot-long suspension bridge, a track with a switch, a crossover track that allowed a figure-eight track layout, and even a bumper to install at the end of a dead-end track.

And the train and trolley could now be operated either by batteries or, in those few homes that had it, by household electric current.

All of this was merely prelude. The signal year in Lionel's history was 1908, when the firm introduced its first locomotive. Again, Cowen wasn't quite on target. Instead of copying the romantic steam engine that then and now fired the imagination, he replicated a Baltimore & Ohio *electric* locomotive. Whether that was done because it seemed appropriate that an electric toy imitate an electric original, or because the engine seemed more modern, or simply was easier to reproduce is not known.

In 1908 Lionel also introduced a derrick car, with a derrick that actually worked. At this early date Lionel already realized that children love toys with parts that work.

In 1905 Lionel had sold eight thousand dollars' worth of toys, an amount sizeable enough in those days to make Cowen comfortable, and by 1909 Lionel was advertising its trains as "The Standard of the World."

Naturally, competition developed. In addition to Carlisle & Finch, which, as we have noted, had been on the scene since 1896 with its brass streetcar (and which also produced a wet-cell-powered toy car in 1901, selling for $3.50), such firms as Voltamp, Knapp Electric (founded in 1890 with $200 cash and $400 in borrowed funds, staffed by Mr. Knapp and one employee), and American Flyer began producing electric trains. And a year after Lionel first sounded its "Standard of the World" clarion, Harry Ives decided to see what he could do about changing that designation. His firm had been peripherally involved with electric trains as early as 1883, when it furnished figures and other parts to the Novelty Electric Company. Also in the 1880s, Ives manufactured toy electric motors, and in the

Horizontal Steam Engine, with Solid Brass Boiler.

Weeden's Horizontal Engine is a miniature type of the engine commonly found in manufacturing establishments throughout the country. Has all the parts for generating steam and converting its power into work. Has boiler and casing, steam dome, whistle, safety valve, cylinder, steam chest, slide valve, eccentric, eccentric rod, piston, cross head, pitman, driving shaft and fly wheel, and a solid brass boiler. The base and boiler casing are of strong Russia iron. It is both a fascinating toy and an instructive piece of scientific apparatus. Size of Engine 3½ x 4½ x 5½ inches.

The Engine given only to Companion subscribers for one new subscriber and 25 cents additional, with 30 cents for postage and packing. Engine sold for $1.25, postage and packing 30 cents extra.

- - - - -

Electric Motor and Battery, Complete.

This Motor is run by an electric current generated in its base. It develops a high rate of speed, and can be used for running light toy machinery. We give with the Motor sufficient chemicals for running it a number of times. The 4-inch Aluminum Fan is not given with the Electric Motor, but will be sent for **25 cents extra.** Notice "Village Blacksmith" offer below. Why not order it?

Given only to Companion subscribers for one new subscriber and 15 cents additional, with 40 cents for postage and packing. Motor and Battery sold for $1.00, postage and packing 40 cents extra.

The Leclanche Electric Bell Outfit.

All modern houses are supplied with electric door bells and call bells. They are easily put up, and not expensive in use.

The Outfit consists of a large Leclanché Battery, with Chemicals, a nickel-plated Electric Bell, mounted on a maple base and having a maple cover; a Push Button with porcelain knob; 50 feet insulated Copper Wire, Clamp Tacks, and full Directions for putting up.

Given, complete, only to Companion subscribers for two new subscribers; or for one new subscriber and 50 cents additional. See Conditions, page 522. Sold for $1.50. Sent by express, charges paid by receiver. Shipping weight of the Outfit 10 lbs.

Model Motor.

This Motor is 2½ inches high, has a 3-pole armature with no dead centres, adjustable brushes, small pulley for running toys. We furnish all the parts for putting the motor together, including the castings, wire and explicit directions for winding.

Materials only given to Companion subscribers for one new subscriber and 15 cents for postage. Sold for $1.00, postage and packing 15 cents extra. The Motor wound, and ready to run, for one new subscriber and 25 cents additional, with 15 cents for postage. Price, $1.50, postage and packing 15 cents extra. Carbon, zinc and package of salts for battery, by mail for 25 cents.

- - - - -

Locomotive, with Tender, Car, Track and Station.

Description.

This is a perfect steam Locomotive. The Train, 22 inches in length, is made entirely of metal, and very handsome in appearance. The Engine alone is 7½ inches long, and uses alcohol for fuel.

"Village Blacksmith."

This toy is designed to be set in motion by an electric motor or steam engine. This is easily done by simply connecting the two with a belt or cord. When in motion the "Village Blacksmith"

The Car has swivelled trucks. The Track, when put together, forms a 12-foot circular railroad. The Station, Truckmen, etc., are lithographed in colors on paper for pasting on wood.

hammers away at his anvil, while a boy at his side operates the bellows, as natural as life. We will include the "Village Blacksmith" with a motor or steam engine for **50 cents extra**, post-paid.

This Locomotive, together with a Tender, Car, Track and Station, given only to Companion subscribers for four new subscribers; or for one new subscriber and $1.50 additional. See Conditions, page 522. Sold for $3.75. Sent by express, charges paid by receiver. Shipping weight 5 lbs.

Price-List of Steam Toys. We can supply an Illustrated Price-List of Steam Toys which range in price from $1.00 to $10.00. These Toys are made by the well-known Weeden Manufacturing Co. This Price-List will be sent to any address on receipt of a two-cent stamp.

Weeden's steam-operated toys were big sellers for years. The "Dart" locomotive at the bottom of the page is shown elsewhere in this chapter. From *The Youth's Companion* magazine, October 31, 1895.

A clockwork Ives Destroyer, "3009." (Sotheby's, New York)

next decade sold some rudimentary electric trains. However, once Ives moved into full-scale production of these toys in 1910, the company became such a force in the field that it was generally thought at the time that it had been Ives who had invented the electric toy train.

Ives introduced its new trains in January 1910 with a master stroke. It offered a means of converting its original mechanical trains to electricity by adding a third rail to the old tracks and a new electric engine to pull the cars. (Ives never phased out the mechanical trains, however, which continued to sell right up till the company's end.)

Ives, long known for quality, didn't let customers down with its new electric trains. Many believe Ives reached its zenith with them. Like all Ives toys, the trains were unconditionally guaranteed, a practice that may have contributed to the eventual demise of the firm.

The Ives electric train line became extensive, soon including a wide assortment of accessories. Ever inventive, in 1915 the company added something called the Controlophone, a device that started and stopped trains and motors by a simple voice command. Many decades ahead of its time, it wasn't successful, but did provide yet another example of Ives's commitment to progress in quality toy making.

Unfortunately, in 1915 Ives expanded into a new line of toys, clockwork ships inspired by a sense of patriotism that prompted the high-minded Harry Ives to stick with them even after it was obvious that the boats had all the sales floatability of an anchor.

Another major firm that began to produce toys during this period was the Dowst Manufacturing Company, of Chicago. The firm had its origins in 1876 as the Dowst Brothers Company, a publishing house that churned out the *National Laundry Journal.* Dowst Brothers took an interest in toys beginning in 1893, when Samuel Dowst attended the World's Columbian Exposition. There he spotted a newly designed typecasting machine, the Linotype, purchased it, and soon after began experimenting with it, finally adapting it to make lead collar buttons and promotional miniatures, such as flat irons, related to his publication. Very quickly, die-casting became Dowst's principal business (which presumably constituted no loss to the world of literature). The firm's early output consisted of lead trinkets to be sold as party favors, as penny jewelry, and as political giveaways and candy-box premiums. Tiny cars, trains, and aircraft were among the items produced, and soon Dowst began selling his products to five-and-tens across the country. His first big success came in 1906—a miniature Model T Ford. Eventually over fifty million of them were sold.

By 1911, Dowst produced his first toy with free-turning wheels, a limousine, and in 1914 added a Ford touring car and a matching pickup truck. The company was fully on its way, but it wasn't until 1922 that it got the name it is known by today. Dowst introduced a line of metal doll furniture, and named it after a granddaughter of

one of his brothers. She was called Tootsie, and the Tootsietoy was born.

Another long-lived toy outfit, the Gibbs Manufacturing Company of Canton, Ohio, began making toys in 1896 (it had been in business from around 1830 as a manufacturer of wooden barrels and tubs and later produced a very successful improved metal plow). The company's first toy was a political giveaway. William McKinley's campaign manager—McKinley was from Canton—asked the company to come up with a novelty that would help publicize the presidential candidate. Lewis Gibbs, the owner, came up with a new version of a top that was operated by a spring. He slapped pictures of McKinley and his running mate on the tops, along with the slogans "McKinley on Top" and

Attractive turn-of-the-century lithographed wooden buildings. The two end structures are by Bliss, and the middle is also possibly a Bliss effort. The Bliss fire pumper belongs to the Fire Station behind it. (Sotheby's, New York)

A wooden horse pull toy, 12¼ inches long, maker unknown, ca. 1900. (Wilkinson Collection, Detroit Antique Toy Museum)

"I Spin For McKinley," and probably couldn't help feeling a bit smug when McKinley spun his way through the Electoral College and into office.

Wood and tin were the company's basic materials, and in the early days color was provided either by paint or nicely lithographed paper. Since the company had begun with tops, movement remained a large part of its line, with tops a staple, but push-and-pull toys also figured prominently, a major feature being moving legs on the horses and other animals that pulled various wagons and carts. Other items included an Irishman dancing a jig and a cat with a head that nodded, both of them pull toys.

Although Gibbs was never a giant, it managed to keep going until 1969, when foreign competition helped force the company out of toys. What finally made the firm decide to abandon them completely was the government's new safety guidelines for children's toys; the exposed

metal spring in Gibbs's tops would have to be eliminated, the same spring that had powered Gibbs's very first toy.

Another company that worked principally in wood was not as long-lived as Gibbs, but was better known in its time and even today. The firm was A. Schoenhut Co.

Albert Schoenhut had immigrated from Germany to the United States shortly after the Civil War. His first job seems to have been with Philadelphia's John Deiser & Sons, toy importers and jobbers. While working there he found that the toy pianos the company imported from Germany frequently arrived broken. At first Schoenhut spent his time repairing the pianos. Then it dawned on him that there might be profit in designing and producing American-made pianos of quality. In 1872 he opened his own business and did well with the pianos; unlike their competition, his produced a pleasant, on-pitch tone.

But it was in 1903 that Schoenhut made his

major mark. In May he ran an ad in *Playthings* magazine, a double-page spread introducing The Humpty Dumpty Circus.

Schoenhut didn't invent the circus set. The credit for that goes to a man who walked into Schoenhut's office with the invention, for which he wanted one hundred dollars outright. Schoenhut assured him royalties would pay him far more in time, but the man refused. He wanted to leave his wife, and one hundred dollars was all he needed to get away from her. Schoenhut finally agreed, began producing the circus, and despite its worldwide success, never heard from the man again.

The first circus set, constructed from wood, leather, and rubber, was simple: a few clowns, donkeys, and elephants, plus a ladder, two chairs, and a pedestal. But it was more than enough for the wonder-struck children who received it. The clowns and animals had articulated arms and legs and could be arranged so that they balanced in an infinite variety of positions. Furthermore, their slotted hands and feet enabled them to be stood on the rungs and railings of ladders, chairs, and whatever else the child could find.

The Humpty Dumpty Circus was an instant hit and quickly expanded. The original pieces were joined by a Ringmaster, a Hobo, a Chinaman Acrobat, a Negro Dude, a Lion Tamer, and a Lady Rider. All sorts of accessories were introduced, as well as a variety of animals, including alligators, giraffes, horses, camels, and buffalo.

Additions to the line of jointed figures soon sprang up, with Max and Moritz of early comic-strip fame the first to arrive, joined shortly by a Farm Set and a Mary Had a Little Lamb set. A real eye-catcher was the highly elaborate Teddy's Adventures in Africa, a 1909 toy version of Theodore Roosevelt's African safari. At the same

Columbian Wheel.

MALLEABLE IRON AND STEEL.

No. 5. Crank Movement.
Pat. Applied for.

Diameter of wheel, ... 14 inches.
Extreme Height, ... 17   "

This is a well constructed toy throughout—strong and durable. The wheel is stamped from steel, the design of the centre being a six point star, all lines of which are heavily embossed. The axle is of steel. The columns, base, toy men and crank are of malleable iron.

The carriages which are of steel are hung on the brace pieces, and maintain a perpendicular position throughout every point of the revolution of the wheel.

We take pleasure in presenting this toy which in this year of Columbian celebration we have fitly named the Columbian Wheel.

The design of the star is finished in vermilion, while the circle enclosing it, as well as the columns and base are of black. The carriages in which are seated life-like miniature figures show a strong contrast in yellow.

Each toy carefully tested, and in perfect working order before leaving the factory.

Price, ... $18.00 Per Dozen.

A Hubley ferris wheel, ca. 1893–94. This one operated by a crank. Hubley also offered a clockwork version, almost twice as expensive. Note the very early numbering.

The Schoenhut Humpty Dumpty Circus set, ca. 1910, was one of the most popular toys of the era. (Sotheby's, New York)

A delightful Strauss circus tin wind-up, ca. 1910. (Bizarre Bazaar, New York)

time, Schoenhut was also making pianos, dolls, boats, toy guns, toy uniforms, blocks, shooting galleries, and a variety of other playthings. Among them were toy soldiers. In the May 1903 *Playthings*, Schoenhut advertised a "U.S. Armory" that came complete with eight composition soldiers, about 4½ inches high, wearing the *pickelhaub* helmets of the time, which today look startlingly foreign.

In the same year that Schoenhut's classic circus set appeared, J. Chein & Company was formed. Founded by Julius Chein (pronounced

"chain"), the company became a force in lithographed sheet-metal toys. Lithographed tin is printed (both design and color) first and then pressed into shape. The process is inexpensive, and lends itself to basic forms. New Jersey's Chein specialized in mechanical toys, all of them brightly colored, inexpensive, and well made of their type. Still in business today making decorative metal housewares, the firm continued to make toys until 1979. Among its better-known tin windups were ferris wheels, merry-go-rounds, drumming toy soldiers, roller coasters, and various animals.

One of the great names in American toys, Kenton (originally Kenton Hardware), of Kenton, Ohio, manufactured its first cast-iron toy in 1893, a Columbia bank, honoring the 1893 exposition. Toy stoves were soon added, and eventually the firm became the leading producer of cast-iron toys in this country, selling hundreds of different toys (over six hundred in 1921), including cap pistols, fire engines, bakery wagons, circus wagons, plantation carts, sulkies, surreys, chariots, drays, and wheeled vehicles pulled by such odd animals as boars (with an Egyptian driver), greyhounds, rhinoceroses, and rabbits. By its own account, Kenton brought out its first line of toy autos in 1903, calling it the "Red Devil" line, since in those early days most cars were painted red, and raised the devil with horses as they sped past them. Kenton's toys were well made and sturdy, produced—according to 1930 ad copy—not by a manufacturing company, but by a guild of "efficient toy makers." According to the story, "For forty-seven years many of them have been engaged in perfecting toy quality and are now teaching their sons the same craft. Their enthusiasm, combined with modern equipment and pleasant working conditions, is the reason why Kenton Toys enjoy

▲ Kenton Happy Hooligan police wagon ("Happy's Patrol No. 762"), 17 inches long and cast iron. The man with a tin can for a hat was a popular early comic-strip character. The toy was produced from 1911 to 1926. (Phillips, New York)

▲ cast-iron English Trap pull toy, possibly by Kenton, 15 inches long. (Sotheby's, New York)

Two Kenton cast-iron fire toys from about 1900. (Phillips, New York)

Quadruple Cs here: Camel, Circus Chariot, Clown. A 1911 cast-iron toy from Kenton. (Ed Hyers Antique Toys, Asheville, North Carolina)

an enviable reputation. This reputation is jealously guarded by each man in the company." In 1930, L. S. Bixler (of Jones and Bixler) was the president of the company.

Another firm that soon had a reputation for quality toys was Kingsbury, of Keene, New Hampshire, which began in 1887 in a small one-story wooden building. Its owner, Harry T. Kingsbury, bought the Wilkins Toy Company in 1895, and seems to have operated it under the

original name until about 1918. The original Wilkins firm had begun not long before as the Triumph Wringer Company. Wilkins had intended to sell wringers, but the tiny model he made to promote the wringer brought so many requests for the miniature that he abandoned his original idea and plunged into toy making.

Kingsbury employed steel as the primary material, for the most part using spring motors, starting with a sealed clockwork motor he patented in 1902. Kingsbury's toys employed "high grade baked enamel or automobile lacquer" and were striped and decorated by hand. Cars, racers, farm equipment, and fire engines were primary Kingsbury toys. The firm's Silver Arrow Flying Planes were made of balsa wood and aluminum; they were powered by "elastic motors" —presumably rubber bands.

In November 1902, when Theodore Roosevelt traveled to Mississippi to help settle a border dispute between that state and Louisiana, a classic toy was born. Roosevelt's mission was to

"draw the line" between the two states, but while in Mississippi the vigorous president decided to get in a little bear hunting as well. On the hunt, he encountered a bear cub and decided to spare its life. Clifford Berryman, the *Washington Star*'s editorial cartoonist, came up with a drawing showing Roosevelt's tender-hearted act, the caption reading "Drawing the Line in Mississippi." The sketch was reprinted in a number of papers, including one in New York. Morris Michtom, who owned a Brooklyn toy shop in which he occasionally sold some stuffed animals that he and his wife made, saw the cartoon and decided to try selling a brown plush bear with button eyes and moveable arms and legs. He put the first one in his store window along with a copy of the cartoon and a sign that read "Teddy's Bear." It took about a year for the bears to take off. By 1906, with the president's blessing, Michtom's teddy bears had become a national rage, achieving a niche in the toy world they've yet to relinquish.

A cast-iron Wilkins horse-drawn trolley from about 1895. (Mapes Auctioneers, Vestal, New York)

Author-artist Palmer Cox had a tremendous influence on the toy industry at the turn of the century. His *Brownies: Their Book*, published in 1887, was hugely popular and spun off a raft of toys beginning about 1892. Among them were printed cloth dolls (by the Arnold Print Works of North Adams, Massachusetts), paper toys backed with wood, cast-iron toys, and even, in 1898, a train set—two cars and a locomotive, all of them crammed with Brownies, who were workaday-looking elves.

Johnny Gruelle was another artist who made a lasting contribution to the world of toys, though tinged with sad irony. In 1915, when he was a political cartoonist for the *Indianapolis Star*, his daughter Marcella was ill with tuberculosis. He found a handmade rag doll in his attic and, naming it Raggedy Ann (after the James Whit-comb Riley characters "The Raggedy Man" and "Little Orphant Annie"), gave it to Marcella.

Gruelle began telling his invalid daughter stories about Raggedy Ann. A year later, clutching her doll, she died. In 1917, Gruelle put out a book of the stories, along with copies of the Raggedy Ann doll to promote the book. A year later, P. F. Volland Co. took over production and also published Gruelle's books. In 1934–35 Volland stopped publication and sold the doll manufacturing rights to The Exposition Doll Co., for Raggedy Ann, and to Mollye's Doll Outfitters, for Raggedy Andy; Mollye's soon took over Raggedy Ann as well. In 1938 the Georgene Novelty Co. took over both dolls, producing them until 1962, when Knickerbocker (a company founded some time in the 1930s) seems to have taken over. By 1974, about half of Knick-

Teddy bears, named for Theodore Roosevelt, have been perennial favorites. The maker and era of this specimen are unknown. (Mapes Auctioneers, Vestal, New York)

An impressive Wilkins-Kingsbury tin fire station and cast-iron pumper from the early 1900s. The pumper is 10½ inches long. (Phillips, New York)

erbocker's sales were coming from six different styles of Raggedy Ann and Andy.

New toy manufacturers continued to emerge early in the century, many of them names that would endure for decades. One firm was headed by Alfred Carlton Gilbert—A. C. Gilbert, who seems to have been as much of a whirlwind as the era into which he was born. He was a medical doctor (though he never practiced), broke the world record for pole vaulting at the 1908 Philadelphia Olympic Trials, tied for an Olympic gold medal the next year in London, changed the sport of pole vaulting by removing the spike at the end of the vaulter's pole and substituting "the box"—the slot in the ground that receives the vaulter's pole. In addition, he was an accomplished magician while still in school.

It was magic that led Gilbert into the toy business. About 1910, at the age of twenty-six, he began producing magic kits, selling them under the name of the Mysto Manufacturing Company. The firm was quite successful, with stores in New York, Philadelphia, and Chicago, but Gilbert wasn't satisfied. On his many rides to New York from his home base in New Haven, Connecticut, he observed the steel girders being erected to carry power lines for trains; somewhere along the way, he decided children would be fascinated with toy girders that they could put together. That, anyway, is the official story. It's likely that Gilbert was influenced even more by England's Meccano line of steel-girder construction toys, which had been patented in 1901.

In the autumn of 1911 Gilbert had miniature steel girders made for him, tested them out, and found they didn't work; they kept slipping. Then he got one of those simple but brilliant ideas: a lip placed along the edge of the girder would prevent slippage. When his partners in Mysto proved reluctant to add the girders to the line, Gilbert and his father bought them out and introduced the Erector Set at New York's Toy Fair in 1913. The toys were successful from the start, partly because of another Gilbert touch—an electric motor (in many of the sets) that powered drawbridges, windmills, vehicles, and even elevators. For the inventive, mechanically minded child, the toy was a godsend and continues to be such today. Despite hordes of competitors, the Erector Set remains the preeminent toy of its genre and is one of the oldest continually produced American toys.

Still another enduring company that claimed original inspiration—but may well have lifted the idea from a predecessor—is Lincoln Logs. The man who started it had the right bloodlines. John Lloyd Wright was the son of America's most famous architect, Frank Lloyd Wright. Supposedly, Wright got his inspiration when he was with his father in Tokyo and saw the construction techniques employed in the foundation of the earthquake-proof Imperial Hotel. However, much earlier, in 1866, Joel Ellis had sold toy logs that worked almost exactly like Lincoln Logs—and so had one or more companies after him.

Wholly original or not, Lincoln Logs, first produced in 1916, were immediately successful. In 1943 the firm was purchased by Playskool, which has manufactured Lincoln Logs ever since. Playskool obviously made a good acquisition: in 1975 alone, nearly sixty years after Lincoln Logs first appeared, one million sets were sold.

Still another construction toy—this one for younger children—was the Tinkertoy, which became one of the most successful toys in history. An Evanston, Illinois, tombstone cutter named Charles Pajeau got the idea for this toy as he watched a baby play with wooden spools and

Erector Set No. 1, from the first year of production, was sold as a "Structural Steel and Electro-Mechanical Builder." The patent date is 1913. (Arlan Coffman)

sticks. After two years of tinkering, he brought a prototype of his new toy to the 1914 or 1915 (accounts vary) New York Toy Fair. His booth was in an out-of-the-way corner, and he attracted little attention. Desperate, he offered the manager of two drugstores forty cents on the dollar for every set sold. Both drugstores were in New York, one at Grand Central Terminal and the other on Thirty-fourth Street, near Macy's department store. Tinkertoys aren't known for animation, but Pajeau hid an electric fan in the window display, which made his Tinkertoy windmills turn. He also hired men to sit in the windows, demonstrating what could be done with Tinkertoys. The crowds that gathered were so great that Pajeau was asked by police to remove the demonstrators.

Three hundred sets a day were sold for five consecutive days at the Grand Central location. When a similar setup was arranged at Philadelphia's John Wanamaker department store by Henry Keuls (one of Pajeau's partners and the designer of the distinctive cylindrical Tinkertoy box), over fifty gross were sold in one day. By the end of the first or second year (again, accounts vary) 900,000 Tinkertoys were sold. And it was only the beginning. By 1975, over 100 *million* Tinkertoys had been sold, with sales averaging 2.5 million pieces a year.

A company that might be of interest to fanciers of the toys of a latter-day firm, Fisher-Price, is Cushman & Denison Mfg. Co., of New York. An August 1909 *Playthings* ad shows three of the company's pull toys, which appear to be wooden and very much like Fisher-Price's product, which they may have inspired. The dog, lion, and duck depicted all had "voices" when they were pulled, and their mouths, tails, or heads moved, features Fisher-Price was later noted for.

World War I presented American toy makers with both a challenge and an opportunity. Beginning sometime after the 1830s, most of the toys sold in this country were produced domestically, but that changed during the early 1900s, when Germany began exporting toys so cheap that many American manufacturers couldn't compete. Imports of toys and games totaled about three million dollars in 1900; by 1908 they topped seven million, by 1912 imports captured 40 percent of the market; and in 1914, they constituted exactly half. The coming of war drastically reduced imports, but when the United States declared war on Germany on April 6, 1917, the toy industry suddenly found itself threatened with restrictions of materials. (One company was so desperate that it first gathered all the wood and metal it could find, and then designed a toy that could be made profitably from what it had on hand.)

The Toy Manufacturers of the United States emerged to cope with the situation. Other toy guilds and trusts had been tried before, but this one took. It became a lobbying group that convinced Congress of the need for a continuing supply of toys to American children, war or no war, and for tariffs against imports that would encourage a native industry. (This second objective was achieved with some chicanery, as the toy makers presented themselves as a struggling "new" industry, which was hardly true.) The organization—still in existence—did much to strengthen the position of American toy makers, particularly by having secured an initial 75 percent tariff on imports.

As was hoped, the legislation strengthened existing manufacturers and encouraged newcomers. One of the fledglings was Ferdinand Strauss. Strauss was born in Gollheim, Bavaria, and immigrated to America at the age of eighteen. He first worked as a sample boy for a wearing apparel concern, for the miserable salary of three dollars a week. He soon quit this job and went

into business for himself with a line of harmonicas. This naturally led him into the field of toys. He was a toy importer in the early 1900s. When war interfered with the stream of German toys he depended on, Strauss went into business for himself, becoming known in the process as the "Founder of the mechanical toy industry in America."

The production of tin windup toys is so tangled among manufacturers that it is often difficult to determine just who did what, but among the toys known to have been produced by Strauss are such classic lithographed windups as The Alabama Coon Jigger, Ham and Sam the Minstrel Team, Jazzbo Jim the Dancer on the Roof, and Jackee the Horn Pipe Dancer. Though Strauss advertised the sale of 3,600,000 mechanical toys in 1923, it seems to have gone partially or wholly out of business in the late 1920s and then

A friction beaver,
by Animate Toys, ca. 1918.
(Mapes Auctioneers, Vestal,
New York)

recovered to some extent, as the firm was still turning out windups and other toys at least until the outbreak of World War II.

Another firm whose way into the business was eased by the lobbying of the Toy Manufacturers Association is the Ohio Art Company, founded in Archbold, Ohio, in October 1908. The owner was a dentist, H. S. Winzeler, who, with the instincts of an entrepreneur, operated a grocery business while practicing dentistry. The combined income was meant to finance an idea he had—the marketing of metal picture frames that would enclose religious scenes, landscapes, and Cupids "awake and asleep." Beginning in 1908, these items were being sold in Woolworth's, Kresge's, Sears, Butler Brothers, and other outlets.

In March 1917 Ohio Art bought a toy company, C. E. Carter (Erie Toy Plant), and began turning out, among other products, a galvanized tin windmill. Later, it produced a climbing monkey on a string for Ferdinand Strauss. Eventually Winzeler sold the Carter plant to Louis Marx, one of the toy-making giants, who, according to the Ohio Art corporate history, used it as the foundation of his Marx Toy Company.

Ohio Art, which retained a name more appropriate to a purveyor of framed pictures, is still making toys today. Over the years, it introduced a huge variety of tin toys, among them tea sets, which it debuted in 1918, and an extensive array of sand pails, which first saw the light in 1923.

Unique Art Manufacturing Company of Newark, New Jersey was another name in tin toys, mainly windups. Although not much is known about it today, Unique Art took out an ad in 1945 that indicated it had been in business since at least 1916, when it introduced its Merry Juggler and Charlie Chaplin. The ad went on to list its other significant toys: Jazzbo Jim, introduced in 1920; Ham and Sam, 1921; Jenny the Balky Mule, 1922; its Krazy Kar in 1923; and, Christmas of 1945, its Li'l Abner Band. Since several of these toys, with similar or even exactly the same names, appear to have come at approximately the same time from Strauss, Marx, and possibly others, it is hard to know if Unique was an original, a pirate, or, perhaps, like its competitors, sometimes one, sometimes the other. In any event, Unique Art, though never a major name, lasted in the business at least until 1952. One clue to its murky history is the 1922 announcement that Ferdinand Strauss had acquired and controlled exclusively the entire output of Unique Art. But in 1925 Unique was noted as being distributed by Louis Marx and Louis Wolf (who was solely a distributor), with no mention at all of any tie to Strauss.

The term "Kiddie Kar" is no longer a household phrase, but forms of that toy exist to this day. It was invented in 1915 by the H. C. White Company of Bennington, Vermont. The idea was simple—and had been anticipated in 1879 in a patent for a similar invention—basically a bicycle that a small child could move with his feet and steer with a steering wheel attached to a single front wheel; it had a seat, and two wheels in the back, and was low enough to the ground so that the young girl or boy could get sufficient traction. The Kiddie Kar was one of the most popular toys ever invented, and one of the few loved by educators and parents as well as the children themselves, as it gave very young children a chance to prepare themselves safely for the tricycle, while helping to coordinate still-uncertain muscles.

For the most part, elaborate metal toy ships were produced by European companies; when American firms, like Ives and Lionel, did get into ship making, it was only as a minor part of their line. The leading exception to this pattern emerged sometime during or just after World War I. Samuel Orkin, of Cambridge, Massachusetts, liked to bill himself as "The Toy Wizard." He built a large working model of a toy ship during the war, and the response he got from displaying it convinced him to manufacture them. His ships were modeled after the real thing—U.S. Naval super dreadnoughts, cruisers, destroyers, and submarine chasers. They were relatively inexpensive and big, ranging in size from about fifteen to thirty-five inches from stem to stern. The firm was later bought by the president of the Waterman Pen Company. Another maker of at least one toy ship during this period was the Walbert Mfg. Co. of Chicago, which in 1915 advertised a "Sinking Battleship With Torpedo"; the ship split apart and sank when struck by the torpedo.

Tin toys cannot be discussed without mentioning the Sandy Andy; virtually anyone who's played at a beach has played with one, or one of its variations (these days usually in plastic). The original was patented in 1909 and turned out by the Sand Toy Company of Pittsburgh. It was simple, but incorporated the kind of action children love. As an early ad by the Sand Toy Company's successor, the Wolverine Company (also of Pittsburgh) explained, "Pour sand in the hopper and Sandy Andy does the rest. The car is drawn up the track by the weight until it opens a swinging shutter on the bottom end of the hopper, allowing the sand to run into the car. When the car is nearly full the added weight of the sand causes the car to run down the track and automatically dump the sand.

"The weight then again pulls the car up for another load and this operation is automatically continued as long as there is sand in the hopper. Great fun for the children." And great fun it was,

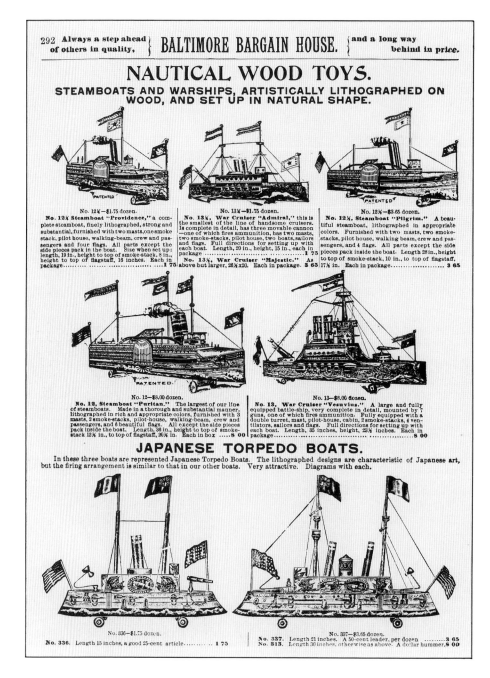

and still is. Wolverine also put out a number of nicely lithographed tin toys, some of them windups, like its famous Drum Major and a well-done diving submarine of the pre–World War II pe-

Dent's cast-iron "Adirondack" steamboat from the early 1900s is 15 inches long. (Sotheby's, New York)

Wooden ships from 1898. The top five ships are probably all Reed's. The two "torpedo boats" don't appear to be Japanese, as they're dubbed *Yankee Doodle* and *Spreadeagle*. OPPOSITE

riod, but its Sandy Andy, in all its variations, is something very special in the history of the American toy industry.

By 1919, that industry, fully matured, bright, energetic, inventive, and continually attracting fresh young blood, seemed to be at an ever-expansive zenith. There would be little in the coming decade to contradict that impression.

TWENTIES BOOM TIME

By most accounts, the 1920s was a glorious decade, and this was certainly true of the toys of that time. The country was more prosperous than ever, and even more on the move. As usual, the toys reflected their period. Toy trains, cars, trucks, and buses led the way.

In the field of vehicles, two names stand out: Arcade and Buddy "L." Arcade had been founded in 1868 as the Novelty Iron Works, located in Freeport, Illinois. The company turned out agricultural products in the beginning—plows and the like, later adding water pumps, coffee mills, and so on. In 1884, when the name was changed to Arcade, one of the firm's officers, E. H. Munn, decided to make toy coffee mills out of the scrap left over from the "real" thing. This was Arcade's first venture into the toy line.

But the company made no real stir in the toy world until the secretary and sales manager of Arcade noticed the profusion of Yellow Cabs on the streets of Chicago. He approached the taxi company owners with an offer: Arcade would get sole rights to reproduce their cabs, and Yellow Cab would gain exclusive rights to use the toy in its ads. The deal was struck, and on December 27, 1921, the Arcade Yellow Cab was kicked off in a public display at Chicago's Sherman Hotel.

It was an instant success. In the words of one Arcade account, "The Yellow Cab seemed to drop like a bolt of lightning from a clear sky." Soon, two thousand cabs a day were being shipped. Seeing what it was on to, Arcade started turning out a line of cast-iron cars, trucks, and buses that have never been surpassed and only occasionally equaled.

A particular favorite was its array of Mack trucks. Everything about them spoke of ruggedness; especially effective were those without windshield supports, suggesting a hard-bitten driver gloriously indifferent to such minor annoyances as rain, wind, hail, and sleet. No doubt because of its past and its proximity to farm country, Arcade also turned out a large line of toy farm equipment: doughty cast-iron tractors, harrows, plows, planters, binders, and the like. Its line of Ford Model T's was another hugely popular offering, and when Ford began making Model A's in 1928, so did Arcade—in coupe, sedan, stake truck, and express truck versions.

Buddy "L" toys, like the tongue-and-groove playthings of Charles M. Crandall, got their start because the owner of the manufacturing company had a child. The man was Fred Lundahl; his son was

"**T**oots and Casper" was a comic strip that began on December 17, 1918. On December 12, 1920, they had a baby, who, after months of agonizing, they finally named Buttercup. The strip was around until at least 1956. This Buttercup and Spare Ribs pull toy is from about 1921. (Bizarre Bazaar, New York) OPPOSITE

A Mack "Lubrite" Gasoline Truck by Arcade, 13¼ inches long, and weighing in at a hefty 7 pounds. (Phillips, New York) INSET

An Arcade Mack Gasoline truck, ca. 1925, cast iron, 13½ inches long. (Mapes Auctioneers, Vestal, New York)

called Buddy L, to distinguish him from the other Buddys in the neighborhood. According to a 1925 company account, when Buddy was four he kept unintentionally breaking his toys. His father sat down with him, and they discussed the kinds of games Buddy would like to play and the type of toy he'd like to play them with. At the end of the discussion, Fred Lundahl promised his son he'd make him a toy that would "last and last."

Lundahl owned the Moline Pressed Steel Company of Moline, Illinois, manufacturing auto and truck parts—fenders and the like. Using the plant equipment, he made a toy truck, all steel, two feet long. It looked very much like the real thing and was an enormous hit. The next year, when Buddy "L" was five, Fred Lundahl brought home a dump truck. Soon, as the Buddy "L" collection grew, and Buddy's playmates clam-

ored for toys of their own, the neighborhood's fathers began asking Lundahl to make them trucks for their own children. What started out as a special present from a father to his son became the foundation for one of the largest and most prestigious toy firms in America.

Buddy "L" toys were known for their accuracy, their size, and their strength. The cars were about a foot long, the trucks two feet or

Arcade's cast-iron 1925 Chevrolet Coupe was one of its more popular toys. (Ed Hyers Antique Toys, Asheville, North Carolina)

more in length. Grown men could stand on them and do no damage. They could be abused and left out in all sorts of weather; though they would show wear, the steel held up. The vehicles came in four groups: trucks, fire trucks, Model T's, and construction equipment. There were also two trains, equally tough and durable. The company is still in business today, without the quotation marks around the *L*.

Lionel had something in common with Buddy "L." Its locomotives were made of sheet steel, the wheels of nickeled steel, and, like the heavily enameled Buddy "L" cars, they were built to last.

A steel auto from about 1920, manufacturer unknown, possibly Turner. (Bizarre Bazaar, New York)

A standard-gauge Lionel freight-train set from the 1920s. (Sotheby's, New York)

But, in advertising and promotion, Lionel went far beyond Buddy "L"—in fact, beyond any toy company of its time. Advertising as we know it today was coming of age in the 1920s, and Lionel's owner, Joshua Lionel Cowen, seemed instinctively to understand all it could do for him. The company launched eye-catching national ad campaigns, with art and copy that packed a punch. Beautifully printed catalogs were also part of the Lionel hype. Those catalogs more than paid their way. The 1920s were a time of monied indulgence, and children got their share of indulging. Electricity was in vogue and giving one's children a set of electric trains at Christmas seemed exactly the thing to do— particularly with Lionel's ads chirping away in the background.

The basic train sets were just part of it; there were also the accessories: headlights that actually lit, individual track switches, automatic crossing gates, automatic warning signals, a huge power station, streetlights, and bungalows and villas that could be arranged around the tracks and which, like the headlights, lit up. In the 1920s Lionel was the largest maker of toy trains in the country, with profits increasing nearly ten times over the level of the previous decade. In 1927, for example, profits were nearly half a million dollars.

There were, of course, competitors. In addition to Ives, was Dorfan, founded in 1924 by two brothers, Julius and Milton Forcheimer, who had worked for a German toy train company known as Fandor. Arriving in Newark, New Jersey, in 1923, the brothers and John C. Koerber, a toy designer they had convinced to immigrate with them, reversed the name of their former employer and set themselves up in business. Dorfan became legendary with train collectors, both for its quality and for its innovations, more

than twenty of which were subsequently picked up by other companies. In its heyday, the firm employed 150.

The fourth big name in trains during the 1920s was American Flyer, of whom we'll hear more later.

A toy that crossed over into two territories —track toys and cartoon toys—was the quaint and colorful Toonerville Trolley, which came out of the popular comic strip "Toonerville Folks." The strip by Fontaine Fox began in 1915, but it was in the 1920s that it reached the height of its popularity and became a boon to toy makers. At least five different manufacturers—three of them American—turned out Toonerville Trolleys, in tin, in lead, and in cast iron.

Other comic-strip characters of the period that had lives as toys included the Gumps, Barney Google, and Maggie and Jiggs of "Bringing Up Father." There were also some Krazy Kat toys, but these were disappointing, as they didn't at all resemble the marvelous feline created by

Schoenhut's Train To Build, ca. 1928. The box uses the red and yellow colors the toy industry has found are the surest grabbers. (MacNary Collection)

Ives No. 703 Electric Train set, with Ives accessories, from the 1920s. (Sotheby's, New York)

the one comic-strip artist universally credited as a genius, George Herriman.

What was probably the most popular cartoon toy of the decade didn't originate in the funnies, though he quickly branched out into them. Created by Otto Messmer, Felix the Cat began about 1919 as a character in animated cartoons produced by Pat Sullivan. The comic strip started up in 1923. Interestingly, Felix failed to reflect the tenor of his time; instead of being buoyant, energetic, and optimistic, he was generally alienated. Carry on he did, but almost always enveloped in an aura of hopelessness.

Despite this, by the 1920s he was being turned out in a variety of forms. Unlike Krazy

Kat, Felix in toy form generally bore a strong resemblance to his movies/strip appearance: an all-black body with a rounded, white-and-black face, and a long, thick tail. Many jointed wooden Felixes were turned out, some by Schoenhut, some distributed by George Borgfeldt, but there were also cast-iron Felixes, pot-metal Felixes, gong-bell Felixes, and tin windup Felixes.

Yet another animated cartoon character popular at the time was Koko the Clown, created by Max Fleischer, better known later for Betty Boop. Koko was born about 1917, but didn't get his name until 1923, evolving from a series called "Out of the Inkwell." The one known American

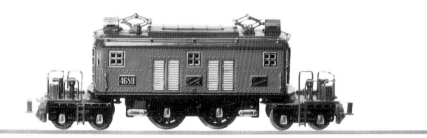

toy version of Koko was produced by Schoenhut, which did a nicely designed, eleven-inch jointed figure in 1925.

The movies were more popular than ever in the 1920s, although individual films rarely gave rise to toys because pictures came and went too quickly. Arcade's 1929 Showboat, made to come out with the movie of the same year, was a rare exception. Film stars, however, had durability. In the 1910s Ferguson Novelty Co. of New York made a Charlie Chaplin doll called Zig-Zag Chap; Louis Amberg, also of New York, had its own Charlie Chaplin doll and in 1914 sold two John Bunny dolls, based on the first comedy star of the silents.

By the 1920s Chaplin came as a bell toy, a windup, a composition doll, and a tin puppet. Harold Lloyd stood in for Marx's Funny Face windup walker in the late 1920s, though there is no evidence he ever authorized the toy. Jackie Coogan emerged as a glass candy container, and Tom Mix had his 1928 Rodeorope. Walt Disney's first successful screen character, Oswald the Rabbit, grazed the toy area as a 1927 celluloid pin-back button and a 1928 stencil set. Later, when Disney was no longer associated with the character, Irwin Toys issued a wood-and-cardboard windup that had stuffed arms and legs, and cloth clothes.

One striking characteristic of toys during

this period was the enormous variety turned out by any given manufacturer. The 1927 Tinkertoys catalog, for instance, had a stunning array of items, all based on the simple Tinkertoy principle of brightly colored turned wood. There were Belle Tinker, a seven-inch-high doll; Belle's twin brother, Tom Tinker, called by the manufacturer "without doubt one of the most successful wooden dolls ever created"; and the Follo-Me Tinker, a pull toy with extra wheels so arranged that no matter how often it turned over, there were always wheels to keep it rolling. The Whirly Tinker featured two whirling sailors (another pull toy), and there was the rather odd Siren Tinker, a series of beads ascending in size to a face that suggested mascaraed eyes and eyebrows and a lipsticked mouth. Two balls (or perhaps bells) hung from the siren's nonexistent

ears. There were Enameled Tinker Beads, which came in three different-sized jars; necklaces could be made from them. The Jump Rope Tinker was obviously for the young and reckless, since it featured wooden beads strung over the length of the rope, presumably resulting in more than a few sharp raps to the head.

This was hardly all. There was a Choo-Choo Tinker, consisting of locomotive and passenger car; a Necklace Tinker; and a Drag-on Tinker pull toy depicting a crawling animal, which, it was advertised, would "invariably right itself." Still they came: the Rowly Boat Tinker, the Pony Tinker, the Clown Tinker, the Surf Boat Tinker, the Lanky Tinker (a skinny wood doll with leather arms and legs), the Seven in One Tinker (a construction toy that could be turned into a locomotive, a wagon, a truck, etc.), Tinkerpins (which consisted of an elevated track and a gyroscopic spinner that knocked down pins), Bunny Tinker, Tinker Fish, a Steam Roller Tinker, a Spinning Jack Tinker, Tinker Dogs, and, about halfway through the forty-eight-page catalog, the Tinkertoy set itself.

Old firms survived only by changing with the times. By 1926, for instance, Gong Bell, which was still making push-and-pull bell toys, made sure that half its line consisted of some variation on a telephone.

Playskool is unusual in that it was one of the few toy companies—and apparently the only successful nondoll company—founded by a woman. Lucille King, a former schoolteacher, worked for the John Schroeder Lumber Company in Milwaukee, Wisconsin. There she originated the idea of marketing wooden toys for preschoolers, basing her designs on teacher aids she and another teacher had developed for use in their classroom. The two teachers formed the Playskool Institute, a division of the John

Two more comic-strip toys: Arcade's cast-iron Andy Gump Car was a good seller, staying in the line from 1923 to 1931. Hubley's cast-iron Popeye Patrol, however, didn't bring in the spinach after its 1938 introduction. (Clinton B. Seeley Collection)

Schroeder Lumber Company. By the end of the decade, Playskool Institute was manufacturing some forty items, mainly wood beads, blackboards, blocks, desks, dollhouses, pegboards, pounding benches (much beloved by preschool boys), and sand and water toys.

Playskool continues to this day. In 1935 it became a division of Thorncraft, Inc., and moved to Chicago. In 1938, the Joseph Lumber Company bought it. Manuel Fink, who had been a buyer for a leading Chicago department store, was hired to run Playskool for Harry Joseph. In 1940 Robert Meythaler joined the company, and within a few years Fink and Meythaler bought the firm and established the Playskool Manufacturing Company, which in 1968 became a subsidiary of Milton Bradley. The firm still turns out versions of some of its earliest toys.

Fully twenty-four years after the Wright Brothers made their historic flight at Kitty Hawk, North Carolina, the toy airplane finally

established itself as a permanent fixture on the toy scene. Before 1927, production had been spotty; there is good reason to believe no American airplane toys were made before 1909. The Wright Brothers, after all, were hardly overnight sensations. There was a period from about 1905 to 1907 when the pair went for nearly a year and a half without making a flight; they were too busy trying to convince the British, French, and German governments to buy their aircraft. Further dimming the spotlight was the Wrights' general avoidance of publicity. As a result, extensive press coverage didn't begin till about 1908. That was the year the U.S. army ordered its first Wright-built airplane. Even then the news was hardly dazzling; the first one crashed in September of that year. It was rebuilt by the Wrights (designated Model B) and delivered in 1909—precisely the year American toy airplanes first appeared in the toy trade magazines.

The May 1909 *Playthings* carried an ad for the Aero Miniature Flying Machine, made by the H. J. Nice Co. of Minneapolis. Like many actual planes of the day, it bore virtually no resemblance to modern aircraft. The top wing (if that's what it was) curved down and touched the bottom wing (if that's what *it* was). Two struts supported the wings, and what vaguely appeared to be a propellor was attached to an appendage hanging from the plane that housed a rubber band or something like it. According to the ad, the Aero was "developed in the making of a successful man-carrying machine." Furthermore, "If started upside down it will right itself and continue flying." It was also "based on scientific principles" and "acknowledged by leading students in Aeronautics as the most wonderful invention of the age." The toy sold for one dollar retail, and measured five inches high and six inches long. The patent date was February 2, 1909.

One of the reasons why people get confused about who made which tin wind-up: Wood's Mechanical Airplane from the 1920s was made by Girard but distributed by Louis Marx. (Perry R. Eichor)

Possibly the most impressive of all toy airplanes is Hubley's trimotor America. The massive cast-iron flying machine has a 17-inch wingspan, and was on sale at least as early as 1928. (The plane at bottom is a German-made tin wind-up). (Sotheby's, New York)

In July of that year, what may have been the second American-made toy plane, the Lee Toy Aeroplane, was advertised by the Baber Toy Aeroplane Mfg. Co. of Dayton, Ohio. This sold for only fifty cents and was sixteen inches long with a twenty-four-inch wingspan. According to the ad, "When wound up it will by its own power scribe two or three circles in the air, total length of flight being about 100 feet."

In September, the final new airplane adver-tised that year was sold by F. E. Fuchs, of 38 Park Row, New York City, which, according to the ad, had its factory and "proving grounds" in St. Albans, Queens. Called the Aeroplane Flyer, it was very simply made, with three American flags attached. (Those flags weren't fanciful; in July, 1908, "Farman's biplane"—wingspan 32.8 feet—flew at Brighton Beach, Brooklyn, two fluttering Stars and Stripes attached to its tail section.) From the looks of it, the Aeroplane

Flyer, patent pending, worked like a kite, lifting off as you ran before it, holding the string attached to its front.

Another early starter was Tootsietoy (then known as Dowst), with three 1910 versions of a Bleriot monoplane.

Then, on May 20, 1927, Charles Lindbergh became the first man—and an American to boot! —to fly alone from New York to Paris. Lindbergh's feat, combined with his boyish good looks and self-effacing charm, became a major symbol of the 1920s, and toy manufacturers quickly took note. Hubley turned out a cast-iron version of the *Spirit of St. Louis*, marking it "Lindy." Tootsietoy, its lawyers apparently chary of getting too Lindy-like without authorization, marketed its version as the "Aero-Dawn," while Barclay slush-cast its own unmarked puddle-jumper. Dent issued a cast-iron "Lucky Boy," American Flyer produced a monoplane adver-

tised as "A pull toy created to meet the youngster's dream for toys like 'Lindy's,'" and Marx made at least two *Spirits of St. Louis.*

As records continued to be set and noted in the nation's newspapers, toy-airplane production accelerated. Shortly after Lindy's historic flight, the *American* and then the *Friendship* flew the Atlantic; Hubley commemorated them both. In 1928, Germany's *Bremen* made the more difficult east–west crossing (more difficult because of the adverse prevailing wind direction), and Hubley and Barclay quickly issued their versions of the plane, each of them retaining the oddly striated fuselage of the original. Other airplane manufacturers included Kingsbury, Keystone, Boycraft, Strauss, and Arcade.

It wasn't only airplanes making headlines in the 1920s. Dirigibles and zeppelins, like the *Graf Zeppelin*, the *Los Angeles*, and the *Akron*, were made in steel, tin, iron, and lead by such companies as

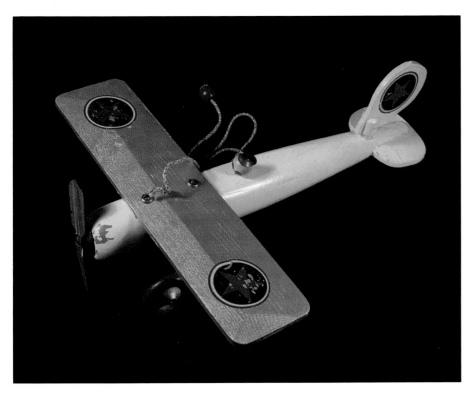

Marx, Strauss, Dent, Steelcraft, Boycraft, and Barclay.

All in all, it was a great era for toy makers (and toy buyers!). Quality was the watchword.

Cast-iron toys were almost exclusively American, and two concerns that consistently came up to Arcade's high standard—or nearly so —were Hubley and Kenton.

Hubley, of Lancaster, Pennsylvania, was founded around 1892 by John E. Hubley, a bank teller who started by making toys for his own children in the basement of his house. Hubley died in 1900, but the firm retained his name. Its early toys included trains, ferris wheels, coal ranges, and mechanical banks. In 1922 it introduced one of its greatest lines, a series of horse-drawn circus wagons known as the Royal Circus. They were beautifully done, with much decorative detail, and included such esoterica as bandwagons, calliopes, a Monkey Trapeze mirror

van, a wagon that held a clown on a trapeze, and the Farmer Van, in which a huge farmer's head revolved, appearing and disappearing at the top of the wagon as it was drawn along. It was also in the 1920s that Hubley designed and manufactured what many believe to be the finest cast-iron toy ever made: a Packard Straight 8, an eleven-inch-long, low-slung beauty. Its front doors opened, it had a driver figure, detailed seats, an engine hood that opened to reveal a nicely done cast-iron engine, and overall detailing that was rare in cast iron.

The Packard headed an extensive line of well-designed cast-iron cars, trucks, buses, fire engines, road-building equipment, and motorcycles. For some reason, perhaps because Hub-

A Chein tin wind-up Ferris Wheel, from the 1930s. (Don Hultzman)

Hubley's Royal Circus was generally a popular toy, but these two cast-iron items seem to have attracted few buyers, judging by their rarity: the Giraffe Cage and the Farmer's Van just ahead of it. The farmer's head bobs up and down as the rear wheels turn. (Sotheby's, New York)

ley was so large a company that it could afford to take chances with toys that skirted the fringes of popularity, the firm had the motorcycles area almost entirely to itself. Virtually without exception their models of the racy two-wheelers were rugged-looking affairs that inspired all sorts of small boys' games.

Hubley was also a leader in "exclusive right" toys, and in that area again ventured into fields few other makers cared to risk. Among them were its Old Dutch Cleanser woman and its Jantzen Beach Patrol and Jantzen Surf Girl. Among its wide range of other toys was a very popular and extensive line of cap pistols.

In the early 1920s, Kenton featured an attractive line of animal-drawn cars, wagons, and fire equipment, but stopped production of them in the mid-1920s to concentrate on more modern toys. Kenton was one of the first companies to realize the attraction toy cars might have for children, and quickly became one of the leaders in that field, with those toys becoming its predominant line.

After the Big Three of Arcade, Hubley, and Kenton, there were a number of other makers of quality cast-iron toys. Dent, of Fullerton, Pennsylvania, was one of the best, offering a number of nicely modeled planes, zeppelins, animal-drawn toys, cars, cabs, fire engines, trucks, road equipment, and buses. Dent was also one of the first toy companies to offer aluminum playthings, though ultimately without success. Aluminum had been around since the 1860s, but was slow in achieving acceptance; in 1886, the world production of aluminum was less than one hundred pounds. Even in the 1920s it was still a wonder metal. Aluminum also meant far lighter castings, which translated into much lower freight charges, a concern of toy companies since the early days. But there was a problem with aluminum in toys. To the child used to cast iron, an aluminum truck felt too light, and (unlike the equally light plastic of later years) aluminum didn't offer exquisite detailing to offset this defect.

An almost wholly anonymous manufacturer of cast-iron toys during this period was Grey Iron, of Mount Joy, Pennsylvania, which poured out a stream of trains, pistols, soldiers, and vehicles during the 1920s. No later records seem to exist, but it is known that in 1921 Grey Iron had seventy employees, who were paid nineteen to thirty-seven cents an hour. Since the company marked none of its toys, it inspired little loyalty from the children who bought its products, and until the rise of interest in old toy soldiers in the 1970s and 1980s, the company was ignored by historians. We'll return to Grey Iron in a later chapter.

Better known in the cast-iron field were J. & E. Stevens of Cromwell, Connecticut (established 1843), Kilgore, and A. C. Williams. Stevens during this period was still churning out its mechanical banks and cap pistols. Kilgore, of Westerville, Ohio, seems to have begun making toys in the 1920s and very quickly became one of the major names of its time, turning out a number of nicely done cast-iron toys. Cap pistols

were the mainstay of the company, with cars, fire engines, and trucks among its other popular toys. A Ford Tri-Motor airplane, with a thirteen-inch wingspan, was one of Kilgore's standout toys, as were a Chris Craft boat, a Stutz Roadster, and an Airport Gasoline Tanker. Most of Kilgore's toys were low-priced. The first owner of the company was a Mr. Kilgore. In 1921 he sold out, and W. L. Payne became the firm's president.

A. C. Williams was one of the largest pro-

An impressive cast-iron motorcycle variant by Hubley, late 1920s. (Ed Hyers Antique Toys, Asheville, North Carolina)

This rugged four-cylinder Indian motorcycle was made about 1929 by Hubley. (Ed Hyers Antique Toys, Asheville, North Carolina.

Dent's cast-iron Parcel Express truck from the late 1920s. Arcade made a very similar version. (Ed Hyers Antique Toys, Asheville, North Carolina)

ducers of small cast-iron cars and trucks. The company had been founded in 1844 by John Williams, whose son, Adam Clark Williams, took over the business in 1866, on the death of John. First located in Chagrin Falls, Ohio, the firm moved to Ravenna, Ohio, in 1892. Like many cast-iron companies, Williams made hardware as well as toys. Sad irons seem to have been the earliest A. C. Williams toys. Toy banks, airplanes, cars, trucks, tractors, and horse-drawn vehicles followed, most selling for a dime. Toy production seems to have stopped by the end of 1938, though the company itself continued.

A 16-inch-long cast-iron truck by Dent, ca. 1923. (Sotheby's, New York)

Buddy "L" had its competitors in the pressed-steel line. There were the three K's—Kelmet, Keystone, and Kingsbury—plus Turner, Steelcraft, and Structo among the better-known names.

Kelmet, also known as Trumodel and Big Boy, was founded in January 1925 by several of Chicago's wholesale toy representatives, who decided to manufacture steel toys that could compete with the large-sized steel trucks and construction equipment of the era. They subcontracted with A. C. Gilbert, who found them some existing tooling for a Burdette-Murray toy dump truck, and Gilbert workers did the actual assembling. White trucks (White was the name of a manufacturer) were a highlight of Kelmet's

▲ Kenton cast-iron Fire Pumper with Gong, ca. 1920 (Mapes Auctioneers, Vestal, New York)

▲ 1929 horse-drawn cement mixer by Kenton in cast iron. (Ed Hyers Antique Toys, Asheville, North Carolina)
OPPOSITE

Fire patrols were popular cast-iron toys. This one is from Kenton, ca. 1929. (Ed Hyers Antique Toys, Asheville, North Carolina)

Open double-decker buses are always eye-catching, and Kenton made several particularly attractive ones. These two cast-iron toys were sold in the 1920s. (Clinton B. Seeley Collection) RIGHT

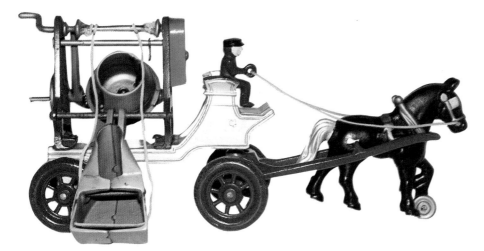

plane, as well as some construction equipment. Keystone helped popularize its products by picturing a 250-pound man standing atop one of their toys.

Kingsbury was strongly oriented during the 1920s toward automotive toys built of steel and, for the most part, windup-motor-driven.

The John C. Turner Company of Wapakoneta, Ohio, concentrated mainly on friction-powered automotive toys. Turner was one of the few manufacturers to offer mail-order toys directly to the public, advertising in national mag-

production. The trucks were all in the neighborhood of two feet long, with an average weight of about ten pounds.

Keystone, of Boston, Massachusetts, had started out by making toy movie projectors and 8 mm films that featured stars of the period like Chaplin and Tom Mix. Later, like Kelmet, deciding Buddy "L" could use some competition, the firm secured rights from Packard to copy its trucks. The Packard truck hood, radiator, and logo were standard items on Keystone's line. They also made Packard-type fire trucks, dump trucks, mail trucks, and a nicely done mail

azines. One of its notable models was a 1926 Lincoln sedan, which measured twenty-seven inches long and weighed ten pounds. It sold for about fifteen dollars.

Structo, of Freeport, Illinois, was founded in 1908 and by the 1920s was best known for its automotive kits, which included trucks, fire engines, a tank, and a tractor. Structo had gotten into the toy business as a maker of Erector-type sets. After World War I it began to concentrate on cars and trucks, originally in the form of construction kits. For a while, in the late 1920s and early 1930s, A. C. Gilbert acted as the firm's distributor. The automotive kits of the 1920s were copied from Stutz models. Structo also sold a range of ready-made wheeled toys, some with windup motors. A number of these toys were painted a very bright red (red and yellow have traditionally been considered the best eye-catchers in toys).

Tin windup toys were all the rage in the 1920s, and if any toy personified its era, it was Marx's eccentric-motor College Boy cars—Whoopee Cars, Limping Lizzies, and Jalopy Fords—most with bywords of the era scribbled on them: "So's Your Old Man," "Don't Bring Lulu," "My Lizzie of the Valley," "Is Zat So!" and "Hotsie Totsie." The toys were so popular that they were still being issued—and *still* as Model T's—in the 1950s.

Louis Marx began working for tin windup king Ferdinand Strauss about 1915; by the next year, at age twenty, he was an officer of the company. A falling out with Strauss resulted in his going out on his own, and in 1921 (Strauss went into brief receivership in 1921 which may have prompted the move), teaming with his brother Dave, he began making his own toys (buying dies from Strauss, who had temporarily gone out of business). The personable Marx became such a favorite with commercial toy buyers that he had little need for other salesmen or even sales catalogs.

His odd little cars were only a small part of the Marx line in the 1920s. There were Climbing Monkeys, Coon Jiggers, Spic and Span (a black musical duo), and the Charleston Trio, with its dancer, fiddler, and small dog holding a cane and nodding to the beat. There were chicken snatchers, racing cars, and the eye-catching Honeymoon Express. The latter featured a tiny train

A handsome Keystone No. 49 Fire Truck from the late 1920s. Heavy-duty steel, 28 inches long. (Joe Freed)

Kingsbury's steel Record Cars from 1927–31 were models of actual record-setters. (Bizarre Bazaar, New York)

that raced around a track, through tunnels, and past a building and simulated terrain. Continually updated, this toy lasted for decades.

Similar to the Honeymoon Express but more expensive were a series of panoramic windups like Main Street, Busy Bridge, and Big Parade, all of which featured moving traffic along a narrow tin street, road, or bridge. Main Street,

for instance, included cars, streetcars, trucks, a traffic cop, a statue, a fruit vendor, a little lady waiting to cross the street, and a barbershop.

In 1928 Marx revived the yo-yo, selling millions. There was also a whole array of push cars and trains, plus colorful accessories like gas stations, and a cheap, jaunty-looking line of windup tin trains. These, known as the Joy Line,

The usual Marx phantasmagoria, this time from 1928. (MacNary Collection)

Strauss's Bus de Luxe from 1927—a tin wind-up and a very happy-looking boxtop. (Bizarre Bazaar, New York)

Strauss's Tip Top the Walking Porter tin wind-up from 1920. The box is fun, too. (Bizarre Bazaar, New York)

first appeared in 1927 or 1928, manufactured for Marx by the Girard Model Works.

The history of Girard, like the histories of so many tin windup outfits, is tangled and murky. What *is* known is that the firm was located in Girard, Pennsylvania. C. G. Wood founded it in 1906, making patterns, models, and special machinery. His son, Frank, was made a partner a few years later. In 1918 they began making mechanical toys for "a large firm in New York" (otherwise unidentified). In 1920 they marketed them under their own name, as "Wood's Mechanical Toys." By 1922 they were making eight different mechanical toys and employed twenty men and sixty women. That same year men from Girard and Erie bought into the firm; the new president was S. Boyd, the secretary Stan Connell, and the secretary-treasurer Fred Ziesenheim, with Frank G. Wood a director of the company along with the other officers.

Lithographed tin wind-up trucks by Strauss, ca. 1925. Accessories made toys more fun. (Bizarre Bazaar, New York)

Strauss's appropriately colorful Santee Clause tin wind-up, ca. 1921. (Bizarre Bazaar, New York)

Strauss's Yell-O-Taxi tin wind-up. (Wilkinson Collection, Detroit Antique Toy Museum)

Louis Marx was in charge of marketing. About 1925, Fred Ziesenheim and Stan Connell bought the business, and all patents were assigned to them. Connell left in 1928, moving to California with a friend, John Katzeman. For a while they manufactured toys there. Ziesenheim continued on in Girard, and in 1933, Katzeman returned from California and joined (or rejoined) him in the business. The firm had as many as a thousand employees by 1931, with Louis Marx serving as their salesman or distributor. Further confusing things, Marx seems to have manufactured toys for Girard using the Marx trademark.

During the Depression, Girard began struggling. Unwisely, the company decided to drop

Two Marx tin wind-up Army Trucks from about 1925. (Bizarre Bazaar, New York)

Two Marx tin litho wind-up trucks from the late 1920s and early 1930s. (Bizarre Bazaar, New York)

Louis Marx to save his 8 to 10 percent commission. Told he'd been fired, Marx bought a plant in Morgantown, West Virginia, where he hoped to produce toys that would take the place of the ones he had sold for Girard. In the meantime, he stalled Girard's customers as he waited for his new plant to get into operation. The buyers knew Marx better than they did the people at Girard, and they fell into line. Its sales slumping disastrously, Girard declared bankruptcy in 1934. Marx, to whom the firm owed much money, took the company's common stock in payment. He then told the employees, who owned the firm's preferred stock, that he would fold the plant unless they turned their stock over to him, fifty cents on the dollar. They did, and apparently without rancor: their jobs were saved, and they seem to have found Marx to be very intelligent and a savvy businessman. Archie Marcus, a CPA friend of Marx's, was installed as overseer. He turned out to be even better liked than Marx.

Girard began making electric trains in 1938 and stayed in business until 1980, though its last toys seem to have come off the assembly line in 1975. Many of Girard's and Marx's toys are

A Girard painted tin touring bus, ca. 1920, 12 inches long. (Mapes Auctioneers, Vestal, New York)

Toy grocery stores have long been favorites with children. This 1920s set from Wolverine is a particularly attractive version. (Don Hultzman)

Wolverine assortment, including Sandy Andy toys, 1928. (MacNary Collection)

interchangeable, since the Girard and Marx tin windups, including cars and trucks, were all made at the Girard plant during that period. Among the windup toys identified as Girard products (the company often neglected to mark its toys) are Flasho, the Mechanical Grinder from the 1920s; Mailplane, a high-wing monoplane also from that period; Gobble, the Gobbling Goose; a bus; a man pushing a wheelbarrow; and a railroad handcar.

Lindstrom, which made windups of light pressed steel as well as tin, was located in Bridgeport, Connecticut. Its full name was Lindstrom Tool & Toy Company, and it began making toy cars about 1913. In addition to windup cars, it also made boats, planes, walking toys, and a Coney Island–type bumper car.

Also keeping busy in the field was Wolverine, maker of the Sandy Andy line of beach toys. Wolverine was founded in 1903 in Pittsburgh by B. F. Bain, who hailed from Wolverine, Michigan. Among the company's toys of the 1920s were a Sandy Andy mechanical tank, a mechanical tractor and trailer, a Gee Whiz horse race, a Kiddie Kampers group of mechanical kids who looked like Boy Scouts and Girl Scouts; and a Sunny Andy Fun Fair, which featured boys and girls on mechanical carnival rides. Wolverine eventually became a subsidiary of Spang Industries and moved to Booneville, Arkansas, in 1970.

To the purist who feels toys should educate and encourage imagination, tin windups are not the ideal toys. But they were a major part of the toy field for decades, because of their ingenuity, their range, their eye-catching color lithography, their humor, and—a most important consideration—their generally low prices.

What a decade it had been! By 1929 there were 539 toy factories in the United States, which had become the world's leading producer of toys. Imports totaled just four million dollars, while U.S. output of toys exceeded ninety million dollars. Things could only get better, couldn't they? And yet . . .

And yet there was Ives.

Ives was still in business and still the most beloved of toy companies. The company had reached a crest, with about one hundred regular employees and another two hundred or so taken on during the busy times. The firm's main lines were now their trains and their clockwork ships. In 1918, Edward N. Hurley, then chairman of the United States Shipping Board, had convinced Harry Ives that it was his patriotic duty to produce toy ships that would inspire boys to

make U.S. shipping their future. The first vessel was issued in December 1918, with Ives scrapping costly new dies and redesigning them along the way to ensure the absolute authenticity of his fleet.

Alas, the ships didn't sell, and Ives executives continually urged Harry to phase out the line. But he stubbornly refused, still imbued with Hurley's admonition that the ships would do much to enhance the future of the country's shipping industry. There were other problems, too. Prices in the 1920s were soaring, but competition forced Ives to keep its prices down. Again, executives suggested sacrificing quality, but Ives refused. Quality had always paid off for the company before, and in a time of such prosperity it

Orkin produced this impressive Cabin Cruiser about 1928. (Bizarre Bazaar, New York) OPPOSITE

A tin wind-up toy from 1921, the Walbert Ferry by Walbert Manufacturing Company, 13¾ inches long. (Bizarre Bazaar, New York) OPPOSITE, BOTTOM

In 1925, Rich Toys helped Bloomingdale's celebrate itself with this wooden toy. (Bizarre Bazaar, New York) BELOW

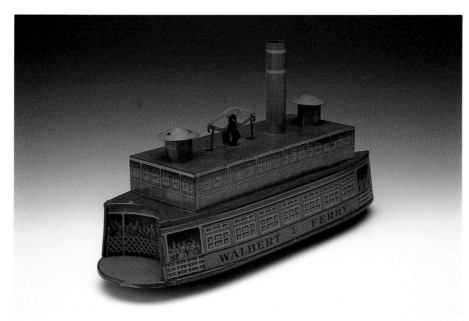

must have seemed that quality could only prove even more of a lure.

But on a dreary September day in 1929, Harry Ives walked out of the factory for the last time. He had lost it to his creditors. Despite the problems, there had never seemed to be any chance of the company's going under. Then, suddenly, after sixty-one years, it did. There have been many explanations, but none has been completely satisfactory.

Ives was a veteran company that produced some of the greatest toys in the history of this country and was still producing them on the day Harry Ives left. In an era as buoyant and monied as the 1920s, the bankruptcy shouldn't have happened. But it did. Was there anyone on that day in 1929 who wondered if it could be a harbinger?

DEPRESSION PLAYTHINGS

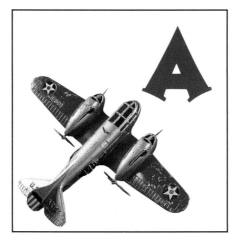

A small boy walks purposefully into a five-and-ten. He moves quickly across the plain wooden floor and pushes up to a counter topped by a double-tiered glass case. There he stares at row upon row of toy soldiers. After considerable staring and even more mulling, he points firmly toward a single soldier. "I want that one," he tells the salesgirl. She reaches for it.

Before it arrived in the store, that toy soldier was individually hand cast. Then it was trimmed by hand. After that it was hand sprayed with a base lacquer, taken (by hand) to be dried, and, once dry, returned for spraying the other side. That done, it was taken off again to be dried and then started down an assembly line, where it was hand painted by a number of girls and women, each attending to a specific operation. Flesh tones were added to face and hands, the stand was painted green, puttees orange. A single brush stroke painted the rifle red or blue. Someone added dots of yellow for buttons.

The process still wasn't over. Lips had to be daubed in, and finally, by those with the surest touch, the eyes delineated. A clip was inserted by hand into a tin helmet, and then the helmet placed atop the soldier's head. Somewhere before or after this, the soldier was carted away once again to be dried. After an hour or so, it was individually wrapped in paper and placed, with a number of its similarly shrouded fellows, in a gray chipboard box. The box was numbered and shipped out.

If that soldier arrived at W. T. Grant's about 1935, a label, preprinted with "W. T. Grant Co. 25¢ 50¢ $1.00 Dept. Stores," was put into a typewriter, and the date that the individual soldier had been received, its model number, and its price were typed on it. The label was then pasted to the underbase of the soldier. Finally, the soldier was carefully set into the glass case our imaginary boy had been staring into. Once he made his choice, the salesgirl removed the soldier, wrapped a scrap of thin paper around it, and then put it into a paper bag.

The price for this hand-painted, hand-manufactured, hand-wrapped, hand-bagged soldier? Five cents. Welcome to hard times.

But let's stay with the child for another moment or two. Because something revolutionary was going on here. Our child came into the store alone, or maybe with a friend or two. He didn't come in with a parent—or any other grown-up.

Marx's Charlie McCarthy and Mortimer Snerd Private Car tin wind-up from 1939. (Bizarre Bazaar, New York) OPPOSITE

Kids fought all kinds of battles before and during World War II with Hubley's Airacuda, whereas the actual plane almost never got off the ground—and certainly never left the U.S. New in 1941. (Perry R. Eichor) INSET

The Depression was almost as hard on children as it was on adults, but it did give that generation of kids something quite magical, a gift that would last more than two decades: a degree of control and self-sufficiency. From the 1930s until about the middle part of the 1950s—when more and more children found themselves in suburban areas where toy stores couldn't be walked to, and more and more mom-and-pop shops found they couldn't compete against the growing number of discounters—children had far more discretion over their toy-buying money than anytime before or since. The Great Depression had created a new world, a penny, nickel, and dime world. For some children there was the occasional excursion to a department store or "good" toy store, but for the most part during those long, ill-lit years (who could afford a high-wattage light bulb?), children's toys were purchased at the five-and-ten, and usually without adult supervision. No mother saying, "What would you do with *that*?" or "You already *have* one of those." No father putting in his two cents' worth about the toy *he* was attracted to. A young boy or girl walked in on their own, and walked out of the store with exactly the toy he or she wanted. *Freedom.*

Possibly the greatest toy symbol of the era was the soldier. It was about as cheap as a toy could get, almost wholly confined to inexpensive stores, and, as war clouds inexorably gathered, it was very much a product of its time. During this period the soldier reached its apex, selling in the millions.

The first important company to produce what is known as a dimestore soldier (roughly 3 to 3¼ inches in height) was Grey Iron, whose origins go back to 1840. On August 4, 1917, the firm had been granted two patents for 40-millimeter solid cast-iron Grey Klip armies. For some reason, the dishlike steel helmets that were introduced late in World War I (much more evocative than the soft headgear they replaced), don't seem to have made an impression on the early postwar soldier makers. All of Grey Iron's tiny figures—marching troops, flagbearers, drummers, buglers, shell-loaders, mounted and foot officers—wore uniforms and hats that seemed more properly to belong to the Spanish-American War of 1898. Nevertheless, once the soldiers found their market, they were popular and lasted in the same form through 1938, a modernized version of them taking over between that year and 1941.

However, aside from the Grey Klips, American-made metal soldiers seem to have gone into a decline in the 1920s and early 1930s. The Connecticut-based Ideal Toy Co. tried a small array

An example of attractive packaging—boxtop, box contents, and the colorful ads on the trucks. Lindstrom produced these tin trucks about 1930. (Bizarre Bazaar, New York)

of approximately 54-millimeter-high hollow-cast lead soldiers from about 1920 to 1924. Their crudeness as castings was only partially offset by their attractive paint jobs, and they made little impact on the market.

Another maker of hollow-cast lead soldiers was New York City's Pearlytoys, which set up shop by 1928. The firm offered an array of mounted and foot figures, of which at present only the mounted officer is known. Black Friday, 1929, may have done the company in, because in March 1930, it was supplanted by Soljertoys, captained by the same owner, S. Rosenberg.

Soljertoys' figures were crude (the company produced the Pearlytoys mounted officer with most—but not all—of the "Pearlytoys" marking removed) and not particularly well painted. However, some of the figures, crude as they are, contain exceptionally sharp and fine detail. The firm marketed doughboys, sailors, cadets, marines, and cowboys and Indians, selling some in Paint-A-Toy kits, which allowed the purchaser to do the painting himself. Soljertoys seems to have remained in business until 1936 or 1937, but judging by the few examples of its soldiers that turn up—and by the general lack of nostalgia for the company's products—it must have been a marginal manufacturer through all of its history.

As early as 1930 a maker of rhinestone ornaments, New York's Cosmo Ornament Co., Inc. (also known as Cosmo Novelty Co.), produced what seems to have been the forerunner of the dimestore toy soldier proper—a hollow-cast lead soldier in a three-inch-plus size. Cosmos were crudely designed—almost certainly pirated from German composition soldiers—and dismayingly painted; and, from all evidence, the firm sank from view by 1932.

Fortunes for the American metal soldier

began to look up in January 1933, when Grey Iron announced a new line of thirty-five different cast-iron soldiers. These were approximately three inches high, with rather frail-looking physiques. They were designed simply but pleasingly and from all indications were at least a modest success. Then in 1934, whether because of increasing intimations of war or a development in the public taste perhaps fostered by Grey Iron's new figures, toy soldiers were suddenly hot items.

One company that took advantage of this trend was the Barclay Mfg. Co. of New Jersey, which had been producing military toys since 1924 (possibly a year or two earlier) with indifferent success. (In the early 1930s, its biggest seller was a tiny racing car, one of its many non-military vehicles.) Barclay geared up and, in 1934 or early 1935, produced a soldier that became the giant of the American toy-soldier industry. At first glance, the figure was hardly prepossessing: very stiff looking, with childlike proportions, and odd eyes that always stared to

Ideal Toy Co. of Bridgeport, Connecticut, produced approximately 2-inch-high soldiers, sailors, Indians, figures for train sets, and ballplayers from about 1920 to 1924. The cannon was also produced by Ideal. (Ed Poole)

Barclay's pre-World War II civilian figures seem to have been about as popular as its soldiers.

Various figures produced by New Jersey's Barclay Mfg. Co. from about 1936 to early 1942.

the side. But a good-quality lacquer made it shiny, and a separate tin helmet (glued on in the first couple of years of production) was an attractive innovation. The first line of Barclay's dimestore figures seems to have consisted of twenty-three pieces, two of them simply paint-job variations. In addition to eleven infantry-men, there were two knights, a pirate, a cowboy (with separate tin brim), two Indians, a cadet, three sailors, and two marines. The soldiers sold phenomenally well, and in 1935–36, four more models were added to take advantage of the Ital-ian-Ethiopian War: an Italian officer, an Italian soldier, and their Ethiopian counterparts, which, in 1937, were replaced by similar Japanese and Chinese types.

At first, the soldiers were slush-cast, like Barclay's other toys and novelties. In slush-cast-ing, a mold holds a single impression, and lead is poured into the mold, which is immediately turned over so that most of the lead pours out, leaving behind a thin layer of metal that adheres to the walls of the mold. This is a hollow casting. Later, Barclay turned to injection molding, in which lead is forced up into the mold and the residue immediately sucked out.

By 1937, Barclay changed the look of its soldiers. Sometime during the Ethiopian war, it had abandoned the rather foolish eyes-askance expression; now those eyes gazed straight ahead (Barclay's eyes, incidentally, consisted of a dot touching a curved line representing the eyelid; eyebrows came only on the company's premium-priced 1937 American Legionnaires). The com-pany also began producing what collectors have termed "long-stride" figures, soldiers with far more movement depicted and a much more re-alistic look.

Both the short-stride and long-stride sol-diers were sculpted by Frank Krupp. Until re-

1
2
1

Auburn Rubber's toys were a big dimestore attraction in the 1930s. This racer is an outsized 10½ inches long. (Mapes Auctioneers, Vestal, New York)

Manoil was the second-largest maker of lead soldiers and related toys from the mid-1930s until the mid-1950s, trailing only Barclay. This catalog page, ca. 1939, shows the variety produced during the late 1930s and early 1940s. OPPOSITE

Auburn Rubber's soldier line, ca. 1941, plus three of its popular baseball players, introduced in 1939.

tion. Auburn Rubber of Auburn, Indiana, had been in business since 1910, making auto tires and inner tubes (and later, rubber soles and heels, flyswatters, stair treads, and so on). In

cently, American-made toy soldiers were looked down upon by soldier collectors as crude and inartistic. True or not, the fact is that many dimestore soldiers were created by trained artists. Krupp, for instance, had studied in New York at Cooper Union, concentrating on architectural drafting for four years. Olive Kooken, who followed him at Barclay (yes, a woman, and not the only one to sculpt American toy soldiers), had determined to make her living as a sculptor, and during 1927 and 1928 studied at New York's Art Students League under Edward McCartan.

From 1934 on, Barclay (named for its first location, Barclay Street in West Hoboken, New Jersey) was the largest manufacturer of toy soldiers in the country, growing from a work force of one hundred in 1928 to four hundred by 1940. Barclay produced nearly half a million soldiers, vehicles, airplanes, and other toys every week, almost all of them sold in five-and-tens across the country.

Soon other companies jumped into produc-

65 Deep Sea Diver   64 Sold. Playing Banjo   56 Paymaster   61 Sold. with Camera   68 Sold. Boxing

62 Sold. with Gas Mask & Gun   59 Soldier Writing Letter   63 Sold. with Gas Mask with Flare Pistol   67 Sold. with Gun and Pack Marching   55 Sitting Sold. at Table with Phone & Map   66 Soldier with Gun on Parade with Overseas Cap

51 Motorized M.G.   57 Camouflage Sharpshooter Lying Down   19 Cannon—S.P. 10c

60 Cook's Helper with Ladle   70 Soup Kitchen   72 Water Wagon   71 Shell Carrier with Sold. on Shell Box   73 Tractor

75 Armored Car with Anti-Aircraft Gun   69 Cannon—S.P. 5c   74 Armored Car with Anti-Tank Gun

1935, owner A. L. Murray steamed off to England and came back with a toy Palace Guard. "Let's see if we can make this in rubber" is more or less what he said. In short order, a local artisan made patterns and then original molds in lead. Samples were cast, painted, and presented to buyers. From that day on, Auburn was into toy making.

Its first toys were five soldiers, all of them rather spindly looking, which suggests that if Auburn was aping anyone's product, it was Grey Iron's. Although it's not known just what the first five figures were, the likelihood is that two were Palace Guards, who also doubled as a Foreign Legion officer and a Foreign Legionnaire—though neither wore the standard "Beau Geste" headgear; something like a pith helmet, then in use by the actual Legion, topped each. A doughboy at port arms, a doughboy bugler, and a striking mounted officer in greatcoat probably comprised the rest of the firm's initial offering.

Auburn's dimestore soldiers were a hit, and the line soon expanded, the figures also becoming more robust. Auburn never added the standard cowboys and Indians during those prewar days, but it did come up with an attractive line of baseball players and some football players. Nor did Auburn stop with human figures. It added a line of vehicles, including, first of all, a Cord—a make of car produced in Auburn—airplanes, farm animals, sponge-rubber blocks, quoits, hammers, hatchets, knives, circus sets, bunnies, scotties, and "storybook characters." Auburn's biggest seller was its tractor, which sold in the millions and was seen everywhere in those Depression days.

The fourth of America's Big Four toy-soldier makers during this period was Manoil Mfg. Co., a combine of three forces: Jack and Maurice Manoil, the Rumanian immigrants who owned the

Slush-cast lead cars were usually turned out in a single color to cut costs. With the exception of the trailer, the vehicles in the top two rows were made by San Francisco's Tip Top Toy Co. in the 1920s and 1930s. The yellow Cord is the only vehicle made by New Jersey's Tommy Toy known to bear the mark of its manufacturer. (Clinton B. Seeley)

company, and Walter Baetz, a Moravian from Canada who was its longtime sculptor-designer. The company had begun as Jack Manoil & Co. in 1927, located in Manhattan's Greenwich Village. In 1934 it produced its first toys, four 4½-inch-long die-cast cars—two sedans, a coupe, and a wrecker. One of the sedans and the coupe were startingly original in design, with an art-deco flair, the earliest evidence of Baetz's distinctive talent. It is not known if, like Barclay's Frank Krupp and Olive Kooken, Walter Baetz was a trained artist, but there is no doubt that he was a serious one. In his spare time he painted, and he *sold* his paintings.

A year later, Manoil issued its first soldiers. They were similar to Barclays as far as size and range of figures went, but they were distinctively Baetz–Manoil in design. Their stride, unlike that of the Barclay soldiers, was jaunty from the start (possibly inspiring the changeover at Barclay), and there was corresponding verve to the rest of Manoil's soldiers, sailors, cadets, and cowboys and Indians. The first Manoils, with a concave underbase, soon gave way to a second type, even more jaunty, but distinctly on the portly side. In time they were joined by a third type, leaner and more realistic, but with just as much energy.

Manoil's soldiers, which were soon supplemented by a line of cannon and military wheeled toys, seem to have started off slowly. Few collectors remember anything much about them before 1939 or so. By 1941, however, Manoil was even beginning to crowd the giant in the field, Barclay, in dimestore displays.

Although the Big Four dominated the field, there were a number of smaller companies that sprang up as well. One, Bergen Toy & Novelty Co., also known as Beton, started off as a metal toy-soldier maker, using the molds of a company called Metal Cast, which sold its casting forms to would-be toy makers across the country. But in 1938, the Carlstadt, New Jersey, company became the first manufacturer to turn out plastic toy soldiers. From the start the line was extensive, including soldiers, cowboys, Indians, and cadets, which quickly made their way into the nation's five-and-tens.

Barclay soon found itself being used as a springboard for other companies. Barclay had been founded by Leon Donze, a French immigrant toy maker, and businessman Michael Levy. Levy soon edged Donze out of the business, and in 1935 Donze was associated with a company called Tommy Toy in Union City, New Jersey. Today, no one remembers exactly what his function was; presumably, he furnished the arguments that convinced a doctor and the owner of a taxi fleet to start the business. Quite possibly he also furnished technical expertise and even some of the molds. In any case, Tommy Toy turned out vehicles, soldiers, and a group of ten nursery-rhyme characters that seem to have been the company's biggest seller. All the soldiers and fairy-tale toys were marked "Tommy Toy," while only one of the vehicles, a Cord, was similarly marked, suggesting that the rest of Tommy Toy's vehicle molds had come from Barclay and perhaps other sources, like New Jersey's Savoye.

All of Tommy Toy's figures were created by Barclay's sculptor, Olive Kooken, and her friend, Margaret Ruth Cloninger. The Old King Coles and other nursery-rhyme figures were robust while the soldiers (nicely detailed, even to curved eyeballs) suggested the feminine hands that had crafted them. When Tommy Toy went out of business about 1938 or 1939, Barclay bought it out, including the molds. Barclay experimented with the molds, but never brought out any of the figures, although it did *copy* a couple of them in a larger, healthier-looking size —the sculpting probably done over again by Kooken and perhaps Cloninger.

Another ex-Barclay employee was Frank Krupp. In 1938 he decided to go off on his own, forming a company called All-Nu. All-Nu's are the rarest of all important dimestore soldiers, and one in particular, a newsreel cameraman, may be the most coveted of all. Perhaps because Krupp, busy being the owner, couldn't devote equal and adequate time to all his creations, the quality of their design varies. Particularly well done, however, was a group of nonmilitary figures: Marching Majorettes, four musicians, a flagbearer, and a leader, all of them women. All-Nu also made a number of novelty items, among them a bare-breasted cowgirl on a bucking bronc!

In scattered parts of the country, another group of dimestore soldiers attributed to J. Edward Jones was sold from at least 1938 through —probably—the summer of 1941. Jones's soldiers, cowboys, Indians, and knight in armor were a mix of borrowings from Barclay, Manoil, and even Auburn balanced by some interestingly conceived (if a bit klunky) originals. A machine gunner firing from behind a stump, a motorcyclist with a handlebars-mounted machine gun, and—especially—an officer in greatcoat holding a pistol in one hand and dramatically pointing with the other were among its more striking originals.

Two American toy-soldier firms emerged in the 1930s that eschewed the five-and-tens for department stores. Consequently, they produced soldiers in the range preferred by connoisseurs—54 millimeters, or approximately 2½ inches in height.

Warren, owned by John Warren of Manhattan, sold only American soldiers, plus a cannon and a couple of military cars. The soldiers were nicely modeled, with removable heads and, often, two moving arms. They were, however, terribly expensive for those Depression days, a single soldier selling for 50¢ in 1936; boxed sets ran from $2.50 to $20, also eyebrow-lifting prices for the time. Warren seems to have been in business for only three years, from 1936 to 1939, but its existence did furnish a bit of toy-soldier romance. Barclay–Tommy Toy sculptor Margaret Cloninger was brought in to redesign some of the company's figures and soon thereafter married John Warren.

Comet Metal Products, owned by the Slonim family, probably began in 1940. The Queens, New York, outfit was obviously counting on Britains, the leading European toy-soldier maker, to suspend operations for the duration of the war, in which case Comet's products could serve as replacements. In a year or two, Comet put out an astonishingly large number of different soldier sets—more than a hundred—in great variety, from doughboys to Chinese to Greeks to knights to Japanese, Russians, Swedes, colonials, redcoats, and so on. Less impressive was their design—sometimes out-and-out swipes from Britains—and paint jobs. Furthermore, they were molded of solid lead, often with thin ankles and, sometimes, necks, and perhaps the lead wasn't the best, either. They broke easily, which might have shortened the company's life if the U.S. entry into the war hadn't ended it more abruptly.

If the 1930s and very early 1940s were a heyday for toy-soldier makers, they were hardly that for a lot of other companies. The toy world had changed drastically, and a lot of firms couldn't make the adjustment. As an example of

the conditions all of them faced, take one toy maker that did survive, Lionel. In 1929, Lionel's profits were $363,700. In 1930, the first full year of the Depression, they were in the black by a mere $82,000, a profit drop of nearly 80 percent. But that was paradise compared to what awaited them the following year. In 1931, Lionel, one of the giants of the toy industry, *lost* $207,000; and

Hubley, of Lancaster, Pennsylvania, came close to having a corner on cast-iron motorcycles. Here's an impressive one, ca. 1935, 8½ inches long. (Wilkinson Collection, Detroit Antique Toy Museum)

The most complex cast-iron toy ever made: Hubley's "The Elgin" Street Sweeper, introduced in 1931, 8 inches long. (Chic Gast)

1932 showed no improvement, with $209,000 in red ink. This despite an ongoing promotion program second to none.

How tough had things become? How often do bosses slash their *own* salaries when sales decline? Owner Joshua Lionel Cowen, who had been making $60,000 a year in 1929, was trying to make do on a salary of $12,750 by 1934, the year Lionel, unable to get the bank loans it needed for production, temporarily went into receivership.

Toy manufacturers put on a brave face. In 1931, *Playthings* asked leading names in the industry to predict what business would be like in the coming year. Bubbling up were such comments as, "There is every reason to be most hopeful," or "Expect a substantial increase over last year's business," or "I see distinct signs of a general improvement in business." And those comments were echoed in similar quotes as the grim years went on, each year slashing away at the number of *Playthings* pages. In 1928, the De-

An interesting Hubley toy, the "Say It With Flowers" Indian Motorcycle Cart, from the 1930s, 11 inches long. (Sotheby's, New York)

Some handsome cast-iron
vehicles from the 1930s. At
the top is Hubley's Bell
Telephone Truck. Bottom,
left to right: a Hubley
"General" Shovel Truck, A
Kenton "Jaeger" Cement
Mixer, and a Hubley
"Panama" Shovel Truck, the
latter 13 inches long.
(Sotheby's, New York)
ABOVE

In various versions, Marx's Tricky Taxi wind-up was popular from 1938 to 1954. (Mapes Auctioneers, Vestal, New York)

This particular 1939 Hubley Yellow Cab came directly from the hands of the original die maker at Hubley. (Ed Hyers Antique Toys, Asheville, North Carolina)
OPPOSITE

cember issue ran 404 pages. The December 1929 issue totaled 192. In 1930, the page count dropped to 160 and in 1931, to 130. December 1932? Only 80 pages, as was the case the following year.

All those hopeful toy makers had counted on one idea: no matter what, children have to have their toys. Perhaps so. But that didn't mean they were guaranteed them. And those children who did continue to receive them, often got fewer toys or cheaper ones.

Some firms simply refused to accommodate themselves to the times by lowering standards and prices. Almost without exception, they foundered and disappeared (sometimes entirely, sometimes by turning to nontoy manufacture). Other firms tried to adjust, as did Metalcraft, which adopted the slogan: "Designed and priced for 1931 conditions." Despite that, as the Depression deepened, the company found there was nothing left in the till.

The list of toy companies killed by the Depression is almost endless. Dorfan at its height had about 150 employees; in 1933 it had 30; in 1934 it ceased production, though continuing for the next four years to sell off its huge inventory backlog. Metalcraft, which made a

line of scooters, bicycles, and wagons, as well as a variety of stamped-steel vehicles, paid Depression wages that ran from twenty-five to forty-five cents an hour and changed the styles of its toys only when the dies wore out. The company still had to call it a day in 1937. Republic, a producer of friction vehicles, saw the handwriting on the financial pages, and in 1932 discontinued toy production, becoming a machine shop. Champion, finding its cast-iron toys an increasingly heavy millstone, shrugged its shoulders and turned to full-time production of hardware in 1936. Converse, which, beginning in 1878, had helped make Winchendon, Massachusetts, "Toy Town, U.S.A.," shipped out its last wooden, steel, and tin toys in 1934. In Sandusky, Ohio, J. C. Neff and William "Bert" Moon of Neff-Moon, folded up shop and left town. Sturditoy suffered the ignominy of being shut down by the state of Rhode Island, its tooling used to make license plates. Dayton Friction Works expired in 1935. Schoenhut, long loved by this country's children, gave up the ghost in 1938.

The greatest hope for companies in those times was to get into the nickel, dime, and quarter lines. This meant making smaller, lighter, and cheaper versions of their toys, or getting into materials, like lead, that were inherently cheap. Some firms, of course, were already in the low-priced end of toy making, and for them survival was easier. Louis Marx, for instance, had always run a streamlined operation, not only in the factories but in sales and marketing as well. His firm had virtually no salesmen (Marx and his toys were usually salesmen enough), no expensive catalogs, and its advertising was confined to the relatively inexpensive toy trade magazines. Marx had no compunction about employing the cheapest material possible, so long as it didn't compromise the toy. Accordingly, he used all

▲ Marx Royal Bus wind-up,
ca. 1930. Note the
passengers. (Bizarre Bazaar,
New York)

▲ Marx American Railroad
Express truck, ca. 1930.
(Bizarre Bazaar, New York)

A Marx King Racer tin wind-up from about 1930. (Bizarre Bazaar, New York)

Marx produced this tin wind-up trolley, shown with its original box, about 1930. (Bizarre Bazaar, New York)

the scrap tin he could come by. It was a common (and perplexing) childhood experience to peer inside a Marx product and find evidence of its prior incarnation as a soup can.

Marx also had long been known for his periodic personal surveys of his line, in which he would ask how one of his toys could be made better and cheaper, frequently achieving both goals. In contrast to Harry Ives and his stubborn devotion to his failing line of ships, Marx almost joyously tossed poorly selling items out of the line. No sentiment wasted.

It was the Marxes who survived the Great Depression, the ones who attempted to turn out the best possible toy at the lowest possible price. As one salesman reported to *Playthings* magazine in August 1930, dealers were demanding "quality merchandise cheap, rather than cheap merchandise." It was a buyer's market, the greatest buyer's market in the nation's history . . . when there *were* buyers.

One astute company that enjoyed success finding buyers was Wyandotte of Wyandotte, Michigan, whose official name was All Metal Products Company. Since at least 1920, it had been turning out a variety of steel and wood toys, many of which were weapons: a 1925 full-page ad displayed nothing but popguns, rifles, and automatics, including a pop pistol and a water pistol. Wyandotte continued to produce these toys during the Depression, but in 1935 the firm added something new—streamlined wheeled toys, including wagons, airplanes, and, above all, cars and trucks.

Wyandotte's toys were a bit unfinished-looking, both because of their styling and the necessarily no-frills approach to their production, but they were brightly painted, very

A typical inexpensive Marx train set, complete with station, from the Depression years. Marx trains were usually sold in five-and-tens, while Lionels and American Flyers appeared in more up-scale shops. (Bizarre Bazaar, New York)

An example of Wyandotte's cheap, but beautifully designed toys. (Bizarre Bazaar, New York)

sturdy, and—without obviously looking it—extremely cheap. In a 1935 ad, Wyandotte displayed eight toys, an Air Speed Coupe, a Streamlined Dump Truck, a Streamlined Sedan, a Streamlined Stake Truck, a Rocket Racer (spaceship), a Streamlined Airplane, a Streamlined Wagon, and another Streamlined Airplane. Yes, *streamlined* was the operative word, but so was a figure: ten cents. All but the second Streamlined Airplane went for a dime; the plane sold for a quarter. A year later, Wyandotte displayed five toys in an ad. Four sold for a dime. The fifth, a Mystery Plane, went for a nickel.

Wyandotte produced only a few genuinely attractive toys—a coffin-nosed Cord and a China Clipper airplane among them—but few who grew up in the Depression don't feel a spot of affection for the company, since the likelihood is that only the richest and the poorest of children didn't have a least one Wyandotte in their toy collection.

It should be mentioned here that the

Considered Wyandotte's classic toy, the "coffin-nosed" Cord (1936–37) was usually sold without a trailer. (Bizarre Bazaar, New York)

Depression had one salutary effect on the toy industry—quality materials were suddenly easy to come by. Suppliers who had previously sneered at small orders changed their tune as car and other sales fell off. "You want top-of-the-line sheet steel? You got it!"

Some companies survived by a combination of wit, enterprise, and luck. Lionel was one of them. It was pure luck that, in 1934, streamlined trains suddenly seized the nation's imagination. Pullman built the M-10000, better known as the *City of Salina*, for Union Pacific, and the startlingly fresh design was given exposure by means of a publicity tour to sixty-eight cities. The ever-alert Lionel pounced, copied it, and reaped the benefit of all that ink. Sales zoomed. (Though *streamlined* was a buzz word of the 1930s, Ives was advertising a "stream line design" for one of its trains as far back as 1917.)

Also mending a few holes in Lionel's pocketbook was an item that emerged in that dark

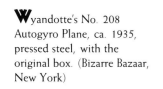yandotte's No. 208 Autogyro Plane, ca. 1935, pressed steel, with the original box. (Bizarre Bazaar, New York)

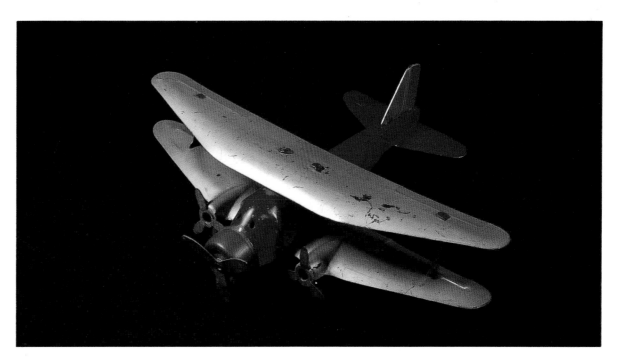

A light steel airplane by an unknown maker—probably Marx or Wyandotte—from the early 1930s. Wingspan, 9⅓ inches. (Perry R. Eichor)

year of 1934: the Mickey and Minnie Mouse Handcar. It was a simple windup toy that ran on the standard toy-train tracks, but it had several things going for it—it was cheap, it looked great, it was fun to watch, and it featured a character who could do no wrong. Lionel, ever attuned to ballyhoo, claimed the toy had saved the firm from bankruptcy. That was hardly the case, but there is no question that this single windup did more than its bit to keep Lionel on track.

The toy was introduced in the fall of 1934, and more than a quarter-million were sold to a public enchanted with both the characters and the price. It was a toy that, all by itself, could make a child's Christmas.

Ever enterprising, Lionel made sure that each of the handcar sets contained a catalog showing the full range of Lionel's output. With revenue and morale rising, Lionel moved ahead, putting out new handcars, adding more stream-

This Wyandotte Gyroplane sold from 1935 to 1940 and was a modification of Wyandotte's twin-engine passenger plane. Wingspan, 12½ inches. (Perry R. Eichor)

This game was sold by Chicago's Hamlin Corp. about 1940, but used Wyandotte's stamped steel Airacuda. The box converted into a hangar, and the bomb-dropping plane was operated via a pulley and a control button, the latter for dropping a bomb on its target. (Perry R. Eichor) OPPOSITE

The kind of toy collectors dream about finding: a mint-condition cast-iron Air Express plane, complete with tag identifying it as a Dent company sample, ca. 1932. The tag reads, "The Dent Hardware Co. Sample No. 668, Fullerton, Pa." (Wilkinson Collection, Detroit Antique Toy Museum)

lined trains, and such innovations as locomotives that could be made to whistle on command and a gateman who automatically dashed out of his shed waving a lighted lantern. It all came in a rush, and by 1935 Lionel showed a profit of $154,000. Meantime, the difficulties of American Flyer, Lionel's distant rival, were not resolved until A. C. Gilbert bought the company in 1937 and turned it around.

Mickey Mouse bailed out a lot of companies during the Depression. The redoubtable rodent first appeared on a movie screen on November 18, 1928, in the sound short *Steamboat Willie*. He was an immediate smash, and his first incarnation as a toy, a stuffed doll, followed in 1930. Despite the apple sellers and the breadlines, by 1931 Mickey had become a godsend to the struggling toy industry. In that year alone, more than fifteen different Mickey Mouse toys were manufactured. Among those offered by veteran

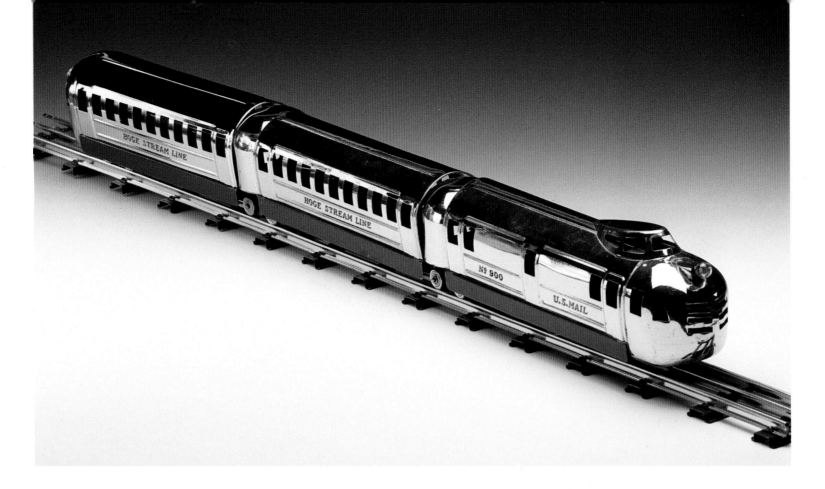

Streamline was a hot word in the mid-1930s. Here Hoge breaks it up into two words on this No. 900 dazzler, ca. 1936. (Bizarre Bazaar, New York)

American Flyer was part of the mid-1930s craze for streamlining. Here are its O Gauge No. 9900 Burlington Zephyr and No. 9900 Railway Mail Engine and Car. (Christie's, New York)

Steelcraft made this attractive Lockheed Sirius about 1931—a very large steel plane with a 21¾-inch wingspan. (Bizarre Bazaar, New York)   RIGHT

Kingsbury's 1934 painted steel wind-up version of the Chrysler Air Flow. The Air Flow did much more for toy manufacturers than it did for Chrysler. (Mapes Auctioneers, Vestal, New York) BELOW, LEFT

Buddy "L"s wind-up version of the revolutionary Scarab. The real car's life was brief, since it sold for $5000 in those mid-Depression years. The toy, ca. 1935, is about 11 inches long. (Continental Hobby House, Sheboygan, Wisconsin)   BELOW, RIGHT

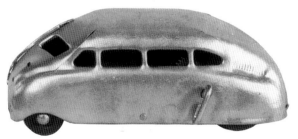

distributor George Borgfeldt were wood figures in three sizes, a Wood Dancer stringed toy, a Sport Ball, a metal drum, a wood walker, a wood express wagon, velvet dolls in six different sizes, a metal sparkler, a metal drummer, a wooden squeak toy, a cricket noisemaker, and a Tumbling Circus Toy, plus several games. By 1932 Borgfeldt was advertising Mickey Mouse toys as the "Toy and Specialty items that have become the

favorites of millions—adults and children."

Minnie Mouse, who had also debuted in *Steamboat Willie*, first appeared as a doll in 1931; in the Borgfeldt ad for that year she also showed up on the side of the metal drum. As time went on, Minnie turned up on—and as—more and more toys, though not nearly so often as her boyfriend.

Nor were Mickey and Minnie the whole ballgame. As important new Disney characters emerged, they became toys as well. There was Pluto, who was born in 1930 and named after the planet discovered that same year; Goofy, who arrived in 1932; and perhaps the greatest of Walt Disney's comic creations, the source of a slew of toys and other merchandise: Donald Duck, who was first seen in the 1934 cartoon short *The Wise Little Hen*.

The famed Mickey Mouse Handcar, which helped steady a very shaky Lionel in 1935. (Sotheby's, New York)

A winning combination: Lionel and Disney. Donald's long bill stamps him as an early Disney toy, and, in fact, the No. 1107 Donald Duck Hand Car was issued in 1936. (Mapes Auctioneers, Vestal, New York)

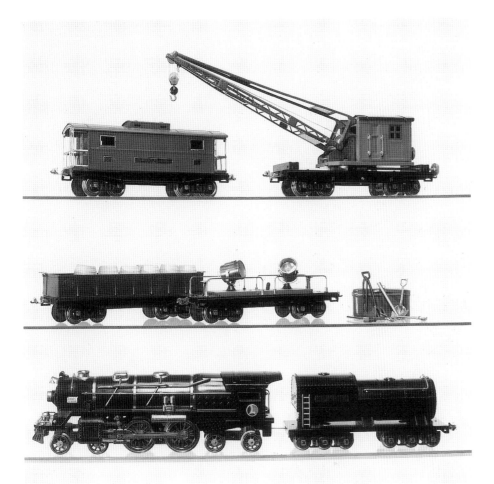

in the toy trade, but in 1940 Pinocchio emerged, joined by Jiminy Cricket and a few lesser characters, who generated profits for those who turned them out as toys.

Some of the manufacturers who fattened on Disney during the Depression included Marx, with a host of windups; Noble & Cooley, musical instruments; Seiberling Latex Products Company of Akron, Ohio, rubber toys; Sun Rubber Company of Barberton, Ohio, more rubber toys; Joseph Scheider, Inc., of New York, tin windups; N. N. Hill Brass Company, pull toys and telephones; Fisher-Price, pull toys; Toy Kraft Company of Wooster, Ohio, wooden push-and-pull

▲ Lionel Standard Gauge 358E Work Train Set from the early 1930s. (Sotheby's, New York)

▲ An 8½-inch wooden, jointed Mickey Mouse doll, ca. 1931. (Mapes Auctioneers, Vestal, New York)

The Three Little Pigs was an Academy Award–winning short in 1933. Though the trio of porkers (along with their nemesis, the Big Bad Wolf) had a shorter lifespan as best-sellers, by the end of 1935 they, along with Mickey, Minnie, Pluto, and Donald, made up the bulk of Disney's toy sales. In 1937, there was another Academy Award–winner, this one feature-length, *Snow White and the Seven Dwarfs*, which added eight more enduring characters to the toy world's population. *Ferdinand the Bull* (1938) picked up another Oscar for Disney without doing too much

toys; Metal Ware Corporation of Two Rivers, Wisconsin, stoves; Amloid Company of Lodi, New Jersey, celluloid baby rattles; Marks Brothers Company of Boston, target games; Kilgore, a Mickey Mouse Bubble Buster gun; and Crown Toy Mfg. of Brooklyn, roly-polys (bottom-weighted toys). And that was only part of it. There were Ingersoll Mickey Mouse watches, there were metal toolboxes, banks, fishing kits, watering cans, tea sets, and on and on—a flood of toys that continues to gush out today.

Naturally, the idea that movie cartoons could spawn big profits kept toy manufacturers on the *qui vive*, and when Max Fleischer's feature *Gulliver's Travels* opened in 1939, it gave birth to a number of toys. Unfortunately, the movie wasn't successful, and whatever effect the toys may have had on cash registers was probably short-lived. There was a book of paper doll cut-outs by Saalfield; jointed wood dolls by Ideal; a wooden boat, a tin sand pail, and a tin drum, by Chein, molded gauze face masks of the movie's

characters; and a wooden castle by Rich Toys that looked like an elaborate version of one of Rich's forts.

A real-life movie star was Shirley Temple. In 1934, she was keeping Ideal very much in business, as 1.5 million dolls modeled after her were sold. Shirley kept selling through much of the Depression, and in the 1960s had a revival of sorts, emerging as one of the stronger-selling dolls of the period.

Radio also had its luminaries, and since the shows often lasted for years, there were far more radio than movie toys during the 1930s. Most of them—in part, a reflection of the times—were free, or nearly so. There was a children's hour during the radio of those days, which generally ran from five to six in the afternoon. Fifteen-minute radio shows geared to children and devoted

This attractive boxed Tootsietoy set was in the company's 1933 catalog. (Bizarre Bazaar, New York) LEFT

Tootsietoy vehicles from the 1920s and 1930s. The general attractiveness of Tootsies and their low price range encouraged a lot of children to concentrate on this company's product. (Clinton B. Seeley) OPPOSITE, TOP LEFT

Tootsietoy's Ford Trimotor Airport set from 1930. (Bizarre Bazaar, New York)

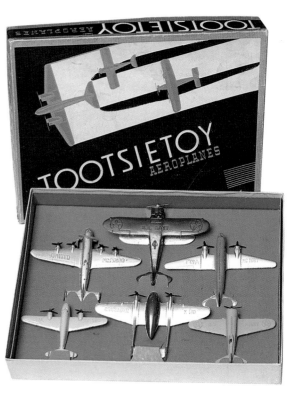

A Tootsietoy display of its Car Transporter, ca. 1932. (Bizarre Bazaar, New York) BELOW

A beautifully designed boxtop for Tootsietoy's "aeroplanes," sold about 1940. (Bizarre Bazaar, New York) RIGHT

BE SURE IT'S A TOOTSIETOY

"WATCH TOOTSIETOYS"
WHEN THE LATEST MOTOR CAR DESIGNS ARE ANNOUNCED

to adventure aired on every network station. Three of the most popular were "Tom Mix," "The Lone Ranger," and "Jack Armstrong, the All-American Boy," all of which debuted in 1933. But there were many others—"Little Orphan Annie," "Captain Midnight," "Terry and the Pirates," "The Shadow," "Tennessee Jed," "Tarzan," "Buck Rogers," "Chandu the Magician," "Dick Tracy," "Don Winslow," "Jimmie Allen," and "Superman." All of them at one time or another offered premiums, small toys that sometimes appeared in boxes of the cereal that sponsored the show, but more often had to be sent away for. Sometimes only a proof of purchase—the label of the product—was needed. Sometimes a dime had to be added to cover the cost of postage and handling. Rarely, as with the coveted "Shadow" glow-in-the-dark ring offered about 1940–41, a simple postcard would do.

all opportunities. Who wouldn't be proud to show off a Jack Armstrong Secret Egyptian Coder Siren Ring? Or a Tom Mix Mystery Ring —with an actual photo of Tom and his horse Tony "magnified 100 times"? Who could resist wowing the gang with one's very own Buck Rogers Solar Scouts Spaceship Commander Badge?

Radio, of course, gave birth to nonpremium toys as well, though not nearly as many as television would. Charlie McCarthy was particularly popular, both as a star and as a toy. In addition to a bunch of ventriloquist dolls, he was turned out several times as a tin windup, as was his companion, the goofily agreeable Mortimer Snerd. Both were also issued as dolls, and there were Charlie McCarthy face masks, play money, and paper puppets.

"Amos 'n' Andy" gave birth to a tin windup

Two beautifully accurate representations of big radio names from the 1930s: Baby Snooks (played by Fanny Brice) and the ever-agreeable bumpkin Mortimer Snerd of the Charlie McCarthy Show. Ideal Novelty & Toy Co. produced them both, about 1938. They're each about a foot tall. (Wilkinson Collection, Detroit Antique Toy Museum)

Radio premiums were colorful, wonderfully evocative, and necessarily small and inexpensive. All sorts of rings (some with the ever-intriguing "secret compartment"), badges, decoders, compasses, and periscopes were issued—even telegraph sets that actually worked (in a limited way). Premiums were true wonders of their time; entrancing, alluring, exciting, captivating, and they provided one singularly excruciating experience: the weeks upon weeks it took for the premium to arrive. For small boys and girls, the waiting was almost unendurable. Perhaps for their parents, forced to listen to the daily whines of *When's* it gonna *come?*" it actually was. When the premium finally did arrive, it was immediately shown to the less fortunate: those who had never gotten around to ordering, or who listened to the wrong show, or—the worst—had yet to receive *theirs*. Before school, during lunch hour, after school, on weekends, it would be shown at

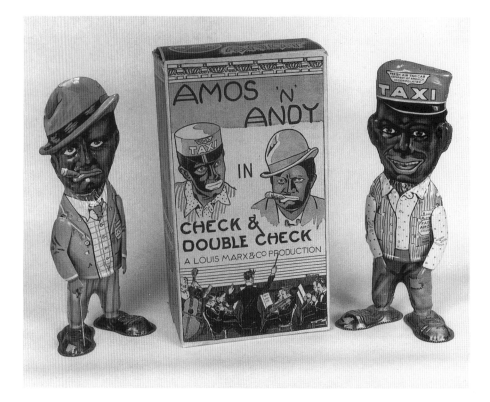

Unique's eye-catching Pecking Goose, Witch, and Cat. (Mapes Auctioneers, Vestal, New York)

After comic Joe Penner ceased to be a household name, the ever-enterprising Louis Marx changed the face of his Penner wind-up and the duck's slogan from "Wanna Buy A Duck?" to "Eggs To Order." Thus the toy became The Butter and Egg Man, ca. 1940. (Scott Smiles)

All of America stopped dead when "Amos & Andy" was heard on the nation's radios in the early 1930s. These tin wind-up walkers were by Marx, shown here with the original box. (Wayne Pratt & Co., Marlboro, Massachusetts) OPPOSITE

Fresh Air Taxi—a dud at the time, but now much-prized by collectors—as well as wood-jointed dolls, tin "walkers," and a few other toys.

Radio's Bob Burns inspired both a toy and the name for a brand-new military weapon. It was a long, tubelike musical instrument (of sorts) called a bazooka. But perhaps the oddest of the radio toys was the Joe Penner "Wanna Buy A Duck?" tin windup—odd because today Joe is virtually unknown (his vogue was very brief), while his highly sought-after metal effigy is known to thousands of toy collectors.

Comic strips continued through the 1930s to provide toy makers with a market. Daisy kept sales of its air rifles high by latching onto Red Ryder, a cowboy who first appeared in the funny sheets in 1935 as Bronc Peeler, evolving into Red by 1938. Although a long-lived character, Red was strictly a secondary strip hero, and it's possible, because of the ubiquity of the Daisy ads, that he was better known to millions of kids as the cowpoke who had a rifle named after him.

Probably the two most popular comic-strip toy characters of the 1930s were Popeye and Buck Rogers. Popeye was the squint-eyed sailor who had been seen first as a subsidiary character in E. C. Segar's "Thimble Theatre" strip in January 1929. Readers and cartoonist alike were immediately intrigued by the salt with the mammoth forearms, and in 1932 he became the strip's eponymous hero, inspiring toy after toy, as did other characters in the strip. One, the cuddly Jeep, even provided the name for a now world-famous vehicle. Popeye fared especially well in the tin windup area. Marx, Chein, and Hoge all grew fat on such toys as Popeye in a Rowboat, Popeye Express, Popeye Puncher, Popeye the Pilot, and on and on. Popeye has also been done over and over again as a doll, and the Popeye Spinach Patrol was a cast-iron Hubley toy featuring the sailorman on a motorcycle cart. There were (and will no doubt continue to be) all sorts of Popeye musical instruments, ball toys, puppets, pull toys, and battery-operated toys. Though the strip is no longer nearly as popular as it once was, the toys continue to come out in new versions.

Lots of vigor here: Hubley's Popeye Patrol from the 1930s. (Ed Hyers Antique Toys, Asheville, North Carolina)

Chein (pronounced "chain") produced at least two Popeye tin wind-up punching toys. This one, with an overhead bag, stands 9½ inches high. (Phillips, New York)

Marx's circa-1935 "Popeye the Champ" wind-up. The toy is 7 inches wide and is all tin, except for the celluloid figures, the wooden posts, and the string "ropes." The box is almost as much fun as the toy. (Phillips, New York) RIGHT

The Thimble Theatre Mystery Playhouse, with Wimpy, Olive Oyl, and one of the leading stars of comic toys, the "I Yam What I Yam" man, Popeye. New in 1939, from Harding Products, Philadelphia. (Phillips, New York) OPPOSITE

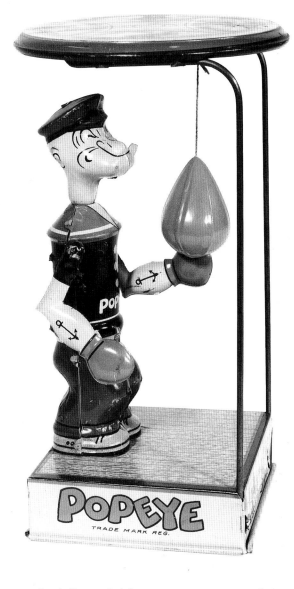

Buck Rogers's lifespan as a comic-strip hero was shorter, and most of the toys he spawned were issued during the Depression. We have already noted that the strip, which began in 1929, gave birth to a number of premiums. But toy stores also discovered that the twenty-fifth-century spaceman could keep the ledger ink running black. There was a line of space-type pistols, most of them in pressed steel, by Daisy. Tootsie-

toy issued a whole set of Buck Rogers spacecraft in 1937, with names like Flash-Blast Attack Ship and Venus Duo-Destroyer. The ever-alert Louis Marx sniffed the wind and came out with a series of Buck Rogers tin windups, including a Rocket Ship in 1934 and a Rocket Police Patrol in 1939. Another toy that could race the pulse of a small boy was the Buck Rogers Chemical Laboratory by Gropper Toys in 1937.

Other comic-strip characters who occasioned the creation of toys during those days included Flash Gordon, Blondie, and Dick

Tracy. Then, at the end of the decade, there emerged another four-color adventure hero. But this one didn't get his start in the strips. Instead, he came to life in that new invention, the comic book. His name was Superman.

The first regularly published monthly comic, *Famous Funnies*, began in 1934. Four years later, Superman burst forth in the premiere issue of *Action Comics*. It took a while for his publishers to catch on to just what they had. After gracing the first cover, Clark Kent's alter ego didn't appear on another until the seventh issue, and he

A Buck Rogers wind-up space ship from Louis Marx, first issued in 1935. (Don Hultzman)

Dagwood's Solo Flight, a Marx turnover airplane wind-up from 1941. Although "Blondie," which began in 1930, has long been more popular than "Popeye" and is syndicated by the same company, it has spawned far fewer toys. (Bizarre Bazaar, New York)

There have been so many Popeye toys that it was almost inevitable two would show up with the same name. The other "Popeye Express," also by Marx, had the squint-eyed sailor pushing a cart, topped by a parrot. Both tin wind-up toys were produced in the 1930s. (Bizarre Bazaar, New York)
OPPOSITE

part were the frivolous, even bizarre, "Cupids," "Fidos," "Jokers," and "Peaches," replaced by the sterner "G-Man," "Hero," "Invincible," and—beginning in 1938—guns bearing the names of current-day movie cowboy heroes. Cowboy stars Buck Jones and Buzz Barton may have started the trend in 1934, when both became Daisy air-rifle names. Movie star Gene Autry and radio, movie, comic-strip, and comic-book hero the Lone Ranger were the first in a parade of celebrity-named revolvers and automatics. Kilgore turned out the cast-iron Lone Ranger six-shooters, and Kenton kept even with Gene Autry sidearms.

One way of staying in business during the Depression was to make everything you could think of that might sell and then hold your breath. In 1933, for instance, Kenton's catalog featured eight construction toys, nineteen trucks, two airplanes, two dirigibles, three buses, two tractors, two tanks, twelve stoves, seven fire

Ideal was one of the few toy companies sufficiently prescient to jump on the Superman bandwagon in 1939, just a year after his birth. Supe's hands and midsection might have seemed a bit of a letdown to a young admirer, but it's unlikely he'd have been disappointed with the very nicely done face. Jointed wood and composition, 13 inches high. (Danny Fuchs)

Fisher-Price did a nice job on this wooden version of the DC-3 transport. New in 1941, it has a 20-inch wingspan. (MacNary Collection)

didn't become the automatic cover boy until the *nineteenth*. But by 1939, Superman provided the inspiration for at least four toys—two by Marx in the form of tin windups; a jointed wooden doll by Ideal; and a Daisy Krypto-Ray Gun.

More conventional versions of the ever-popular toy gun were also in demand, and the 1930s saw a continual stream of cast-iron cap pistols. Hubley, Kilgore, and Kenton were the three biggest names of the day, pushing out pistols of all shapes and sizes. Some of their guns fired a single cap at a time, some held a whole roll, and at least one was double-barreled, and could fire two caps, either simultaneously or alternately. Unlike the toy pistols of the turn of the century, these weapons were almost uniformly realistic-looking affairs. They also sported less eccentric names. Gone for the most

This very impressive riding toy was made of pressed steel by Keystone, ca. 1940. (Bizarre Bazaar, New York)

engines, two trains, eleven banks (including a Franklin D. Roosevelt bank), four pistols, and a few other miscellaneous toys.

Incredibly, some firms actually began in the Depression years, and even more incredibly, prospered. One of these was Fisher-Price, of East Aurora, New York, founded on October 1, 1930, by Herman Fisher and Irving Price. Both men were certain that quality wooden toys, colorfully lithographed and aimed at very young children (aged six months through six years) would succeed. Sixty years later, it's obvious that they had a point—though it took them six years to show a profit.

Fisher-Price toys for young children were, and are, happy-looking (with the occasional ex-

ception of an irascible Donald Duck), mostly animals, and they make a noise (a most important feature) when moved. From the beginning they were sold to dealers as toys that would sell throughout the year. Helping get the company off the ground was the skilled artwork of Price's wife, Margaret Evans Price, the firm's first artist and designer, who had previously illustrated postcards, valentines, and books for Rand McNally and Harper & Brothers.

Milton Bradley had started the whole theme of educational toys, Playskool had followed in the 1920s, and about 1930 Holgate got into the act, with results comparable to those of its predecessors—enough success to keep it going right up to this writing. Cornelius Holgate had established the Holgate Co. in Philadelphia, turning out such wood products as brush and broom handles. About 1930 the daughter of the company's treasurer married an educator/child psychologist, whose ideas had a great influence on the firm, turning it toward the production of educational wooden toys. Holgate hired Jerry Rockwell, brother of famed Americana painter Norman Rockwell, to design its toys. Jerry Rockwell was as influential in his way as Norman, inventing a stream of innovative, simple, and practical toy designs. Wooden pounding benches, nesting blocks, kindergarten blocks, lacing shoes, colored beads, and ring stacks poured forth in profusion. In 1958 Holgate and Playskool merged, with Jerry Rockwell continuing to design for the new amalgamation.

Also wooden were Halsam's American Logs, which went into production in 1934, obviously inspired by Lincoln Logs. Unlike most copies of a product, Halsam's logs actually improved on the original, notched indentations making them look far more realistic. The company was in business for years, though always in the shadow of Lincoln Logs (in fact, kids often called its product Lincoln Logs, once the original identifying box was gone).

By 1940 the cast-iron toy, due to foreign competition and the increased cost of freight, was slowly becoming a thing of the past. Hubley, now the largest producer of cast-iron toys and cap pistols in the world, began to replace iron with die-cast zinc alloys. In 1940 and 1941 it issued two classic toy pistols. The 1940 toy was the Texan, a huge (9¼-inch-long) cast-iron revolver, so heavy that any child under eleven must have had a hard time holding it up as he fired off its caps. A year later, there was the Pirate Pistol, popular but not as ubiquitous. It was even longer—9⅜ inches—but lighter, since

only the two hammers and the trigger were iron. The rest was die-cast zinc, except for the plastic grip.

Plastic, as in that grip, was increasingly employed in the closing days of the Depression. As early as 1937, Kilgore started to issue plastic cap pistols (three automatics, one resembling a German Luger), cars, trucks, planes, and buses. As previously mentioned, Beton's soldiers debuted a year later, and by 1941 Dillon-Beck Mfg. Co., of Irvington, New Jersey, was issuing Wannatoys—plastic submarines, battleships, freighters, and airplanes. Columbia Protektosite (which cast Beton's figures) had a child's tea set. Ideal advertised a doll with a plastic head, and Monsanto was offering building blocks of the new material. Once more, the lightness of plastic and what it saved in shipping charges, was an important factor. The Bakelite Corporation,

Arcade's World's Fair Bus sold in 1939 and presumably 1940, the second and last year of the New York fair. (Bizarre Bazaar, New York)

pushing hard to get toy manufacturers to employ its product, stressed this heavily in its ads. But despite its lightness and other advantages, plastic, like aluminum, might have faltered, given its inherent problems at the time—brittleness in many cases, indifferent color for the most part, and little of the striking detail that later characterized it. However, something took place in 1941 that suddenly and dramatically added a new, major advantage to the use of plastic in toys. The Japanese attacked Pearl Harbor, and the United States entered World War II.

Plastic toys of the period immediately prior to World War II: The figures are by Beton (also known as Bergen Toy and Novelty), and the vehicles and planes are either by Kilgore or Lapin Products. (Beton factory files)

WORLD WAR II: MAKING DO

In the absence of metal airplanes, these Jack Armstrong–Wheaties cereal premiums were widely welcomed. Shown here are relatively accurate versions of Germany's Focke-Wolfe Fw. 190 *(left)* and Britain's famous Spitfire. (MacNary Collection) OPPOSITE

Built-Rite's World War II cardboard toys, with drab colors and uninspired art, came nowhere near the mark hit by their forts. Still, in the absence of anything much better, they sold. (MacNary Collection) INSET

The era shaped by World War II was a heightened time for children. Patriotism was rife. Good and evil would never again be so black and white.

But there was a flip side to the coin. And that side was as gloomy as the other was charged.

In 1937, the aspiring writer John Hersey was earning a living as secretary to Nobel Prize–winning author Sinclair Lewis. Perhaps because he was having problems with his own writing, Lewis suggested to Hersey that it was becoming increasingly difficult for young people to make their way as writers. The thing for Hersey to do, Lewis went on, was to study the manufacture of lead toy soldiers. War was coming, and when it arrived small boys everywhere would want their own regiments of toy soldiers.

Artists are celebrated for their vision, not their business sense. In this instance at least, Sinclair Lewis followed the pattern. Yes, war did come, and when it came, small boys did seek out toy soldiers, and lead soldiers were what they wanted most of all. But no lead soldiers were available. The government had prohibited the use of this important war material in the manufacture of toys.

Nor were the restrictions limited to lead toys. Soon Marx tin windups began to disappear from the five-and-tens and department stores. So did Wyandotte steel trucks, Auburn Rubber tractors, Hubley zinc-alloy cap pistols, and Grey Iron cast-iron toy soldiers. Production by these companies had already been cut in half as war first reared its head; by mid-1942 production of all toys made of metal and rubber was stopped completely. The actual regulation, as it applied to soldiers, decreed that "no lead toys can be fabricated after April 1st [1942], and the quantity of lead used during the first quarter of 1942 must be restricted to 50% of the amount used in either the 3rd or 4th quarter of 1941." Toys made of other strategic materials had until June 30, 1942.

Some of the companies coped successfully with the exigencies of war. Hubley began producing M-74 bomb fuses. Grey Iron capped its cupola and turned out torpedo trucks, bomb racks, and bomb skids. Marx made shell casings, and Fisher-Price manufactured ship fenders, first-aid kits, cots, bomb crates, and aircraft ailerons. Comet used guard dogs to patrol its premises as it reproduced warships in miniature for military identification purposes.

Other companies, however, went out of business—or simply floundered. Manoil, for instance flailed about fruitlessly for the first three years of the war, first trying to survive as a warehouse and then, with equal lack of success, as a chicken hatchery. Others, like Auburn Rubber, which was busily producing soles, gaskets, and the like for war use, also kept trying to find substitute materials for toys. Sawdust and glue, excelsior and lime—even old battery cases—were tried. But nothing worked, and finally Auburn discontinued the manufacture of toys for the duration.

But all of that was the toy companies' problem. The era's kids had more important things on their minds. Whole categories of playthings had disappeared. Bicycles were gone. Steel wagons were gone. Ice skates, sleds with metal runners, roller skates, all gone. Even balloons. Where were the rubber squeak toys? And the types of toys still left—too often they were less than enchanting, because what was available now came mostly in wood, plastic, and paper.

To the children of the time, the wooden toys were probably the worst offenders. Most were crude and sadly lacking in detail (it didn't help that the better grades of wood were reserved for war use); few of them made use of the paper lithographs that had made so many turn-

A wooden tank in the usual elemental form of the period, manufacturer unknown, and a wooden landing barge, which looks as if it might have been designed for the Playskool set, manufacturer unknown. (MacNary Collection)

All-Nu's 3¼-inch-high lead soldiers had a brief life, probably introduced in 1941 and terminated by government material restrictions in April 1942.

A page from a 1942 "Billy and Ruth" catalog. Boston's Keystone manufactured the U.S. Coast Defense Fort. Presumably the other forts and the garage are also by Keystone. However, in 1943, Philadelphia's Melco was making very similar forts also of "hard pressed wood with solid wood towers."

of-the-century toys attractive. Most offensive were the weapons boys desired so avidly. Rifles, pistols, and tommy guns were dispirited symbols rather than accurate representations, and they didn't hold up all that well, either.

About as fragile, but far more attractive, were the paper and cardboard toys. Built-Rite, of Warren, Ohio, provided handsome cardboard forts that were just the right size for the dime-store soldiers of the prewar days. Companies like Whitman, Lowe, and Merrill, which had con-

centrated on paper dolls before the war, began turning out books of soldiers, airplanes, tanks, antiaircraft guns, nurses, WAVES, WAACS (later, WACS), and women marines.

The advantage of cardboard was its capacity for detail and brilliant coloring; the disadvantages were its lack of dimension, light weight, and fragility. Thus, more from lack of competition than any inherent quality at the time, plastic began to come into its own. Early plastic vehicles may have been brittle, small, and light-

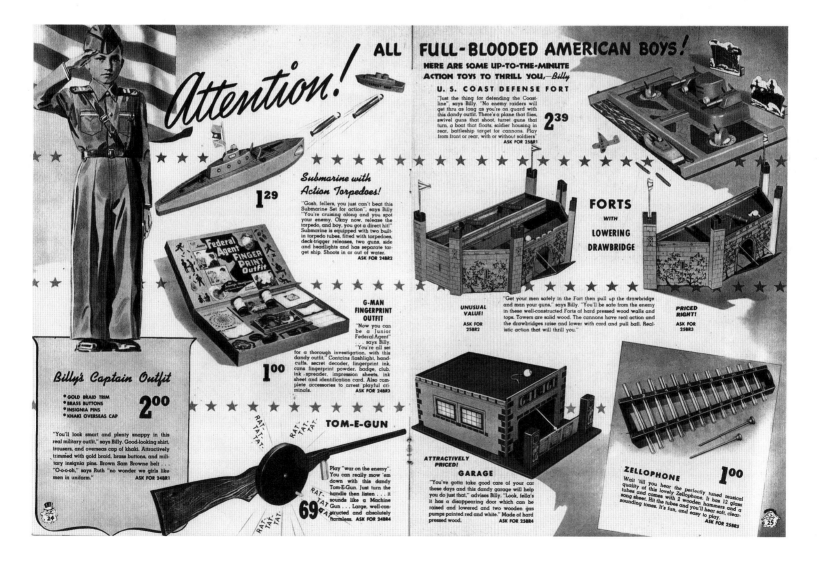

A handsome pressed-wood and solid-wood fort from the period of World War II. Most forts of this type bore no manufacturer's mark, but some features suggest this was made by Rich Toys, of Clinton, Iowa, which manufactured toys from about 1923 until about 1962, when the company was destroyed by a flood (by then the firm was in Tupelo, Mississippi). (Mapes Auctioneers, Vestal, New York)

All-Nu's Frank Krupp was just getting his toy company off the ground when World War II deprived him of lead. A trained artist, Krupp tried to cope with the situation by designing these cardboard soldiers, but the market wasn't there.

A circa 1942 cardboard toy set. Toys like this tended to be flimsy and spontaneously disassemble themselves at a discouraging rate. (John D. [Jack] Matthews)

One attempt to make up for the lack of metal toy soldiers was this 1942 set of paper toys from Electric Corporation of America. (The Paper Soldier, Clifton Park, New York) BELOW, LEFT

Though originally issued in the late 1930s, sales of Built-Rite's cardboard Fort 25A peaked during the war since it was one of the period's few attractive toys. Built-Rite's cardboard soldiers are shown on the fringes, with Barclay's lead soldiers inside the fort. It's not known if Built-Rite and Barclay formally cooperated. (Ed Poole) BELOW, RIGHT

weight, but they were there. Beton's soldiers were out of scale with the dimestore lead, iron, and rubber soldiers and with the 54-millimeter "connoisseur" figures. But they were there. As bad as some of the war toys were, they *were* toys, and the nation's income was rising. The makeshift and the substitute sold as quickly as they were made.

Buddy "L," involved in war work, set up a factory in Glens Falls, New York, which produced (from "the crudest of pine") station wagons, taxicabs (with "sky views," roof openings), a Greyhound bus with opening doors, a Railway Express truck, a Coca-Cola truck (now highly valued by collectors), a milk truck, a two-piece circus trailer, and a retractable hardtop convertible that actually anticipated the retractable tops of postwar years.

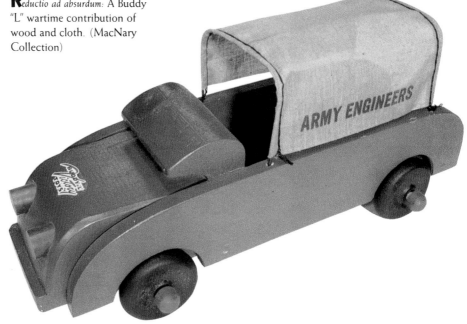

Reductio ad absurdum: A Buddy "L" wartime contribution of wood and cloth. (MacNary Collection)

This Buddy "L" truck appeared in the firm's 1943 catalog, when the company turned to wood as a manufacturing material. (Wilkinson Collection, Detroit Antique Toy Museum)

Molded Products' soldiers were turned out during World War II with the same extruding equipment that had produced the Mickey Mouse figures for Lionel's famed handcar. OPPOSITE

World War II toys made from composition: The jeeps and probably the plane were by New York's Well-Made Doll and Toy Co. An ad showing one of the jeeps appeared in the January 1943 *Playthings*. The company also made composition submarines, PT boats, a P-40 pursuit plane, tanks, aircraft carriers, and destroyers. (MacNary Collection)

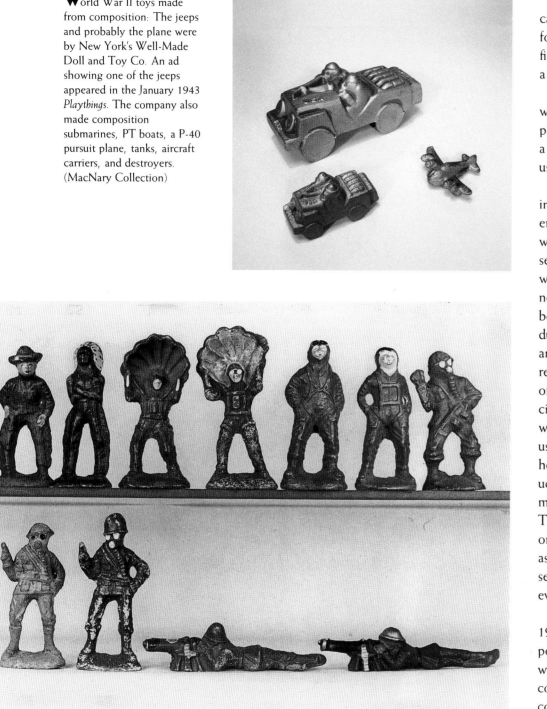

Rayco, also of Glens Falls, was founded because its owners couldn't find any Christmas toys for their children. From 1942 through 1946 the firm produced wooden dump trucks, army tanks, a train, and a lawnmower.

Fisher-Price, strenuously involved in the war effort, turned out a very limited toy line patched together from scraps of wood and using a few metal parts, such as bells; the metal was usually painted rather than plated.

Another company, Molded Products, came into being because of war shortages. The owners, Leslie S. Steinau and his son, Leslie, Jr., were in the advertising display business. They sensed that, when war came, consumer goods would be so hard to get there would be little need for advertising. So, late in 1941, they bought the extruding equipment Lionel had used during the Depression years to make its Mickey and Minnie Mouse Handcar figures. Through a relative of the Steinaus, Barclay's salesman heard of the purchase and hurried over. He was prescient enough to know he would soon be out of work at Barclay and convinced the Steinaus to use their equipment to make toy soldiers, which he would sell. Beginning in 1942, Molded Products worked at full capacity, turning out soldiers made of wood flour, starch, whiting, and water. They were crude and they dissolved in the rain or bathwater, but at least their scale was the same as the old dimestore figures. How well did they sell? According to Leslie, Jr., retailers "grabbed everything we could send them!"

Molded Products began production late in 1941 or early in 1942. A year later, another composition soldier company, Transogram's Playwood Plastics, emerged with soldiers that were concoctions of triple-zero wood flour from Wisconsin, 20 Mule Team Borax, water, and unbleached white flour that had been condemned by food inspectors, who marked it with chicken blood. Playwood's soldiers were just as clumsy as those of Molded Products, and just as vulnerable to water, but they, too, were in the right scale and were greedily gobbled up by buyers for the nation's five-and-tens.

Dolls, for the most part long made of composition (basically sawdust and glue), were less affected by the war than most toys, but still there was the sudden shortage of workers and some restrictions on materials. The same applied to stuffed toys. Model airplane kits sold by companies like Strombecker, Megow, and Joe Ott enjoyed a boom, both because of the heightened interest in aircraft and the lack of competition from metal or rubber planes.

Strombecker was a particularly popular company. When it was solely owned by a Mr. Strombeck, the Moline, Illinois, firm had made wooden handles for knives and axes. In 1935, an employee attended the Chicago World's Fair and began making copies of the trains he had seen exhibited there, using cast-off wood from the handles. A Mr. Becker (Strombeck + Becker = Strombecker) was brought in to sell the new line of models, which was innovative in that the parts were precut. Dedicated model people turned up

Dolls had an easier time of it during the war, as they'd long been made from composition. One of the era's popular Story Book Dolls, in this case No. 152, Mary Had a Little Lamb. (MacNary Collection)

StromBecker's pre-cut wooden models were particularly popular during World War II. (Perry R. Eichor)

Hubley's "Roy Rogers" cap pistol from 1941, 8¼ inches long. (Charles W. Best)

COME ON—GOOD LITTLE *Sports*

Billy on SPORTS Be physically active and you'll keep vitally fit!

Shooting!

Archery!

ARCHERY SET

This set has a double target board. You'll have twice as much fun. You also get a big Hickory Bow, varnished, with velour grip, waxed bowstring, and 3 feathered arrows with rubber suction tips.
ASK FOR 38BR4

1²⁵

1⁰⁰

50¢

RAID GUN

"Take aim . . . FIRE! you'll route out the enemy with this nifty Raid Gun," says Billy. "It has a swell repeating action. Makes loud popping noises when you move the pistol grip handle backward and forward." Made of wood and has an imitation walnut finish, red cartridge case and black trim.
ASK FOR 38BR1

SUB-MACHINE TOM-E-GUN

"Exciting! . . . Boys, you'll go for this nifty Sub-Machine Tom-E-gun," says Billy. "Made entirely of wood, and it has a new and realistic design . . ." Varnished stock with black enameled drum barrel and grip. Has "Brr" sound.
ASK FOR 38BR2

1⁰⁰

ANIMAL ARCHERY TARGET

"Want the thrill of a Big Game Hunt?" ask Billy and Ruth. "Here it is. Colorful, life-like Target. High grade, big Hickory Bow with velour grip and waxed bowstring. Three arrows with safety suction cups, and feathered shafts for straight shooting."
ASK FOR 38BR5

1⁰⁹

ALPHA BASEBALL GAME

Different! . . . Exciting! "Imagine, every letter in the alphabet represents a play, based on real Baseball and each play controls the action of the batter as well as any men on bases," exclaim Billy and Ruth. "The playing field is cut out for placing Base Runners and keeping score of Balls, Strikes, Outs and Runs."
ASK FOR 38BR3

their noses at this, but there were plenty of others who were delighted to skip all the tedious cutting the other kits involved. The Strombecker models seem to have been a hit from the first, retailers often having to settle for only a portion of their orders. With the advent of World War II, the company was in even better shape, scooping up all the boys who had previously bought Hubleys and Tootsietoys.

Strombecker continued to make knife and axe handles as well, but after the deaths of Becker and Strombeck, much of the life went out of the firm itself. Eventually, a portion of it was bought by Shure (which owned Tootsietoy), and the rest by Chicago Cutlery, which wound up with much of the toy tooling (later bought by Polk's Hobbies).

No matter what the category, the story was the same. Toy trains were now either wood or cardboard (Lionel's sole wartime entry), toy xylophones now had glass tubes or wooden tone bars, and a sturdy-looking Rum-Tum drum turned out to be made of cardboard (and must have lasted a good five minutes in the hands of a future Jo Jones).

In short, from mid-1942 till the late fall of 1945, war, for young toy buyers, was heck.

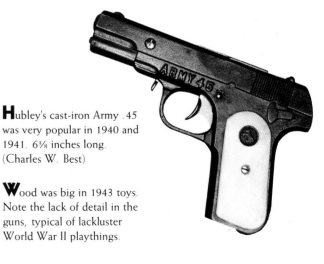

Hubley's cast-iron Army .45 was very popular in 1940 and 1941. 6⅜ inches long. (Charles W. Best)

Wood was big in 1943 toys. Note the lack of detail in the guns, typical of lackluster World War II playthings.

POSTWAR AND THE FIFTIES

eelings toward toys in the immediate postwar era can be summed up by a single, simple symbol: the black rubber tire.

The black rubber tire had been used earlier on a few toys but was quickly abandoned because it left marks on floors and furniture. The postwar tires no longer offended in this way, but that was only a minor reason for their now extensive use. Four long years of newsreels, graphic photos, and Hollywood's endless stream of war movies made black rubber tires essential on toys. Where did kids see white-tired vehicles? White rubber tires made toys look *goofy;* they weren't *realistic.* Black tires *were* realistic—even those made of plastic or wood.

Realism was in. Green stands on soldiers suddenly looked absurd; wars were fought in mud, not on lawns. Toy trains that didn't look precisely like the real thing? *Come on.* Wyandotte's trucks, with their austere, blank look? *You've got to be kidding.* The war had engendered an increased awareness of the world, a sharper eye, a certain sophistication. Which meant that, for a time at least, some companies got lucky.

C. W. Doepke Mfg. Co. of Cincinnati (and, later, Rossmoyne), Ohio, had been a manufacturer since 1940, making ammunition containers and tank-tread components during the war. The war ended in August 1945, and as late as December of that year, the company was still uncertain about its future course. Christmas was coming, and Frederick Doepke brought a dilapidated toy into the shop (toys were still in short supply), hoping to restore it and give it to his children on December 25. His brother Charles, the firm's co-owner, watched. A light bulb lit up. It was a 300 watter. And soon the company was producing Doepke's Model Toys line, a group of steel vehicles that has been called "the finest line of toys of the postwar era."

For the most part, Doepke concentrated on scrupulous reproductions of heavy construction equipment. Each toy was an authorized replica. Even the color schemes were accurate, and equally authentic were the metal treads and the tire sizes, complete with brand names (Goodyear or Firestone, depending on the model). *Perfection* probably sums it up. The Barber-Greene high-capacity bucket loader operated exactly the way the real thing did; the Adams diesel road grader's blade adjusted to all angles, perfectly aping its prototype; the Heiliner earth scraper loaded, dumped, and operated on four wheels, just as it should have. The toys were stunningly expensive for the day, ranging from $10.75 to

Mr. Potato Head, when he really had a potato head. Introduced in 1952, this was the first toy advertised on TV. (Hasbro) OPPOSITE

Unique Art's "G.I. Joe and His Jouncing Jeep" from the middle to late 1940s. (Scott Smiles) INSET

$20.75, but dealers, once they took on the line, found that it moved.

Similar inspiration struck the Santa Monica, California, firm of Smith-Miller (later, Smith-Ironson) at almost exactly the same time. Only it was Smith-Miller's plan to craft perfect duplicates of trucks and tractors in cast metal and aluminum. Smitty Toys, as they were sometimes called, came in two price ranges, neither of them cheap for the time. The lower-priced range consisted of toys that weren't exact replicas; the higher-priced toys were. Prices ran from about $6.95 to $27.85, for an aerial ladder truck. "Cost More Because They Give More" was the slogan, and for a time, in those reality-is-everything days, it worked.

Still another toy manufacturer obsessed with accuracy and detail was Fred Ertl, Sr., of Dubuque, Iowa (later, of Dyersville). The Ertl company likes to call its origins "a real Cinderella scenario," and with good reason. Ertl was unemployed in 1945 when, with help from his family, he began making toys in the basement of his home, pouring molten aluminum into sand molds. (Ertl had learned about sand-casting in his native Germany.) Very early in his toy-making career Ertl began working directly from original blueprints for tractors, trucks, and other vehicles he was copying. His specialty was farm toys, and he contracted with such manufacturers as John Deere and International Harvester to allow him to issue toy replicas at the same time

A very impressive-looking convertible sold by New York's Irwin Toy Co. about 1953. Metal with minor plastic trim. (Bizarre Bazaar, New York)

The bus at front is from Arcade, and sold in the 1930s. The two at rear were produced by the Realistic Toy Co. and appear to be from the 1950s. (Bizarre Bazaar, New York)

Not many toy manufacturers came out of Marietta, Georgia. In fact, the only one known is Grimland, which made the truck in the foreground about 1940. The Ralston Pfizer was made about 1950. (Bizarre Bazaar, New York)

as they unveiled their new models to the farm trade. Deere and Harvester and other farm equipment manufacturers quickly saw the promotional possibilities of such a scheme and just as quickly agreed. Today, Ertl is the largest manufacturer of toy farm equipment in the world, supplementing the line with other wheeled toys, including cars, trucks, and airplanes, some of them related to television series.

A couple of years after Ertl began operations, Tonka came along. The firm had started in 1946 as Mound Metalcraft, Inc., stamping out metal tie racks and garden tools. In 1947 it took over the tentative toy business of L. E. Streeter Company. Streeter had shown a steam shovel at the 1946 Toy Fair (held every February in New York City) with poor results. Lynn F. Baker, Avery F. Crounse, and Alvin F. Tesch, Mound's co-owners, worked out the bugs in the toy while conducting a survey to find out what boys wanted and what it would take to get retailers interested.

In 1947, Mound showed two pressed-steel toys at the Toy Fair, the No. 50 Steam Shovel and the No. 150 Crane and Clam (so much for those who believe all toys were numbered consecutively). Each bore a logo that read "Tonka Toys by Mound Metalcraft Incorporated, Mound, Minnesota." Tonka (named for nearby Lake Minnetonka) had done its homework well; thirty-seven thousand toys were made and sold that year.

In 1948, Tonka introduced its third toy, the No. 200 Lift Truck and Cart, and in 1949 expanded its line to fourteen items, including a doll hospital bed with mattress. The bed and four of the other toys were soon dropped, but Tonka was on its way, and by 1955 employed 355 people. The company, which in 1956 changed its name to Tonka Toys, was never as scrupulous

about accuracy as Doepke, Smitty, and Ertl, but did earn its reputation by producing good-looking models that were very tough and relatively low-priced. Another firm in the Tonka mold is Nylint, whose steel vehicles have been coming out of Rockford, Illinois, since 1946.

The end of the war brought other changes. Though production of metal toy soldiers resumed, they were featured in far fewer stores, perhaps as much a victim of the retailers' desire to forget war as of children's changing interests. There were also few science-fiction toys: Flash Gordon and Buck Rogers had become old hat. Cast iron was extinct, or nearly so. Plastic was increasingly in, and the new plastics were holding up better than the old. Postwar exuberance gave birth to a number of new companies, many of which—like Thomas Toys, Ajax, Banner, and Lido—dealt almost exclusively in plastic.

The new taste for realism had a marked impact on trains. HO, the smallest of the three most common gauges of model trains (the largest was Standard, with O in the middle), had ap-

▲ Keystone garage made from pressed wood, with one of Keystone's own plastic cars, from the late 1940s. (Ron Fink)

peared before the war, but in the postwar years increasingly became the gauge of choice, partly because the smaller size was appealing and partly because the trains were much more realistically modeled.

Accuracy in toy trains had, in a more limited way, been important before the war, too. In 1937, Lionel put out a replica of which it was justly proud—a painstakingly accurate copy of the New York Central's Hudson-type steam locomotive and tender. Every part, aside from the throttle in the cab, was reproduced in precise scale. Lionel advertised in one of its brochures that even the rivets on the tender were a 100 percent reflection of the real thing: "Sixteen hundred model rivets dot the sides of the tender, rivet by rivet exactly as in prototype." Quite a claim, and quite a demonstration of concern with accuracy. Lionel had reason to be scrupulous. One day the company received a letter of complaint. A customer had stalked the New York Central's yards, found himself an original tender, and counted rivets. Then he counted Lionel's rivets. Neither version had 1,600. The New York

Central's tender had 1,402. Disturbingly, both to the writer and Lionel, the model reproduced 1,399. An embarrassed Lionel then actually created the post (presumably part-time) of rivet-counter.

It was the engines and tenders that had monopolized attention in the 1930s and early 1940s. Now, however, HO manufacturers were finding that plastic, a material—in its improved form—exquisitely suited to detail, was enabling them to make each car a true miniature of the real thing. The thirst for realism was evident at American Flyer, and not only in HO. In 1938, when A. C. Gilbert purchased the company, he shifted its base of operations from Chicago to New Haven and began to redesign all of its trains. After the war, Gilbert ignored all the earlier tooling and set out to produce accurately scaled trains that ran on a realistic two-rail system (most electric trains, including Lionel's, were three-rail). By 1950, with all his innovations, Gilbert had brought his firm into at least sixth position among toy makers in terms of sales. But there are exceptions to everything, and the new two-track S-gauge trains were one of

The burgeoning interest in HO trains during the postwar years extended to accessories for the train set-ups. Lee Stokes Industries was started in New Oxford, Pennsylvania, in 1945. Lee Stokes created all the original models (except for the first three) and all the molds. Twenty-five different vehicles were sold in HO and just six in O Gauge. The models were made of a compound of plaster and urea formaldehyde, a material so hard and durable that they've weathered better than many metal toys of the same period. The company had eight employees and sold to England, France, Germany, Italy, Brazil, and Japan, as well as domestically. Lee Stokes Industries moved to Bel Air, Maryland, in 1950 and closed in 1955. The kit shown was issued in 1948. (Lee Stokes)

them. Though they remained a staple part of the American Flyer line to the end, sales were consistently disappointing and never came close to those of Lionel's seemingly archaic, unrealistic rail system.

Toy soldiers were becoming more realistic, too. Previously, they were most often considerably out of proportion, the heads too big for the bodies, as if their designers were consciously modeling them on the dimensions of the children who would play with them. The new breed of toy soldier, uniformly molded in plastic, was meticulously sculpted in lifelike, adult proportions, with far more detail than previously found on any toy soldiers.

Metal toys still existed, of course. Restrictions were eased by about the spring of 1945, so that before the fall of Japan in August of that year, a few metal toys had emerged, and new metal molds for plastic toys were manufactured. Many companies that did not resume operations until the war's end were back in time for Christmas. Unique Art had one of its all-time best-sellers, the Li'l Abner and His Dogpatch Band

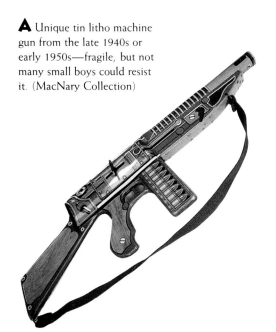

A Unique tin litho machine gun from the late 1940s or early 1950s—fragile, but not many small boys could resist it. (MacNary Collection)

Unique's postwar line of tin litho trains were attractively done. Shown here are its "1950(a)" engine and tender. (Richard MacNary)

Unique's Rodeo Joe Whoopee Car tin litho wind-up. (Mapes Auctioneers, Vestal, New York)

windup, on toy shelves by late 1945; and Man-oil, with new, more realistically designed lead soldiers, was in such a rush to catch Christmas orders that it didn't take the time to paint the figures.

Few prewar firms had trouble coping with changes that had taken place since the war. Some companies, like Barclay and Manoil, whose production had been dominated by war toys, found themselves in reduced circum-stances, but still they survived. Auburn Rubber, perhaps inspired by the prewar success of its tractor, dropped its soldier line entirely and turned more and more toward farm toys—equip-ment, barns, and animals. Perhaps the only major company that faltered was Arcade, which listlessly tried turning out zamac (a hard metal alloy), plastic, rubber, and tin toys before giving up the ghost about 1946.

Those early postwar years were a time of hope and increasing prosperity. The future looked brighter, and parents' hopes for their children—the baby boom had begun—rose cor-respondingly. Their kids were to have all the advantages: more education, better jobs, and a higher level of culture. The time was ripe for a company that catered to such hopes and dreams.

Creative Playthings was founded in Hights-town, New Jersey, in 1950 by Bernard Baren-holtz and Frank Caplan. The two men had the idea of offering toys that helped develop a child's imagination, rather than (as so many thought at the time) stunting it with toys so elaborate the child could bring nothing of himself to them. Creative Playthings' toys were simplicity itself: beautifully designed cars, airplanes, trucks, and trains of immaculately finished, unpainted wood, which essentially symbolized, rather than literally depicted, the objects they represented.

The approach proved successful virtually from the start. Geared to volume sales for preschool and kindergarten programs, Creative Playthings' toys were also scooped up at the better department stores by earnest, enthusiastic young parents.

Soon Creative Playthings had New York and Chicago offices. Much of what the company sold was made for it by other manufacturers, but the firm itself also made tables, cots, swings, and other preschool equipment. As much as parents loved the firm's products in the 1950s and 1960s, the toys don't seem to have made much of an impression on the children who played with them. Were the children too young? Or was the toys' elemental beauty a turnoff, the smoothly turned surfaces offering no kitschy angles to ex-cite a child's affection? Or had the toys done exactly what they had been designed to do: take a child at one stage of his development and help push him onto the next, minus any lingering traces of affection for the objects themselves? In any event, nearly forty years after their initial manufacture, Creative Playthings' toys have in-spired few—perhaps no—collectors.

Milton Berle was the king of television in the late 1940s and early 1950s, and Louis Marx did what he could to make the most of the phenomenon. (Mapes Auctioneers, Vestal, New York)

But something that causes parents to shudder to this day did catch children's eyes and capture their hearts. Television was a postwar phenomenon. In 1946, since few homes had sets, people crowded bars to watch it, but by 1947 sets had become somewhat cheaper, and there was more programming, including, beginning December 27, 1947, a children's show called "Howdy Doody." By 1948, Milton Berle had begun his remarkable run of popularity and was eventually credited with having inspired the purchase of more sets than any other individual or show.

The same year, "Hopalong Cassidy" debuted. Hoppy, a black-suited cowboy played by William Boyd, had been a popular movie hero since the 1930s, but the sense of wonder that was a part of television in its early days invested the Clarence E. Mulford creation with a magic he had never before had. The show became a hit very quickly, and almost as quickly a wide variety of manufacturers leapt aboard Hopalong's bandwagon. There were Hopalong Cassidy costumes, tin windups, toy soldiers, binoculars, dart boards, knives, badges, shooting galleries, and of course a wide variety of guns and holsters.

Gene Autry, who had debuted on the small screen in 1947, the Lone Ranger (1948), and Roy Rogers (1950) also found that television boosted their toy-licensing programs.

Trigger was still being billed as "The Smartest Horse in the Movies," but by the time this 1956 Marx toy came out, television was the famous equine's vehicle, as Rogers had made his last western movie in 1951. (Charles D. Richards, Pevely, Missouri)

New in 1953 was Marx's Disney Television Playhouse. The figures were of soft, flexible vinyl plastic, and the lithographed metal theater was 11¾ inches high. (Ron Fink)

What appears to be a postwar Disney toy: Marx's Mickey Mouse Express tin wind-up, a variation on Marx's long-popular Honeymoon Express. (Bizarre Bazaar, New York)

Goofy usually played second or third string to the other Disney characters, but here he appears to be the star —till you see the name of the toy. From Louis Marx in 1946. (Bizarre Bazaar, New York)

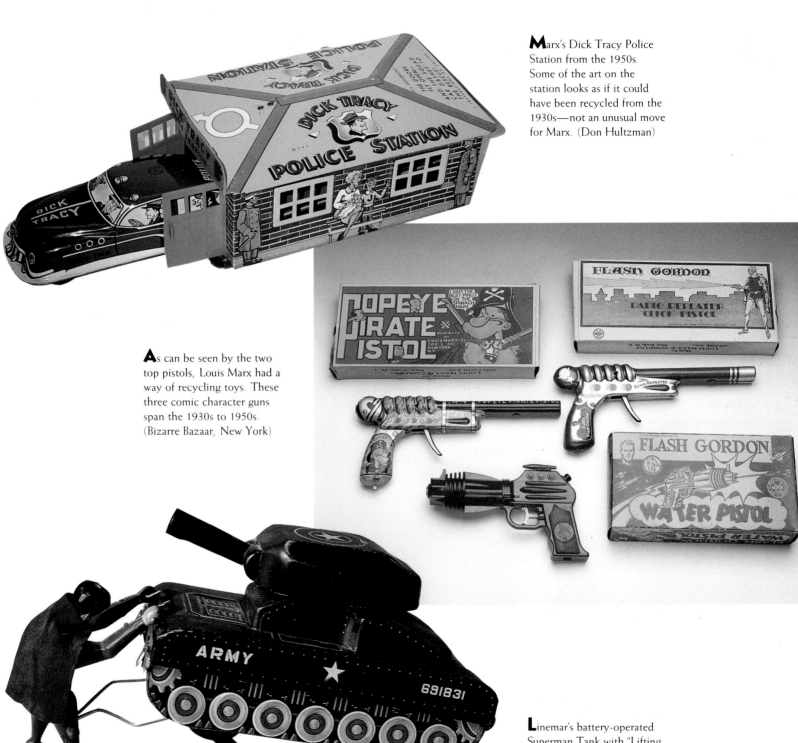

Marx's Dick Tracy Police Station from the 1950s. Some of the art on the station looks as if it could have been recycled from the 1930s—not an unusual move for Marx. (Don Hultzman)

As can be seen by the two top pistols, Louis Marx had a way of recycling toys. These three comic character guns span the 1930s to 1950s. (Bizarre Bazaar, New York)

Linemar's battery-operated Superman Tank with "Lifting Tank" action, from 1958. (Danny Fuchs)

More and more television-inspired toys appeared as the 1940s and 1950s marched on. "Captain Video," which debuted June 27, 1949, featured a stalwart hero operating out of his "secret mountain headquarters" here on earth while fighting against the forces of evil throughout the universe. Despite an absurdly low budget (and it showed), the show caught on, lasted until August 16, 1957, and launched a welter of toys. All or most of them were premiums: a Flying Saucer Ring, a Rite-O-Lite flashlight, a Rocket Launcher and rocket ships, a Secret Seal Ring, a Space Fleet Ray Gun, and a Rocket Balloon.

Howdy Doody was a particular favorite among toy buyers. A freckle-faced puppet, he translated naturally into the toy world, as Charlie McCarthy had before him. For years there were Howdy hand puppets and marionettes, tin windups, squeeze toys, sand molds, dolls, toy TV sets, ventriloquist's dummies, and musical instruments.

Toy musical instruments became a major force in the early 1950s. Mattel, a new California company, purchased the rights to a simple invention that changed the whole approach to toy instruments. It was a rubber belt with bumps.

A fun idea from Marx in the 1950s: a "Fix-All Convertible." The car is a 1953 Pontiac Catalina, all plastic. (MacNary Collection)

Marx is known for its wind-ups, but it also made push and friction toys. This is one of the latter. (Mapes Auctioneers, Vestal, New York)

The 1951 version of Marx's Balky Mule and Cart, a tin litho wind-up. (Mapes Auctioneers, Vestal, New York)

When the belt moved, it struck prongs that played musical tones. The process was similar to that of a player piano, with the advantage of lending itself to low-cost mass manufacturing. Adding to that the intricate detailing plastic offered, the musical instruments of Mattel and others were soon caterwauling across the land.

Another phenomenon that began in the late 1940s and continued until at least 1976 was Louis Marx's legion of Playsets. Until recently, most have considered Marx's greatest toys its line of colorful tin windups. Of late, this opinion has been subject to reassessment, as a growing number of toy fanciers look upon the company's postwar plastic figures and their amazingly numerous accessories as Marx's ultimate achievement. Most of the figures were impressively sculpted (about 90 percent of them probably by Joe Ferriot, of Akron's Ferriot Brothers), in approximately 60-millimeter size. Virtually none of them were painted; they came in a single solid color. But they were so detailed, with distinctive faces and expressions, the children of the day didn't seem to mind. (Virtually no plastic soldiers of the period were painted.)

Marx's early sets weren't particularly inspired as to subject—soldiers, cowboys and Indians, and, a little later on, gas stations and farms—but their quality and the quantity of their components made them catch on quickly. A single Marx set contained more toys and accessories than most of the kids of the 1920s and 1930s had owned throughout the duration of their childhood. Take the U.S. Army Training Center set of 1951. For $5.98 one got a stunning 145 pieces: 100 plastic soldiers in a variety of positions (during the deepest days of the Depression, 100 soldiers alone would have cost $5), a metal headquarters building, machine guns, tents, stacked rifles, bazookas, flags, trees, rocks, an army half-track, a scout car, sixteen sections of fence, and—the kind of equipment details that made so many of the Marx Playsets intriguing— a desk, swivel chair, switchboard, rifle rack, crate, side chairs, map table, bench, and even a file cabinet and a wastebasket.

A year later, the ever-enterprising Marx, always ready to latch on to hot toy trends, issued at least four new sets inspired by TV shows: a Roy Rogers Mineral City and a Roy Rogers Double R Bar Ranch Rodeo, a Tom Corbett 25th-Century Space Academy, and a Super Circus with Mary Hartline. In 1953 Marx added one of his most popular items, the Fort Apache set, which was issued in a bewildering number of variations over the years.

In 1954 Walt Disney introduced "Disney-

land," a weekly TV series that gave renewed impetus to Disney toys. That same year Disney brought Davy Crockett to TV, originally as a set of three one-hour-long shows, aired in December 1954 and January and February 1955. There was tremendous, virtually instantaneous demand for coonskin caps and frontier-type weapons. More than two hundred Davy Crockett items (not all of them toys) were marketed, some with the Disney imprimatur and some without (there was no way Disney could copyright the Crockett name). Among the many manufacturers putting out Crockett toys were Daisy—who issued a rifle, a canteen, and a powder horn—and, of course, Marx. The 1955 Sears version of Marx's Davy Crockett at the Alamo set had one hundred pieces, including a large tin reproduction of the

An example of the superb craftsmanship that went into many of the plastic figures in Marx's Playsets. These are personality figures from the "Ben Hur" set, first issued in 1959. (Gary Linden, River Forest, Illinois)

Alamo with "fighting platforms" and moveable gates, Crockett himself with thirty frontiersmen, thirty foot and mounted Mexicans, plus an incredible assortment of accessories, including a water pump, an andiron, a well, a hitching post, and a stack of logs.

Meanwhile a military police action on the other side of the globe had severely affected the U.S. toy industry. Most people who lived through both World War II and the Korean conflict remember the first as a time of shortages and the second simply as a period when the front page carried a daily account of events too remote to have much impact. But, like World War II, the Korean War created some serious shortages. A Hubley catalog of the period stated, "From the start of hostilities in Korea, the American manufacturer has been put in a position of limited production due to the allocation or scarcity of metal. This factor has brought about a great increase in the output of plastic toys. The Hubley Company at the present time is devoting 20% of its time to plastics." Due to metal shortages, some companies, already struggling, let go. Doepke tried to find heavy-gauge steel but, hurt by the less-detailed and much cheaper toys of Nylint and Tonka, finally gave up its line of steel toys in 1956, turned to wooden toys for a year or two, then expired. Manoil, having floundered for four years during World War II, floundered again during the Korean conflict, and shut down for several months in 1953. Most likely, shortages of materials combined with strong competition weakened Smith-Miller, which bowed out in 1954. Wyandotte followed in 1956.

But the "ill-wind" theory proved true in practice as the J. H. Miller Company of Quincy, Illinois, enjoyed a vogue in dimestores for a couple of years, selling toy soldiers for nineteen cents apiece. These were extremely fragile playthings, made entirely of plaster except for their plastic equipment, but they filled a void. Slik-Toy of Lansing, Iowa, also turned out a series of plaster toy soldiers beginning in mid- to late 1951; at the height of interest in the war, the company churned out hundreds of figures a day.

Another materials problem was giving certain manufacturers fits. It wasn't a shortage, but an overabundance. The material was plastic, which began to flood the toy market in the 1950s. One hundred Barclay or Manoil metal toy soldiers would have cost fifteen dollars in the 1950s, while a bag of one hundred unpainted plastic soldiers sold for a dollar: one cent apiece. Even unpainted, they were an enormous bargain, and children, quick and shrewd in such matters, pounced.

The problem was even more perplexing. Many of the plastic toys—an ever-increasing number of them—were coming from foreign countries, particularly the Far East. There was no way that American companies could compete with the low cost of labor in less-developed nations.

It was, in fact, an invasion, particularly by the Japanese, who not only exploited the use of plastics, but introduced a revolutionary way of powering toys. Toys had used batteries before, but only for illumination, or to power horns, buzzers, and so on. Movement was provided by a spring or flywheel. The Japanese changed all that by developing miniature electric motors powered by one or more batteries. The result was toys that stayed in motion much longer than previous playthings. Battery operation also meant that toy makers could devise all sorts of additional movements, providing as many as six different actions in a single item.

Once they fully realized what was happening, American companies, true to their heritage, tried to leap aboard the new bandwagon. But they met with limited success. Indeed, much that was marketed under such names as Marx, Ideal, Hubley, and Daisy actually was made in Japan. And plenty of the Japanese toys selling here retained their own company trademark, declining distribution by American giants. It was the beginning of a revolution that is still under way—though it is no longer led by the Japanese.

Another trend, inspired in part by the Japanese innovation, began during this period. In September 1954, Republic Pictures released a movie called *Tobor the Great*. There is no evidence that the movie lived up to its title at the box office, but somehow a character from that movie, Robert the Robot, became the first big-selling battery-powered plastic toy robot. Ideal brought out a number of versions of Robert, which encompassed minor design variations as well as major changes. The standard Robert had moveable arms and a face that lit up when a dial was turned. It was operated via a remote-control box. Robert also talked—oddly enough, in a woman's voice. In a major departure from the film Robert emerged as the driver of a bulldozer; in that repressed era, even exotic figures could be forced into mundane lives.

Mundane, but not necessarily standard. One of the more esoteric toys of the 1950s was from Renwal, circa 1957: a Panama Canal set. The plastic toy had a water tank meant to represent Lake Gatun, along with four ships and locks that mechanically lowered, raised, and launched the vessels. The entire thing retailed for six dollars. If Renwal scored the coup of the year with its set, the firm was impressively modest about it.

There was a boom in assemble-it-yourself plastic models in the 1950s (some could be used

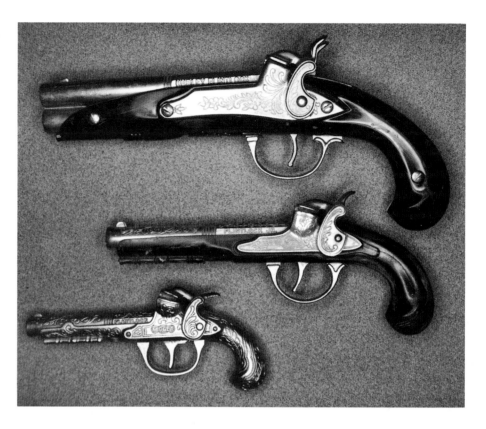

In 1955, Hubley was selling these, opposite, top to bottom: Flintlock; Flintlock Jr.; and Midget. The same year, a kid with poor aim could always follow up with the dagger that was an integral part of the Dagger Derringer from Hubley, 8 inches long, with dagger extended, shown in the picture opposite, below. (Charles W. Best)

Robert the Robot, a 1950s battery-operated toy from Ideal. (Don Hultzman)

A significant robot toy, Ideal's battery-operated 14-inch-high "Robert the Robot," which emerged in 1954. (Don Hultzman)

as toys, some only for display), spurred in part by the development of plastic cements that really did the job of permanently joining parts. Major names included Monogram, Aurora, Pyro, and particularly Revell, which jumped into the field in 1951 and was soon producing more cars than Ford, General Motors, and Chrysler put together, plus more planes than the whole air industry. This flood of models, of which a circa-1950 reproduction of Jack Benny's famed Maxwell was the first trickle, vaulted Revell into the top ten among toy makers and also inaugurated a trend toward nostalgia.

By and large the toys of the 1950–59 period reflected the relative placidity of the times. All the longtime staples were there, both as to manufacturers and the toys they made. A peek at a few 1950s catalogs makes this clear. A 1952 Woolworth's *Christmas Book* shows two pages of dolls; pull toys; a Roly Poly clown; an Alphabet Rattle set; molded-plastic dresser sets (which looked "just like Mother's"); some Sun Rubber toys, including a Mickey Mouse Fire Truck and a Donald Duck Roadster; a page of Auburn Rubber toys, including a tractor, a train set, a fire engine, and a racing car; a plastic ukulele; playballs (oversize rubber balls decorated with colorful designs); a page of Hubley trucks ("all sturdy plastic and metal"); a page of Wyandotte trucks and road equipment (for the most part made of heavy-gauge steel); tin toys by Chein, including an amusement park Rocket Ride, a ferris wheel, and a merry-go-round; tricycles; Bachman Brothers' popular plastic toy village of the period, which fit in nicely with the increasingly popular HO trains; a rifle that shot "6 harmless plastic balls"; a half-page of Fisher-Price's pull-and-push toys; several sets of building blocks; and an American Logs set. A full page of cowboy pistols and holsters concluded the catalog.

Three years later, judging by *The Toy Yearbook*, nothing much had changed: dolls, Disney toys, lots of Fisher-Price, blocks, Hill bell toys, stuffed animals, a Schoenhut grand piano (by a Schoenhut licensee), a wide variety of Playskool toys for young children, Auburn Rubber farm sets, an official Walt Disney Davy Crockett outfit (complete with coonskin cap), pistols, and pistols with holsters. There were also plastic knights, Ramar of the Jungle figures (a TV-series tie-in), doctor sets, plenty of dolls and carriages, Lionel trains, an array of Emenee plastic musical toys, kitchen toys, Walt Disney Frontierland Logs (like Lincoln and American Logs), plastic bricks, Plasticville buildings (HO size), a Tinkertoy set, a tool chest, Gilbert's Erector Sets and chemistry sets, a toy typewriter, plastic model sets, a Jerry Mahoney ventriloquist dummy (another TV tie-in), Daisy and T. Cohn

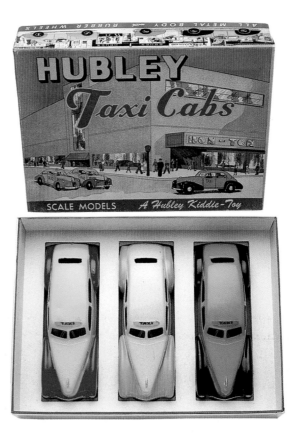

Hubley taxis, mid-to-late 1940s. All metal with rubber tires. (Bizarre Bazaar, New York)

rifles, a variety of Wyandotte, American Model Toys, Product Miniature, Buddy "L," Ideal, Hubley, Doepke, Tonka, Nylint, and Structo vehicles, a Doepke yard train big enough for kids to ride, and various hobby horses, bicycles, tricycles, and pedal cars.

The only indications of future trends in this catalog were a Robert the Robot; a Saunders battery-operated tractor, Marvelous Mike, which was driven by a robot; and a Mattel metal-and-plastic Burp Gun, about which more later.

By 1956, things began to change, but just a bit. A Sears Christmas catalog reveals a sudden jump in battery-operated toys. Whereas the year before there had been just one American battery-operated moveable toy, in 1956 there were seven, including a robot dog and a Brainy Bug.

These three versions of Hubley's approximation to the Seversky P-35 are less than faithful replicas. (Perry R. Eichor)

Likewise, the year before there had been no sub-machine guns; there were now three.

In October 1957, Russia launched its Sputnik, and on January 31, 1958, America's first satellite went into orbit. By Christmas 1958 the space boom—in toys—was on. The new Sears catalog showed a sixty-plus-piece Cape Canaveral Rocket Set, by Marx, and there were a battery-operated Moon Rocket, a battery-operated Moon Space Ship, and a friction-powered Two-Stage Earth Satellite (all Japanese). There were now *seven* submachine guns.

The increased number of Japanese toys in the 1958 Sears catalog underscores a significant event of that year: Charles Marcak, who exactly twenty years before had introduced the first plastic toy soldiers, attended the New York Toy Fair and saw, in the words of an associate, that the Japanese had been "copying his toys," offering them at a far lower price than he could. Marcak saw no way he could compete and, shortly after the fair, closed down his Bergen Toy & Novelty Co.

The handwriting was on the wall. By the end of the decade, a number of companies were out of business, unable to compete with far cheaper toys from the Orient. Among the casualties was New Hampshire's Toy Manufacturing Company, maker of jumping jacks since 1872.

Yet, as the 1950s came to a close, two classic toys premiered, and something that would become a major toy genre in the future was just getting its start. It all happened in 1959.

The first item was an instant success that has yet to falter. But, then, how could so perfect a being *ever* falter? And Barbie *was* perfect. That hair, that face, those legs, those—um—perfectly formed breasts! A true 1950s teenager (as most any boy who wound up in the back seat with one of them could tell you), Barbie made

Here she is, Misses America —Barbie!—mounted, as her publicity blurb breathlessly points out, on her "original pronged stand." The epochal year was 1959. (Mattel Toys)

sure her first two outfits were bras and girdles. According to Billy Boy, author of *Barbie: Her Life and Times*, "they allowed young women to anticipate the structured and difficult-to-wear undergarments of the era."

Eventually, Barbie was to accumulate a total wardrobe Imelda Marcos would envy. She also had a host of friends and relatives, the most prominent of them, of course, being Ken, Barbie's "significant other," who had perfect hair, face, legs, and—um—pecs. If anything embodied the 1950s, it was Barbie. And, in many ways, if any era best reflected what we think of as typically American, it was the 1950s. Perhaps this is why the first successful postpubescent doll is still so very much with us.

In 1959 Marx debuted its classic Ben Hur Playset, timed to benefit from the ballyhoo for the MGM release in November of that year. The larger version of the set, which sold for $12.98, contained an astounding 217 pieces. It was a phantasmagoria that included galleries with plastic columns, an amphitheater, a slave market and bazaar, tents, braziers, tables, lamps, chests, urns, food containers with molded plastic food, portrait busts, a lion, a tiger, eight charioteers, an emperor, an empress, Ben Hur, gladiators, slaves—even a hookah!

The toy of the future in that 1959 Sears catalog came in the form of seven playthings, each eight to ten inches high, of molded plastic. They represented Zorro, Roy Rogers, Marshall Matt Dillon of TV's "Gunsmoke," Jim Hardie of "Wells Fargo," Dan Troop of "Lawman," Paladin of "Have Gun Will Travel," and *Sleeping Beauty's* Prince Philip. They were precursors, of what, in the next decade, would come to be known as "action figures."

But before we move on to the 1960s, let's drop back a year to 1958 to note one of the great toy fads. A California company, Wham-O, had done well the previous year, with a little item called a Frisbie. In May they released a plastic version of a wooden Australian toy. It was a three-foot hoop of polyethylene tubing called the Hula Hoop.

There was no way Wham-O could patent its hoop, but despite a dozen or more companies jumping onto the bandwagon, by September Wham-O had sold two million of its torso twirlers. The fad swept the world and, of course, set off the usual rash of alarm-sounders (perhaps because in action, hula hoopers looked dangerously like Elvis Presley, he of the suspect pelvis). Japan banned the toy from the streets; three million were sold there anyway. In South Africa, free Hula Hoops were given to the poor. A group of Belgian explorers brought twenty hoops with them to the South Pole.

By the summer of 1959 the fad was over. A few months later, so were the 1950s.

OHIO ART's

Etch-A-Sketch

AS NEW AS 1960

No. 505 ETCH-A-SKETCH

Fascinating

FAMILY FUN!

No. 505 Etch-A-Sketch is an absorbing new toy that's fun, and educational . . . truly a toy for all ages. Manipulate the knobs to form letters, pictures, charts, designs — whatever the imagination dictates. Turn the Etch-A-Sketch upside down, shake it, and the printing disappears.

This original Ohio Art toy made of plastic and glass, is approximately 9½″ wide, 7¾″ high and 1¾″ thick. Each in a box. One-half dozen to the carton. 7 lbs.

THE OHIO ART COMPANY, Bryan, Ohio

Manufacturers of Lithographed Metal, Flexible Poly and Rubber-Like Vinyl Toys

New York Office:
200 Fifth Avenue Building
Suite 852
Telephone: CHelsea 2-1432

8

THE SOARING SIXTIES

he 1960s were an exciting time for toy buyers. They were the years when plastic came into its own, and while some die-hard toy fanciers viewed anything made of plastic as junk, toys had, in fact, never been so beautifully detailed. Now that toy makers had solved the problems of color in plastics, the new material was at least the equivalent of its ancestors in providing eye-catching brightness.

Ohio Art started the decade with one of the longest- and steadiest-selling toys in history when it began production of the Etch A Sketch on July 12, 1960. The toy had been invented by Arthur Grandjean, a Frenchman who called his prototype the Magic Screen (the full name for Ohio Art's toy is still Etch A Sketch Magic Screen). It consisted of a rectangular box with two knobs with which one could form letters, pictures, charts, and designs on the screen. Turned upside down and shaken, the Etch A Sketch was once again a blank screen, ready for more. Ohio Art representatives had seen the Magic Screen at the 1959 toy fair in Nuremburg, West Germany, and turned it down. Later, they reconsidered and decided to market it. There were a few doubts when the blueprints reached Ohio; the instructions were in French, and the measurements were metric. But Ohio Art persevered, and "The first indication it was a hit was when some of our company officials were playing with it on the way to New York," a company executive recalls. "Everybody on the plane wanted to play with it. It's the ideal travel toy."

It was also the first toy Ohio Art advertised on television. The toy sold so well that the factory was assembling units up until noon on December 24, 1960, so that a final shipment could be flown to the West Coast in time for very late Christmas shoppers.

In the same year another highly imaginative toy emerged, Ideal's Mr. Machine, a tall, top-hatted windup mechanical man, with forty-four numbered plastic parts that could be assembled and disassembled, a transparent body, and all sorts of colorful gears. He walked, swung his arms, opened and closed his mouth, rang a bell, and every ten seconds a siren in his belly went off. Wound up, he ran for about a minute. Mr. Machine, continuing to wear the ingratiating smile of old, has refused to go away. In 1977, he was revived—though he could no longer be disassembled—and a bellows squeaker playing "This Old Man" replaced the bell and siren. Exactly ten years later, he was back again, still tootling out "This Old Man."

Ohio Art's first Etch-A-Sketch ad. (Ohio Art)
OPPOSITE

Ideal's Mr. Machine, in his 1962 incarnation. INSET

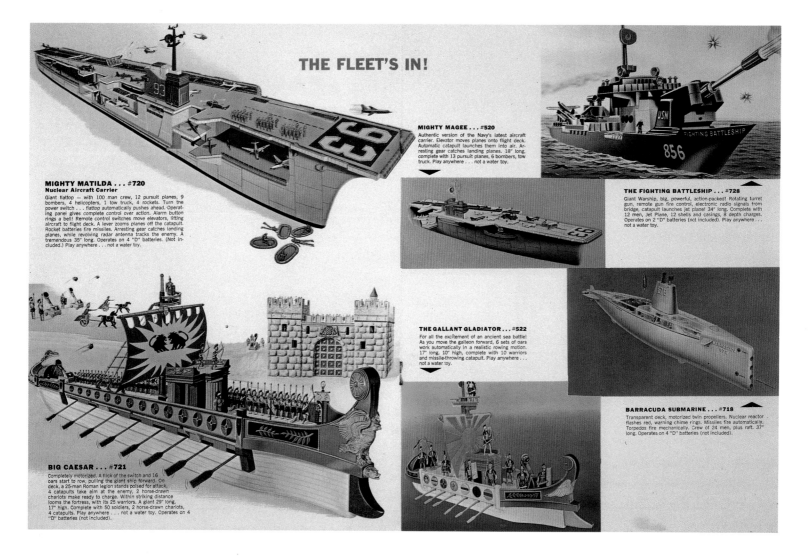

THE FLEET'S IN!

MIGHTY MAGEE . . . #520
Authentic version of the Navy's latest aircraft carrier. Elevator moves planes onto flight deck. Automatic catapult launches them into air. Arresting gear catches landing planes. 18" long, complete with 13 pursuit planes, 6 bombers, tow truck. Play anywhere . . . not a water toy.

MIGHTY MATILDA . . . #720
Nuclear Aircraft Carrier
Giant flattop — with 100 man crew, 12 pursuit planes, 9 bombers, 4 helicopters, 1 tow truck, 4 rockets. Turn the power switch . . . flattop automatically pushes ahead. Operating panel gives complete control over action. Alarm button rings a bell! Remote control switches move elevators, lifting aircraft to flight deck. A lever zooms planes off the catapult. Rocket batteries fire missiles. Arresting gear catches landing planes, while revolving radar antenna tracks the enemy. A tremendous 35" long. Operates on 4 "D" batteries. (Not included.) Play anywhere . . . not a water toy. (Not included.)

THE FIGHTING BATTLESHIP . . . #728
Giant Warship, big, powerful, action-packed. Rotating turret gun, remote gun fire control, electronic radio signals from bridge, catapult launches jet plane! 34" long. Complete with 12 men, Jet Plane, 12 shells and casings, 8 depth charges. Operates on 2 "D" batteries (not included). Play anywhere . . . not a water toy.

THE GALLANT GLADIATOR . . . #522
For all the excitement of an ancient sea battle! As you move the galleon forward, 6 sets of oars work automatically in a realistic rowing motion. 17" long, 10" high, complete with 10 warriors and missile-throwing catapult. Play anywhere . . . not a water toy.

BARRACUDA SUBMARINE . . . #718
Transparent deck, motorized twin propellers, Nuclear reactor flashes red, warning chime rings. Missiles fire automatically. Torpedos fire mechanically. Crew of 24 men, plus raft. 37" long. Operates on 4 "D" batteries (not included).

BIG CAESAR . . . #721
Completely motorized. A flick of the switch and 16 oars start to row, pulling the giant ship forward. On deck, a 25-man Roman legion stands poised for attack, 4 catapults take aim at the enemy, 2 horse-drawn chariots make ready to charge. Within striking distance looms the fortress, with its 25 warriors. A giant 29" long, 17" high. Complete with 50 soldiers, 2 horse-drawn chariots, 4 catapults. Play anywhere . . . not a water toy. Operates on 4 "D" batteries (not included).

In 1960, *huge* battery-operated toys—plastic, naturally—began to take over. The span of their reign was brief—only about four years—but in this time a number of impressive toys were offered. There was, for instance, Remco's Fighting Lady battleship, which was three feet long and sold for $8.88 at Sears. It had a gun that rotated, fired, and ejected shells. It launched a plane and fired depth charges. Electronic alarm signals were sounded from the bridge. Motorized, it had a landing craft and seven men and

was molded of high-impact plastic. The next year Remco sold a Ball Turret Gunner for $9.97; "fingertip control" whipped the gun from side to side, the ammo belt fed automatically, and gun blasts lit up a target.

In 1963, Remco was still turning out its huge motorized sea toys. Among them was Big Caesar, a Roman galleon with a twenty-five-man crew. One flick of the switch, and not only did the twenty-nine-inch-long ship move forward, its sixteen oars began to pull. Big Caesar came

Remco's extraordinarily action-packed ships, as shown in a 1964 catalog.

with four catapults, two horse-drawn chariots, and a plastic fortress with twenty-five defenders.

Remco's Mighty Matilda was a nearly three-foot-long atomic aircraft carrier. An operating panel controled all the action aboard: an elevator lifted aircraft to the flight deck; once placed on a catapult, the plane was ready to spring into the air at the press of a button; rocket launchers shot off missiles; an arresting gear caught landing aircraft; if the gear was missed, the planes hit a crash barrier. There were twelve planes, nine bombers, four helicopters, four rockets, one tow truck, and a one-hundred-man crew. Like virtually all of Remco's ships, it couldn't be used in water.

Meanwhile, Disneyland, which had opened on July 17, 1955, at a cost of seventeen million dollars, had become enormously popular. With the continual appearances of Disney's characters at the park, on television, and in the movies, Disney merchandise continued to crowd the nation's toy counters. In 1961, Louis Marx decided Disneyland itself might be a good bet as a toy. The result was a huge ninety-five-piece Playset to be assembled on a five-foot-by-thirty-inch plastic layout sheet that came with the set. All the various sections of Disneyland were represented: Fantasyland, Adventureland, Frontierland, and Tomorrowland. There was a train, a rocket, flying saucers, cowboys and Indians, animals, boats, and such Disney characters as Dumbo, Donald Duck, and Professor Ludwig Von Drake. Impressive as it was, it was swallowed up in the Disney stream—just one Disney toy among many, including music boxes, windup trains, miniatures of the Disney figures, musical instruments, jack in the boxes, and so on.

Marx also capitalized on another trend that had started in the mid-1950s, when movies like *Godzilla* had begun to seize the imagination of the nation's youth. The ever-creative toy mogul first came out with his own version of a B-grade Japanese monster movie hero-villain in 1961. The creature's name was Garloo, also known as The Great Garloo. He was American-made (of plastic) and battery-operated. Garloo could advance, stop, turn, bend, and pick up and drop things at his owner's remote-control command. Significantly, when Marx later issued two versions of The Great Son of Garloo, each was made in Japan.

A magazine called *Famous Monsters* had hit the newsstands in 1958. Aimed at young boys and teenagers, it devoted itself exclusively to monsters of the movies. It was a huge hit, and intensified its audience's interest in B-grade monster movies just as they were beginning to leave the theaters and appear on television. In 1961, Aurora Plastics took advantage of the trend and came out with the first in a line of smartly designed monster model kits that depicted Universal Pictures monsters. The premiere ghoul was Frankenstein's Monster. Dracula and The Wolfman followed in 1962 and, after them, in 1963, the deluge: The Phantom of the Opera, The Hunchback of Notre Dame, The Mummy, and The Creature from the Black Lagoon. King Kong and Godzilla were next in 1964. Kids were entranced, and the ever-enterprising Louis Marx once again took note. In 1963, he issued one-piece (no assembly required) polyethylene versions, employing the same toolmakers who had fashioned the Auroras.

During the 1960s Aurora also sold its own soft plastic monsters, which stood approximately three inches high. Multiple Toy Products, a firm not celebrated for superb sculpture, issued 2½-inch-high soft plastic monsters that, except for The Phantom of the Opera, were generic witches, mummies, werewolves, and the like.

Nineteen sixty-four was a signal year; it marked the emergence of a whole new category of toy: the action figure. As previously noted, there had been earlier intimations of what was to come, but Hasbro's G. I. Joe was no intimation. He was the real thing.

Hasbro was—and still is—a family-owned business, founded in 1923 in Providence, Rhode Island, by two brothers, Henry and Hillel Hassenfeld, immigrants from Poland. (The name "Hasbro" wasn't used until 1968.) In the earliest days, Hassenfeld Brothers sold textile remnants. Later, they manufactured pencil boxes, economically covered with those same remnants. As the years passed, Henry Hassenfeld gradually took over the reins of the company, while Hillel started another textile business. By mid-1939 Hassenfeld Brothers was making pencil boxes as well as other school supplies; sales reached a half million dollars, an impressive sum in those late Depression days.

Henry Hassenfeld's sons, Harold and Merrill, joined the company in the late 1930s; in 1943 Merrill took over as president, and in 1946 Empire Pencil Company of Shelbyhill, Tennessee, became part of the operation, managed by Harold. It was Merrill's idea to start making toys during slack times in the seasonal school-supply business. The firm's first toys were similar to their school supplies: paint sets and wax crayons, and then doctor and nurse kits. By the end of the 1940s, Hassenfeld Brothers was taking in three million dollars a year. Then came Mr. Potato Head in the 1950s, the first toy to be advertised on television. By the 1960s, the company was really booming.

But all that was only a prelude to G. I. Joe. Inspired by an artist's manikin a Hasbro executive noticed one day in the window of an art supply shop, G. I. Joe hit the stores in July 1964,

Hasbro's wildly popular action figure, G. I. Joe, with "lifelike hair," ca. 1970. (Hasbro)

and the world of boys' toys hasn't been the same since.

The predecessors of G. I. Joe had been fairly static figures, their movement limited. Hasbro's soldier, however, was at least as manipulable as the aforesaid manikin—more so than

MILITARY PERSONNEL — MINIATURE METAL

15¢ RETAIL PRICE

NO. 960 SOLDIER, WOUNDED, W/ CRUTCHES
NO. 962 NURSE
NO. 961 SOLDIER, WOUNDED, HEAD & ARMS
NO. 988 SOLDIER, MARCHING W/GUN ON BACK
NO. 977 SOLDIER UNDER MARCHING ORDERS
NO. 903 SOLDIER SNIPER
NO. 909 SOLDIER BUGLER

NO. 947 SOLDIER MARKSMAN
NO. 948 SOLDIER RUNNING
NO. 919 SAILOR WHITE UNIFORM
NO. 920 SAILOR BLUE UNIFORM
NO. 938 SOLDIER BOMB THROWER
NO. 991 SOLDIER FLAME THROWER
NO. 937 SOLDIER, CHARGING MACHINE GUNNER
NO. 906 SOLDIER CHARGING

NO. 941 AVIATOR
NO. 929 SOLDIER, W/PISTOL CRAWLING
NO. 901 SOLDIER FLAG BEARER
NO. 922 MARINE
NO. 990 SOLDIER W/ BAZOOKA
NO. 928 SOLDIER MACHINE GUNNER
NO. 974 SOLDIER, ANTI-AIRCRAFT GUNNER
NO. 908 SOLDIER OFFICER

PACKED: 2 doz. per box
WEIGHT: 2¼ lbs. per box

COWBOYS — INDIANS — KNIGHTS — MINIATURE METAL

RETAIL 15¢ PRICE

NO. 953 COWBOY W/PISTOL
NO. 800 BLACK KNIGHT W/SWORD & SHIELD
NO. 957 INDIAN W/BOW & ARROW
NO. 955 INDIAN W/RIFLE
NO. 954 INDIAN W/SHIELD & TOMAHAWK
NO. 956 INDIAN W/KNIFE & SPEAR
NO. 950 COWBOY W/PISTOL SHOOTING
NO. 951 COWBOY W/RIFLE
NO. 952 COWBOY W/LASSO
NO. 802 KNIGHT W/ORANGE & BLK. SHIELD & SWORD
NO. 803 KNIGHT W/RED & GRN. SHIELD & SWORD
NO. 801 KNIGHT W/RED & BLUE SHIELD & SWORD

PACKED: 2 doz. per box
WEIGHT: 2¼ lbs. per box

RETAIL 49¢ PRICE
ITEM NO. 5
T-41 ARMY TANK, W/6 RUBBER WHEELS. ATTRACTIVELY BLISTER PACKED ON NEW CARD. PACKED: 1 doz. per box, 6 doz. per ctn. WEIGHT: 30 lbs. per ctn.

RETAIL 69¢ PRICE

RETAIL 59¢ PRICE
CANNON, MOVABLE W/ LARGE RUBBER WHEELS. ATTRACTIVELY BLISTER PACKED ON NEW CARD. PACKED: 1 doz. per box, 6 doz. per ctn. WEIGHT: 25 lbs. per ctn.
ITEM NO. 1

3 PIECE EQUIPMENT SET, ALL W/RUBBER MOVABLE WHEELS. ATTRACTIVELY BLISTER PACKED ON NEW CARD. PACKED: 1 doz. per box, 6 doz. per ctn. WEIGHT: 32 lbs. per ctn.

316 PALISADE AVENUE, BARCLAY UNION CITY, N.J.
MANUFACTURING CO., INC.

A Barclay catalog page from the late 1960s. Barclay reduced the size of its soldiers in the 1950s to try to hold down its prices—and it worked . . . for a time.

most. Made of plastic (of course), his body was jointed at the neck, shoulders, arms, waist, and legs. He was the miracle small boys had dreamed of for decades: he could be dressed, undressed, posed in all sorts of positions, and could hold a rifle, a pistol, or a machine gun. According to

Hasbro, his face was a composite of twenty-three Congressional Medal of Honor winners. If that were true (but apparently it was not), the composite looked stunningly like a rival to Barbie's Ken, and more than a little bland. But Hasbro's designers did add an inspired touch: a scar.

G. I. Joe was available as a soldier, an Action Sailor, an Action Marine, and an Air Force Action Pilot, each in appropriate cloth uniforms. The equipment was there from the beginning, too—a welter of field jackets, ponchos, pup tents, rifles, helmets, machine guns, sandbags, shovels, packs, scuba outfits, sea bags, pilot's helmets, you name it. By the end of the year, rival Louis Marx had issued Stony, a paratrooper with jointed head, shoulders, elbows, and wrists, who stood—could it be?—exactly eleven inches high. The same height as G. I. Joe!

Stony lasted a while, but G. I. Joe's real competition emerged in 1966. "Batman," based on the familiar comic-book character, began as a TV series on January 12, 1966. Done as pure camp, it seized the country for two years. During 1966 alone, Batman merchandising, in the form of toys, games, ice cream, clothes, peanut butter, and so on, grossed $150 million. A variety of superhero toys appeared, and Ideal sprang in to fill whatever breach it could find with Captain Action, ensuring his link with Batman by launching him via TV commercials. Perhaps intentionally, the good captain was an inch taller than G. I. Joe. He was also better modeled, with far more detail. He came in a superhero's costume of cap, jersey turtleneck with chest insignia, pants, plastic boots, a belt, a lightning-shaped sword, and a raygun-like pistol. A nice idea, but it didn't end there. Captain Action could be transformed; you could buy Superman, Batman, Flash Gordon, and Aquaman outfits that fit him. Furthermore, you could add slip-on heads that made our captain look just like the superhero he was supposed to represent. And probably a good thing, too. The one flaw in Captain Action was that his own face was kind of sad-looking, sort of beat-up looking, a bit old-looking. He could have played Barbie's father (and possibly did).

The next year, Spiderman and Captain America costumes were added, and so was Action Boy. Nine inches high, Action Boy could be transformed into Robin, Superboy, and Aqua Lad. At about the same time, Ideal added a truly inspired figure, one that must have raced the pulses of the same types who had scooped up all those Aurora monster kits. His name was Dr. Evil, a marvelously hideous adversary who came with such props as a hypodermic rifle, an almost normal fake face that could be ripped off at the proper time, and other accessories collectively known as Dr. Evil's "evil things."

Captain Action had his own accessories, things like a Secret Chamber and a Silver Streak Car. In time, he also masqueraded as Buck Rogers, the Green Hornet (with Action Boy as Kato), the Phantom, the Lone Ranger, Steve Canyon, and Sgt. Fury. In a kind of reverse spin,

For kids who got turned on by hats as weapons: Oddjob, 1966, from the James Bond movie *Goldfinger*. (Charles D. Richards, Pevely, Missouri)

Captain Action also hatched a comic book, which lasted six issues in its first incarnation.

At about the same time, toy makers discovered James Bond. The first Bond movie, *Dr. No*, had been released in 1962; toy moguls caught up with 007 about 1965 with a spate of Bond toys. Gilbert issued a huge array of 3¼-inch plastic figures: Bond himself, Dr. No, Oddjob, Domino, Largo, "M," Miss Moneypenny, and Goldfinger. One could also buy a scene from *Thunderball*, M's Office, Dr. No's Laboratory, and Goldfinger's Lodge, as well as Bond in a scuba outfit. Bond and Oddjob were also issued as eleven-inch action figures. Perhaps the most fun was Oddjob, the killer whose blade-rimmed hat was a deadly Frisbee-like weapon. Oddjob's arms were spring-operated; when the right arm's spring was released, it flung the hat in the general direction of whatever adversary Oddjob was pointed toward. Release the left arm and—look out!—Oddjob's forearm chopped "downward like an axe."

"The Man From U.N.C.L.E." debuted as a television series on September 22, 1964. It was very much influenced by James Bond and for a time enjoyed as much popularity, both as a show (it ran for four years) and as a fount for toy making. Aurora Plastics added the show's characters to its line of model kits, Gabriel came out with walkie-talkies, the irrepressible Marx sold an U.N.C.L.E. shooting cane, and Ideal produced a target game. Again, it was action figures that were most prominent, with A. C. Gilbert spinning out eleven-inch versions of the show's stars. The most popular was Illya Kuryakin, played by David McCallum, who was known as the "Blond Beatle" because of his mop-top haircut. Like most of the action figures who tried to ape G. I. Joe and Captain Action, he had more limited mobility, but he did wear a black turtle-

neck sweater, pants, and shoes (all removable), and could hold a die-cast metal pistol that actually fired caps.

Naturally, a host of other accessories were available, including a Jump Suit Set, a Target Set, and an Arsenal Set, which consisted of a cap-firing tommy gun and pistol, a spring-firing bazooka, three shells, a bipod, a sight, and a rifle butt for the pistol. All three of the accessory sets were made in Japan. Also generating a few toys was the spinoff, "The Girl from U.N.C.L.E.," which had more limited success, running from 1966 to 1967.

Other notable action figures of the time included the various folks from the TV series "Bonanza," Marx's Johnny West, Jane West, and Josie West (Jane's daughter), and Marx's 11½-inch-high Knights in Shining Armor. Complete with horse, the Knights set consisted of fifty-three pieces—mostly the armor.

Space toys continued to be hot sellers during the 1960s. In 1961 Ideal put out Robot Commando, which obeyed spoken commands, moved forward, turned to its left or right, and fired rockets and three missiles. Another popular American-made robot was the "Lost in Space" gent who wandered about flashing a light where his head should have been. He stood twelve inches high and was made of plastic. In 1963 Marx debuted Big Loo, a three-foot-high moon robot. (*Loo* presumably stood for *lunar*—though perhaps for Louis, as in Marx?) Big Loo came with a variety of weapons, including darts that shot out of his chest, as did water. He also possessed a clicker, a bell, a whistle, and a record that enabled him to say ten different things. Despite all the weaponry, Big Loo was a friendly-looking sort, with an ear-to-ear grin.

As the nation turned more and more toward space, a horde of spacemen were created, some actually made in the United States. In 1966, inspired in part by the "Lost in Space" TV show, Mattell turned out a Lost in Space set, the main feature of which was a motorized Space Chariot. The same year G. I. Joe was issued a space capsule and a space suit outfit. Sears had a spaceman with an accompanying Space Mutt the same year; the canine even had his own space helmet.

The following year, Mattel found itself with a pretty good space seller, Major Matt Mason, a bendable figure that stood six inches high and came with a Space Sled, a Motorized Space Crawler, and a Jet Propulsion Pak. The next year, 1968, Mattel added a four-inch sliding Cat Trac space tractor to Mason's accessories and brought out Captain Lazer. A truly impressive piece of work, Lazer stood thirteen inches high, and his chest, eyes, and "lazer" decoder all lit up. He also contained a buzzer and had bendable legs and moveable arms. But why did he look vaguely Japanese?

At the beginning of the 1960s, Louis Marx was still slinging out his Playsets, perhaps the most impressive of which was the Untouchables set. "The Untouchables" had begun as a two-part television movie on April 20 and 27, 1959. The

FLIES WITH
JET PROPULSION PAK
AND SPACE SLED!

FLEXIBLE SPACE SUIT

BENDS TO ANY POSITION

Punched blister card, 10" x 13".

NEW! [TV] [PRINT]

Major
MATT MASON™

#6300
Blast-off with Major MATT MASON, Mattel's Man in Space! Meeting every challenge of the moon, Major MATT MASON is the adventurous astronaut who lives, works and completes courageous assignments in the Mattel Space Complex!
The six-inch tall interplanetary traveler, with equipment adapted from official space program design, wears a molded space suit with detachable helmet and movable visor.
The spaceman travels the moon surface on a special Space Sled with control column. He makes short space hops with his personal Jet Propulsion Pak, a galaxy gadget manually-operated by a simple mechanism (no batteries needed). Control column and space labels included.
Std. Pack: 1 Doz. Wt: 6 Lbs.

TV series began October 15, 1959, and ran for four years. The Playset, copyrighted 1961, was marvelously well done. Each of the eighteen figures was superbly and imaginatively modeled, each different from the other. In addition to Eliot Ness and Al Capone, there were cops, plainclothes detectives, gangsters, and a woman who could be employed as heroine, innocent bystander, or moll. Virtually all were in a state of action, with the standout probably a gentleman losing his hat and dropping his pistol as he was shot. There were two lithographed tin building facades, one a complex that included a federal building, restaurant, movie theater, and bank; the other was a foot-long warehouse. There were two nicely done tin friction-powered 1920s cars, one of them a convertible, the other a sedan, both made in Japan by a Marx subsidiary. Like most of the Playsets, this one also contained furnishings, most of which, like the figures, were plastic: two chairs, a file cabinet, a desk, a coat rack, a store counter, a bank teller's cage and safe, and a restaurant table with two chairs. That wasn't all. There was a tank for brewing bathtub gin, and all the accoutrements needed for the prohibited activity—a skid with a handle, a barley sack, a handtruck and two fifty-five gallon drums; six small barrels and six boxes were made out of wood. That still wasn't all. There were six telephone poles, two old-timey streetlights, a barricade for closing off a road, barbed-wire fencing, and the one absolute necessity for depicting the illicit side of the Prohibition era—an open violin case with a machine gun (plus a few spare weapons). You say you're still not satisfied? Neither was Louis Marx. There was also a thirty-by-sixteen-inch polyethylene sheet that marked off a street and sidewalks, and a three-inch metal pistol that fired off caps and came with ten plastic bullets, which, if the gun were aimed properly and the proper gods invoked, would when fired knock down a figure.

Marx continued to issue his Playsets through the rest of the decade and beyond, many of them based on TV series. But their heyday was obviously over. Robots and action figures provided too much competition, and some pretty sharp little cars didn't help either.

Some of the figures from Louis Marx's impressive "Untouchables" Playset. Note the variety of positions. (Gary Linden, River Forest, Illinois)

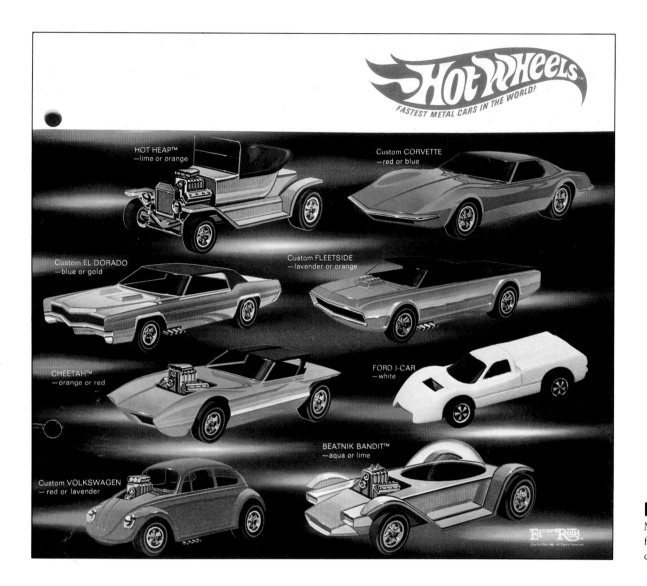

HOT HEAP™
—lime or orange

Custom CORVETTE
—red or blue

Custom EL DORADO
—blue or gold

Custom FLEETSIDE
—lavender or orange

CHEETAH™
—orange or red

FORD J-CAR
—white

BEATNIK BANDIT™
—aqua or lime

Custom VOLKSWAGEN
—red or lavender

Hot from the beginning: Mattel's Hot Wheels, which first appeared in a 1968 catalog.

Possibly the hottest toy of the decade had the right name for it: Hot Wheels. There had been HO-scaled racing cars before. In 1965, for instance, both Aurora and Lionel had put them out. But theirs were electrically powered, while Hot Wheels were gravity powered and billed as "The Fastest Cars In The World!" Pound for pound, inch for inch, they probably were. They came with a plastic track and moved so swiftly they could even drive sideways and upside down when the track was bent or looped. Mattel of Hawthorne, California, was the maker. Not surprisingly, its first Hot Wheels vehicles (1968) all had "California Custom Stylings" and were meant to represent customized collectors' cars. They had "mag" wheels, red-stripe racing slicks, and "dazzling Spectraflame paint jobs." According to their first catalog (1968), they had been built to "out-race, out-stunt and out-distance every other metal miniature car on the track!"

There were custom Cougars, Mustangs, Camaros, T-Birds, Barracudas, Corvettes, El Dorados, Volkswagens—all but the Ford J-Car in a choice of two colors. Most had side pipes, power bulges, raked bodies, detailed undercarriages, rear exhaust pipes, "vinyl" tops, and contrasting interiors. Millions were sold. And helping to fan the flames was a "Hot Wheels" TV show—for a while. In 1969 the Federal Communications Commission banned the show because it had been "designed primarily to promote the sale of a sponsor's product rather than to service the public by either entertaining or informing it." A firm door-slamming—or was it? More later.

Television was now at least as big a takeoff base for cartoon toys as the funny papers had been. On September 3, 1960, a network cartoon series debuted that was to rival Disney in the toys it inspired. The show was "The Flintstones." Bill Hanna and Joe Barbera, its creators, had already had some success with a syndicated cartoon series, "Huckleberry Hound," which had begun in 1958 and birthed a few toys of its own.

But Huckleberry and his pal Yogi Bear were no match for Fred Flintstone and his merry troupe, who were prehistoric versions of Jackie Gleason's "The Honeymooners." By 1961 a man named Louis Marx had issued a fifty-piece Flintstones Playset, with plastic figures of Fred and Wilma Flintstone, Barney and Betty Rubble, stone-age cars, animals, and buildings.

Since "The Flintstones" lasted on network television for a very long six years and has since been in what seems perpetual syndication, the line of toys emanating from the show is a long, long one. There were Flintstone trains, ten-inch-high vinyl dolls, a shooting gallery, a battery-powered dinosaur, a reversible car (Fred and Barney on top, their kids underneath, and vice-versa), tin windups, even a Turnover Tank made by Linemar (a Marx subsidiary that manufactured in Japan), which expert recycler Marx later issued as a Jetsons Turnover Tank, "The Jetsons" being yet another TV cartoon series courtesy of Hanna-Barbera.

Another popular cartoon show (and wittier than most) was "Time for Beany." The Bob Clampett creation had originated in 1949 as a TV puppet show. In 1950, the first hand puppets were sold. The puppet show lasted till 1954, and then in 1962 "The Beany and Cecil Show" was aired. This was a color cartoon series, and by 1963 Mattel was launching a series of toys based on Beany and Cecil (the Seasick Sea Serpent). In addition to hand puppets, there were stuffed toys, helicopter beanies, and talking dolls. Another firm made Leakin' Lena boats.

Beany and Cecil appeared on TV in the 1940s, 1950s, and 1960s, in one of the brighter children's television shows. A number of colorful toys evolved, including this Mattel Jack-in-the-Box from 1961. (Brad Krewson)

Comic-strip characters popping up as toys in the 1960s included the gang from "Peanuts" and the bunch from "Pogo." The most popular of the "Pogo" toys were premiums, plastic figurines that came with Duz detergent. They were faithfully done and included all the main "Pogo" characters—Pogo himself, Albert Alligator, Churchy LaFemme, Beauregard, and Howland Owl.

"Peanuts" had begun October 2, 1950, but had taken a while to get up steam. By the 1960s the strip was spewing out toys left and right, with Snoopy the most popular of all, many versions of him unauthorized.

Popeye, too, was still on the scene, with his King Features TV series doing much to keep him visible. Marx had a couple of Popeye walkers (with Wimpy as a companion to one), Mattel made a Popeye "Getar" ukulele, which could be strummed or cranked (it played—what else?— "Popeye the Sailor Man"). There were also Popeye, Wimpy, Olive, and Bluto sports cars, by Elm Toys.

Other old standard toys were still around. Toy cowboy pistols seem never to go out of favor, and Hubley, Mattel, and others were still popping them off the assembly lines. As with so many toys of the period, a large number of the weapons were TV-influenced. There were pistols based on "Bonanza," "Have Gun Will Travel," "The Rebel," "Wanted Dead or Alive," "Wagon Train," and "Maverick." "Dragnet" inspired more current weapons, and the steady flow of James Bond movies kept toy makers busy selling CIA-type people-mashers. An interesting 1966 weapon was Wham-O's Air Blaster. Cocking it created a vacuum; pulling the trigger sent a puff of air that could be felt some feet away. It was surprisingly effective against annoying pets.

Toy vehicles, too, the kind that were satisfied to traverse as mundane a sphere as earth,

still found favor with children. Many were the old familiar push-'em-yourself kind, in steel or plastic. Tonka, Nylint, Structo, and Ertl were the leaders in the steel category, still producing nicely designed, realistic-looking cars, trucks, farm, and construction vehicles that were dura-

Shades of the old Magic Lantern: Despite color television, kids in 1964 were all agog about this Kenner Give-A-Show Projector. (Charles D. Richards, Pevely, Missouri)

Tinkertoys' Curtain Wall
Builder Set No. 630, ca.
1960, echoed the new
architecture. Painted tin.
(Arlan Coffman)

ble and well painted. Battery-operated remote control was also popular. Ideal had a Dick Tracy Copmobile that could be operated by touching its antenna with a "controstick," and Johnny Express was a huge tractor-trailer truck operated by remote-control levers.

Toy trains were still visible, too, but times were changing. Lionel began to founder in the mid-1950s, when its output declined to less than the combined production of all the various small companies manufacturing HO trains. Belatedly, Lionel introduced HO in 1957, the last year Lionel's electric train ledgers showed black ink.

It was also the year Lionel tried a train set for girls, featuring a pink locomotive. It turned out to be one of the company's major marketing gaffes. Fathers, who bought most of the train sets, turned up their noses at the engine and its trail of cars in robin's-egg blue, buttercup yellow, sky blue, and lilac—powered by a white-and-gold transformer.

Joshua Lionel Cowen retired at the end of 1958. A year later, he and his wife unloaded all their stock. The new owners sold every antique Lionel in the showroom and continued to blunder through a sea of red ink.

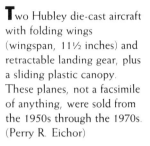

Two Hubley die-cast aircraft with folding wings (wingspan, 11½ inches) and retractable landing gear, plus a sliding plastic canopy. These planes, not a facsimile of anything, were sold from the 1950s through the 1970s. (Perry R. Eichor)

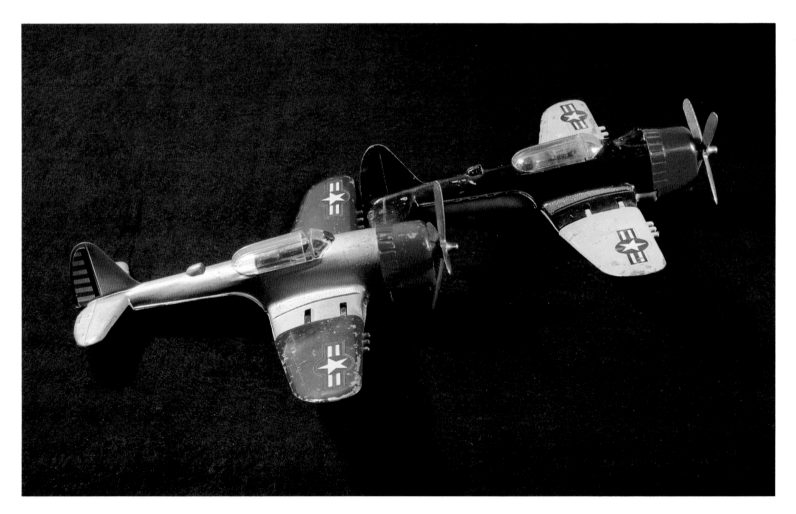

▲ Hubley No. 751 Folding Wing Jet, die-cast with retractable landing gear and a 6-inch wingspan. Sold in the 1950s and 1960s. (Perry R. Eichor)

Not that things were going any better at American Flyer. All the interest in space-age toys and the continuing decline of the American railroads had shifted young boys' interest elsewhere. Not helping any was Louis Marx's low-priced line of trains. In 1961, A. C. Gilbert died, and Jack Wrather (owner of the TV series "Lassie" and "The Lone Ranger") took over, cutting back drastically. Though sales rose 30 percent in 1965, production costs and borrowed capital offset all the good news. In what its board of direc-

tors took to be a positive move, Lionel bought American Flyer in 1966, and stopped production of all of Flyer's trains. It didn't help. In 1969 the company was sold again, this time to General Mills. Train production resumed in 1971, but output was limited.

It was not only the people putting out trains who had problems. *Everyone* in the business was peering anxiously over his shoulder. There was a crowd of newly aroused consumers back there, many of them looking quite angry.

9

THE TURBULENT SEVENTIES

he general activism that had originated in the civil rights movements of the 1950s and burgeoned in the 1960s soon made itself felt in the toys field. The 1970s proved to be a continuation and intensification of that process. There had always been concern about toys. In the very first issue of *Consumers Union Magazine* way back in May 1936, the editors had warned against toys of "a soft metal alloy containing a high percentage of lead" because they were dangerous not only to younger children, "who enjoy their toys with their mouths as well as their hands" but to older kids as well, since lead (once the protective coat of paint is gone) rubs off on the hands and could be "carried to the mouth." But for the most part, a spirit of laissez-faire had prevailed among parents until the second half of the twentieth century, when consumer groups erupted all over the country

In 1970 Remco incurred the wrath of conservationists with its line of Tru-Smok toys. Since they gave off "Smok"—better known as smoke—there were those who decided the toys fostered an acceptance of pollution. Protests followed. In the same year, Consumers Union and the Children's Foundation asked the U.S. Secretary of Health, Education, and Welfare to force removal of eight allegedly dangerous toys. The request was turned down, but the Food and Drug Administration (FDA), prompted by the urgings of citizens' groups, did ban certain dangerous toys, including breakable rattles and dolls, noisemaking toys with dangerous components, and any cap or toy pistols that produced noise levels above 188 decibels. In all, thirty-nine toys were banned from the market in 1970.

In 1971, the Nerf Ball—a light plastic ball that was ideal for indoor use since it was too light to break anything—was declared flammable by the FDA, and Parker Brothers quickly reformulated it. That year also saw complaints about sadistic toys, including guillotine kits and hypodermic needles (the latter connoting use of illicit drugs).

Packaging frauds—false bottoms, oversize boxes, misleading boxtop illustrations—became a new target. And Nabisco found itself picketed by the National Organization for Women (NOW) because of the increasingly macabre monster toys put out by its new subsidiary, Aurora.

Aurora protested, marshalling all sorts of arguments in favor of its little dears, but Nabisco, fearing a potential widespread boycott if it didn't back down, sent an order from on high. The series was discontinued. That same year the FDA banned or ordered the redesigning of two hundred different

A Hubley die-cast P-40 fighter, sold from 1940 into the 1970s. (Perry R. Eichor) OPPOSITE

The Hubley P-38. (Perry R. Eichor) INSET

toys. The next year it proposed new standards for electrical toys.

The protests against unsafe and offensive toys continued. In 1973, the Consumer Products Safety Commission banned 1,500 toys as unsafe and sent out volunteers to toy stores to make sure the order was obeyed. The New Jersey health commissioner, obviously attuned to the times, was responsible for the removal of 437 toys deemed hazardous.

And so it went, a process that hasn't stopped yet. From time to time, one group or another would announce that the industry was now aware and responsible, and there was very little more to fear. Promptly, potentially harmful new toys would pop up, some of them causing deaths. A growing danger were the toys from the Far East, since few or no rules existed in that area. Playthings (usually stuffed) containing flammable or otherwise hazardous materials turned up with distressing frequency, often in counterfeits of top-selling toys.

Things were tough enough when, in 1974, the toy industry was shaken by a totally unexpected problem: the fuel crisis. Fifteen hundred people lost their jobs in Harrison, New Jersey, when Remco, long an industry leader, temporarily went under. Its president, Herbert S. Gerbst, announced that a major reason for the belly-up was a shortage of raw materials; 70 percent of the materials used in Remco's toys were petroleum based.

Mattel, which also manufactured most of its toys from petroleum-based plastic, was quick to attribute to the energy crisis a sudden decrease in the number of toys produced by the industry. In 1975 toy makers faced not only a shortage of materials, but—also linked to the oil dearth—a national recession and unemployment, resulting in decreased sales.

There were other debacles during the decade. In 1977, Ideal found out just how risky the "personality toy"—a plaything based on a real person—could be. Evel Knievel, the most famous daredevil of his time, was convicted of assaulting the author of a book about him; the sale of Evel Knievel action figures plummeted, and Ideal found itself taking a $1.6 million loss.

Many toys were now heavily advertised on television, which resulted in a number of problems, as dealers complained about too many returns when toys didn't perform as the ads suggested they would.

Change was a watchword for manufacturers in the 1970s. Most toys were now retailed in "bubble packs" or other tight-fitting sealed plastic to discourage the increasing problem of shoplifting. In 1974, war toys returned after five years in the limbo created by Vietnam and its aftermath.

Toy supermarkets had appeared as early as 1955, when independent toy shops found themselves in trouble because of an onslaught of price-cutting and promotion by large stores and mail-order houses and heavy promotion of low-markup toys by manufacturers (the big stores could make money on these, but not the mom-and-pop operations, which could not afford to stock large quantities). By the 1970s the supermarkets were making their presence felt in earnest. In 1973, nearly 75 percent of the $4.7 billion in retail toy sales was through discounters, chains, and toy supermarkets. In the latter category the three biggest names were Lionel Corp., Child World, and Toys-'R'-Us.

Battery-operated toys were so pervasive that *Playthings*, as a service to its subscribers in the toy industry, printed an annual survey of "Battery Needs." In 1971 thirty-eight firms were listed; it took five pages of small type to mention the toys and what type of battery each needed.

ITEM NO. 377

LOADED DELIVERY TRUCK — MINIATURE METAL

TRUCKS LOADED WITH 6 BEER BARRELS OR 6 MILK CANS. BLISTER PACKED ON NEW COLORFUL CARD. ASST'D. COLORS. (ASST'D. TO 1 DOZ. BOX)
PACKED: 1 doz. per box, 12 doz. per ctn.
WEIGHT: 44 lbs. per ctn.

ITEM NO. 325

LABELED TRAILER TRUCK— MINIATURE METAL

DECORATED WITH POPULAR EVERY-DAY LABELS, SUCH AS: U.S. MAIL, ETC. 2 SEPARATE PARTS, CAB & TRAILER. ASST'D. COLORS. BLISTER PACKED ON NEW COLORFUL CARD.
PACKED: 2 doz. per box, 24 doz. per ctn.
WEIGHT: 43 lbs. per ctn.

29¢ RETAIL PRICE

ITEM NO. 347

SPORTS CARS—MINIATURE METAL

2 CARS, SPORTS CAR & CONVERTIBLE, W/ DRIVERS. BLISTER PACKED ON NEW COLORFUL CARD. ASST'D. COLORS.
PACKED: 2 doz. per box, 24 doz. per ctn.
WEIGHT: 36 lbs. per ctn.

ITEM NO. 6789

ANTIQUE VINTAGE CARS — MINIATURE METAL

2 CARS, (4 DIFFERENT MODELS) BLISTER PACKED ON NEW COLORFUL CARD. ASST'D. COLORS.
PACKED: 2 doz. per box, 24 doz. per ctn.
WEIGHT: 44 lbs. per ctn.

ITEM NO. 349

FOREIGN CARS— MINIATURE METAL

2 MODELS, VOLKSWAGON & CITROEN, BLIS-TER PACKED ON NEW COLORFUL CARD. ASST'D. COLORS.
PACKED: 2 doz. per box, 24 doz. per ctn.
WEIGHT: 34 lbs. per ctn.

39¢ RETAIL PRICE

ITEM NO. 335

3 PIECE TRAIN SET — MINIATURE METAL

ATTACHES AND DISENGAGES QUICKLY AND EASILY. CONSISTS OF LOCO-MOTIVE, TENDER & PASSENGER CAR. BLISTER PACKED ON NEW COLORFUL CARD. ASST'D. COLORS.
PACKED: 2 doz. per box, 18 doz. per ctn.
WEIGHT: 50 lbs. per ctn.

ITEM NO. 330

ITEM NO. 339

49¢ RETAIL PRICE

AUTO SET — MINIATURE METAL

7 MINIATURE AUTOS, BLISTER PACKED ON NEW CARD. ASST'D. COLORS.
PACKED: 1 doz. per box, 12 doz. per ctn.
WEIGHT: 40 lbs. per ctn.

AUTO TRANSPORT SET — MINIATURE METAL

CONSISTS OF: NEW MODERN CAB, TRAILER & 2 CARS. BLISTER PACKED ON NEW CARD. ASST'D. COLORS.
PACKED: 2 doz. per box, 12 doz. per ctn. WEIGHT: 31 lbs. per ctn.

RETAIL **69¢** PRICE

ITEM NO. 440

DOUBLE DECKER AUTO TRANSPORT SET — MINIATURE METAL

CONSISTS OF: MODERN CAB, DOUBLE DECKER TRAILER & 4 CARS. TRAILER MOVES TO UN-LOAD. BLISTER PACKED ON NEW CARD. ASST'D. COLORS.
PACKED: 1 doz. per box, 12 doz. per ctn.
WEIGHT: 46 lbs. per ctn.

A Barclay catalog page from the late 1960s or very early 1970s. The company closed in 1971.

The 1970s had its fads. In 1972, the Chinese gave the United States pandas, and suddenly plush pandas were everywhere. But they were nothing compared to the storm that began in 1977.

In May of that year a movie called *Star Wars*

opened. The George Lucas space film proved to be a phenomenon, bedazzling children, teenagers, and not a few adults throughout the country and most of the world. It also seems to have inspired a first in the toy business—an IOU for a plaything. Kenner leapt on the *Star Wars* band-

Kenner's *Star Wars* action figures and toys—the George Lucas version of the U.S. Mint. (Kenner)

wagon early, but not quite early enough. The demand for *Star Wars* figures was so high that Kenner couldn't keep up. The firm stood to lose hundreds of thousands, perhaps millions of dollars in Christmas sales because it had—in many stores—nothing to sell. And so someone at the company came up with a brainstorm: Kenner would issue chits that could be redeemed as soon as the toy was available. A frantic public bought the idea. Kenner found itself merrily counting money for toys it had yet to make. In February 1978, nearly two months after the Christmas season was over, the firm began making good on its certificates.

The *Star Wars* phenomenon was truly that. George Lucas liked to think of the film as the first fairy tale of our modern age. The merchandising results make one wonder just what the Brothers Grimm might have salted away if they had been born at the right time. Between 1977 and 1984, Kenner and MPC, which were the two principal makers, sold *three hundred million Star Wars* toys.

The best-sellers in the original line were the 3¼-inch-high action figures of the characters in the movie—Luke Skywalker, R2D2, C3P0, Princess Leia, Darth Vader, Han Solo, Obi-Wan Kenobi, Chewbacca, and so on.

There had, of course, been similar toys before. In 1970, Colorforms of Norwood, New Jersey had introduced a line of seven figures called The Outer Space Men. The spacemen could be bent and twisted, and had removable helmets and futuristic weapons. Among them were such characters as Commander Comet and Xodiac, the Man from Saturn, all but the doughty commander quite bizarre in appearance. The 1960s TV series "Star Trek," which was similar in theme to *Star Wars*, had also generated a few toys. But "Star Trek" had been watched mainly by older teenagers and adults; accordingly, "Star Trek" toys enjoyed only mild sales. (The later success of *Star Wars* naturally sparked a revival of "Star Trek" toys, abetted by the vastly successful series of *Star Trek* movies, which began with 1979's *Star Trek—The Motion Picture*.)

What helped in the success of the *Star Wars* toys was Lucas's insistence that he have approval of every new plaything. He allowed no shortcuts in quality or design, and as a result there was nothing disappointing about the toys; they looked like what the kids wanted them to look like, and they held up under strenuous play— the parts designed so they would be more likely to detach than break. *Star Wars* also signaled a change in the way children were approaching their games. For most of history, kids have played with toys that reflected their times, unconsciously preparing themselves for the future by imitating the actions of their parents and other adults. They "rode" horses and "drove" horse carriages, cars, and trains. They "flew" airplanes. They played house with dolls and played war with toy soldiers. But after *Star Wars*, more and more toys emerged that had nothing to do with the past, nothing to do with the present, and very little to do with the foreseeable future. Children no longer copied their parents, other adults, or anyone else on earth. They were too busy constructing games that took place in different galaxies far, far away. A basic tenet of playthings had been violated, but nobody in the business seemed much to have noticed. Presumably, they were all too busy dreaming up and pushing out more *Star Wars*–type toys.

It was a decade of other milestones. In 1970 Tonka began marketing its toys in food stores through Pillsbury Corporation. It is not clear whether this was a first, but it was certainly an important move by a major manufacturer into a

market then wholly or largely untapped. Pillsbury got into the business itself in 1972 with a surprisingly popular toy, Poppin' Fresh, a vinyl doll that was the advertising symbol for Pillsbury's products. *Playthings* promptly named it "Toy of the Year" in the under-two-dollars category. Predictably, not only did Pillsbury add the female, Poppie Fresh, the next year, but Campbell's soups, seeing both the publicity and sales value of a company symbol in the toy market, came out with its own Campbell Kids dolls, from Grantco Import Services. (Campbell's had actually issued similar dolls earlier in the century.)

In 1970 Mattel, which had been founded on wood scraps and leftover plastic, made toy world news by celebrating its twenty-fifth year. Like Ohio Art and Manoil, Mattel had begun with picture frames on its mind. The owners were Harold Mattson and Ruth and Elliot Handler—hence Mattel: *Matt* for Mattson and *El* for Elliot—and the business began in a Los Angeles garage. (Mattson, an old friend of the Handlers, sold out early due to poor health.)

The firm quickly turned from picture frames

to toys when Elliot Handler decided to make toy furniture from the leftover scraps of wood and plastic. The company was successful with the toys from the start; eight employees by the end of the year and a hundred thousand dollars in sales, with a net of thirty thousand—nice money for the time.

Complications arose the next year when competition emerged, in the form of an injection-molded line of perfectly detailed doll furniture—priced lower than Mattel's. Just breaking even, the Handlers saved their necks by getting into toy instruments. In 1954, the firm realized it needed to expand its line and developed the first automatic cap gun, the Burp Gun. Mattel introduced it at the 1955 New York Toy Fair, and buyers enthusiastically placed orders that were very exciting . . . on paper.

But something happened between the buyers' orders and the actual point of sale. Somehow kids weren't responding the way Mattel and the buyers had assumed they would. It was at this time that Mattel was offered sponsorship of a fifteen-minute segment of TV's hot new show,

"The Mickey Mouse Club." The cost of sponsorship was exactly Mattel's net worth. The Handlers gulped and gave it a try. The results started a revolution in the toy industry. Hasbro may have had the first TV-advertised toy—Mr. Potato Head—but it was Mattel's phenomenal success with the Burp Gun that got that line of competitors forming to the right.

Mattel's next big toy, Barbie, was named after the Handlers' daughter. It was only fair. Ruth Handler had noticed how often her daughter played with teenage paper dolls and their wardrobes, rather than with the toys she had been given. At the time, the *only* teen dolls were made out of paper or cardboard. Mattel hired a Japanese company to make Barbie's clothes at a price far lower than if they had been manu-

factured here. Thus was inaugurated one of the first ties between the Far East and American toy makers.

Some individuals also made toy news. Jerry Rockwell, Norman's brother, retired in 1971, having moved over to Playskool when Holgate merged with it in 1958. Even in his last, forty-first year in the business, he was still known for his beautifully designed toys.

A name that made more noise outside the industry was Louis Marx. The man who had become one of the legends of the business, a man who had manufactured a greater variety of toys than anyone in history, sold out in 1972 at the age of seventy-six to the Quaker Oats Company. Without Marx, the company foundered, and in 1976 Quaker sold it to Europe's largest toy man-

Two Ertl toys from the 1970s: an International Harvester 966 Hydro (IH45A) Tractor and a John Deere Side Chute Wagon. Ertl is meticulous about providing accurate reproductions of farm and other toys. The tractor is 9½ inches long. (Wilkinson Collection, Detroit Antique Toy Museum)

ufacturer, Dunbee-Combex-Marx, which fared no better. What had once been the Marx empire went into bankruptcy in 1980. In 1982, at the age of eighty-five, Marx died.

In 1970, the long-lived Buddy L announced, "There are 30 Buddy L trucks sold every minute of the day all year long!" and Knickerbocker trumpeted it was still "No. 1 in Stuffed Toys." Tonka introduced its heavily advertised (mostly on TV) line of Crazy A's competitors to Hot Wheels. They were modernized or customized versions of Model A Fords. Kenner's SSP racers went up to four hundred self-propelled scale miles per hour, and Topper had its own Hot Wheels variant, Johnny Lightning.

Public TV's "Sesame Street" was a hit with the preschool crowd and with adults, who approved of its mix of education and literate good humor. Gaily colored toy versions of Bert and Ernie, Big Bird, and the Cookie Monster began a parade to the toy stores that continues to this day. In 1972 a stunning nine million "Sesame Street" toys walked off the counter.

That same year saw the debut of a popular action figure, Action Jackson. In his first incarnation, Jackson (put out by Mego) rode a remote-controlled ScrambleCycle, powered by a motor that made a roaring noise. By the end of the year, Action Jackson had proven popular enough to be additionally issued as a sailor, a pilot, and an Aussie Marine—in each case with the proper paraphernalia.

The venerable firm of Ives had once had a toy based on the famous nursery rhyme about the Old Woman Who Lived in a Shoe. In 1972, Questor's Child Guidance came out with a good-looking educational version of the toy. There were six buttons on the side, "picture coded" with the face of one of the characters. When the child pushed the buttons, children popped out

The "good old days" are fun again with the Buddy L Ol'Buddys, replicas of America's famous trucks of the Fabulous Thirties souped-up to become the Soaring Seventies when Buddy L customizes the Ol'Buddys just like the Teens do today.

4252
BUDDY L OL'BUDDYS CUSTOM SURF-N-DUMP

Mod surf buggy eases twin surfboards right into water at the flick of the dump lever • equipped with exposed chromed drag race engine and 8-barrel carb • rugged deep-ribbed dump box with swing-open tailgate real car steering controlled from steering wheel • swing-open door detailed interior • whitewall tires brite-plate grille, bumper, "headlights" and wheel discs • rugged auto-steel construction. Touch-N-Sell™ Package.

L. 12", W. 4½", H. 5¾" Indiv. Corr. St. Pk.—½ Dz./Wt. per Dz.—24 Lbs.

Features:
OPERATING STEERING WHEEL and KNUCKLE STEERING

4254
BUDDY L OL'BUDDYS CUSTOM PICK-UP

Here's a Swinger! Customized rugged auto-steel Pick-Up has open chromed drag race engine, 4 tube header exhausts • cab door really opens, operating steering wheel with knuckle steering, complete cab interior, hinged tailgate and tonneau cover • brite-plate grille, bumper, "headlights" and wheel discs • whitewall tires. Touch-N-Sell™ Package.

L. 10¼", W. 4½", H. 5"
Indiv. Corr.
St. Pk.—½ Dz.
Wt. per Dz.—22 Lbs.

4250
BUDDY L OL'BUDDYS SAND DRAG'N

Go bananas with the "in" crowd over this dune buggy • loaded with giant exposed chromed gas tank, engine, 8-barrel carb, spare tire and follow-me flower on its whip antenna real car steering controlled from steering wheel • whitewall tires brite-plate grille, bumper, "headlights" and wheel discs detailed interior • rugged auto-steel construction. Shopper Stopper™ Package.

L. 10⅜", W. 4¼", H. 4½" Indiv.Corr. St. Pk.—½ Dz./Wt. per Dz.—24 Lbs.

Some interesting 1970 Buddy L vehicles.

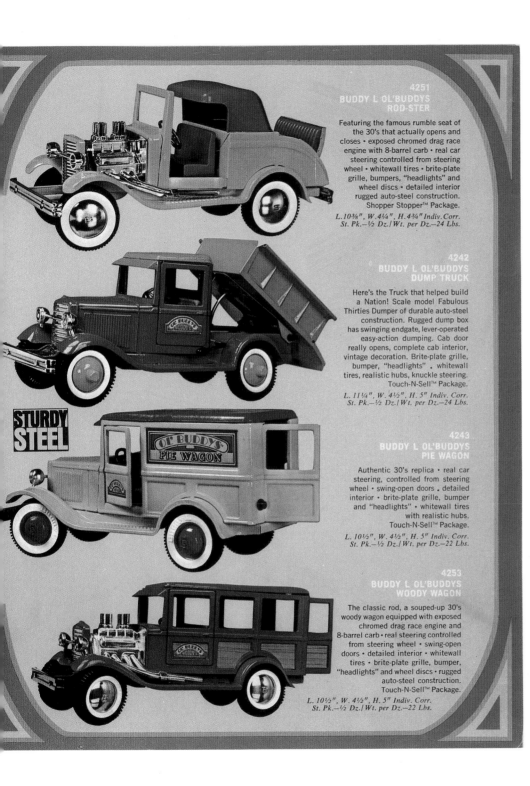

4251
BUDDY L OL'BUDDYS
ROD-STER

Featuring the famous rumble seat of the 30's that actually opens and closes • exposed chromed drag race engine with 8-barrel carb • real car steering controlled from steering wheel • whitewall tires • brite-plate grille, bumpers, "headlights" and wheel discs • detailed interior rugged auto-steel construction. Shopper Stopper™ Package.
L.10⅜", W.4¼", H.4¾" Indiv. Corr. St. Pk.—½ Dz./Wt. per Dz.—24 Lbs.

4242
BUDDY L OL'BUDDYS
DUMP TRUCK

Here's the Truck that helped build a Nation! Scale model Fabulous Thirties Dumper of durable auto-steel construction. Rugged dump box has swinging endgate, lever-operated easy-action dumping. Cab door really opens, complete cab interior, vintage decoration. Brite-plate grille, bumper, "headlights" • whitewall tires, realistic hubs, knuckle steering. Touch-N-Sell™ Package.
L. 11¼", W. 4½", H. 5" Indiv. Corr. St. Pk.—½ Dz./Wt. per Dz.—24 Lbs.

STURDY STEEL

4243
BUDDY L OL'BUDDYS
PIE WAGON

Authentic 30's replica • real car steering, controlled from steering wheel • swing-open doors • detailed interior • brite-plate grille, bumper and "headlights" • whitewall tires with realistic hubs. Touch-N-Sell™ Package.
L. 10½", W. 4½", H. 5" Indiv. Corr. St. Pk.—½ Dz./Wt. per Dz.—22 Lbs.

4253
BUDDY L OL'BUDDYS
WOODY WAGON

The classic rod, a souped-up 30's woody wagon equipped with exposed chromed drag race engine and 8-barrel carb • real steering controlled from steering wheel • swing-open doors • detailed interior • whitewall tires • brite-plate grille, bumper, "headlights" and wheel discs • rugged auto-steel construction. Touch-N-Sell™ Package.
L. 10½", W. 4½", H. 5" Indiv. Corr. St. Pk.—½ Dz./Wt. per Dz.—22 Lbs.

of their respective windows and the old woman raced out "in a sporty red car." The idea was that the child could create his own fantasy by varying the order of the buttons he pushed (sound as well as action resulted with each press-down).

Two especially interesting toys arrived in 1973. One was Owens-Illinois's Super Sleuth, which, believe it or not, was a lie detector for kids. Just how well it worked is unknown, but it was obviously impressive. Kids were known to confess beforehand, rather than allow themselves to be subjected to the Sleuth by siblings or playmates.

The other toy was, of all things, Charlie the Tramp by Kenner. In 1971, after a long period under a political cloud, Charlie Chaplin had returned to the United States and was given a special Academy Award. Most importantly, he was back in the headlines. Licensors, being licensors, quickly sprang into action, so that suddenly, sixty or so years after Charlie's heyday, there was a rag doll that, as the box explained, "waddles as you walk him"; legs and clickers in his shoes simulated "a walking sound."

Toys based on cartoon figures had become a huge area of the business. Disney and Hanna-Barbera were reaping millions in royalties from toys and other products, like Hanna-Barbera's astonishingly long-lived Flintstones Vitamins (still popular at this writing).

In 1978 the most popular cartoon characters were Mickey Mouse, the folks from "Peanuts," the "Sesame Street" gang, Superman, Spiderman, and the Incredible Hulk, the latter three from the pages of comic books. By the end of the 1970s, a third of all toys produced were based on cartoon characters and averaged 10 to 20 percent more sales than other toys. One manufacturer stated that putting a cartoon character on a quality toy could mean sales of three hundred

MORE 1970 MODELS

Johnny Lightning cars, the fastest in the world! With exciting designs. These are the winners, the ones that race on the Johnny Lightning Tracks. Without wires, without batteries. The fastest cars in the world, on the world's fastest tracks. Ride with the winners in 1970!

JOHNNY LIGHTNING TV $5,000,000

JOHNNY LIGHTNING JP JET POWER CARS

The cars that don't know how to lose! The cars with the special racing feature not found on any others! These are the new, the fantas... The JOHNNY LIGHTNING JET POWER RACERS!!

—48 J.P. Car Assortment
Pk.1 Wt.11 Lbs.
Size 20 x 12¾ x 5¾

4009—THE WHISTLER
4064—BAJA
4080—GOLDEN HAULER
4072—CONDOR
4064—TURBINE
4076—ROCKET 500 SPECIAL
4057—MAD MAVERICK
4050—SPOILER
4061—STILETTO
4061—WASP
4054—SMUGGLER
4071—TRACK BAC

Racing Decal Kit
Just what you need to do a far-out "custom" job on your JOHNNY LIGHTNING cars. Competition stripes, flames, numbers, etc.
No. 4023 Standard Pack: 24 Weight: 1½ lbs.
Item Size: 6" x 8¾" x 1"

Carrying Case
No. 4009 Standard Pack: 6 Weight: 8½ lbs.
Item Size: 13¼" x 10¼" x 1¾"

4151—FLYING NEEDLE
4157—FABULOUS FIN
4158—BAZOOKA
4162—THE BRUTE
4161—BULLET
4159—PEGASUS
4152—SCREAMER
4155—WEDGE
4150—MONSTER
4153—GLASSER
4164—JUPITER 7
4154—BUBBLE
4160—MANTA RAY
4156—DART
4163—DYNAMO

---

thousand units instead of one hundred thousand.

Mego introduced its Super Heroes Action Figures in 1972, which promptly landed among the ten best-sellers, remaining in that category through at least 1975. The Super Heroes included such gentry as Batman, Superman, and Wonder Woman, who were joined in 1975 by superfolk of another variety—the Waltons—

who were drawing super ratings on their Depression-era TV series. Action figures of Mom and Pop Walton, John Boy, his sister Ellen, and Grandma and Grandpa Walton emerged, no doubt gazing about in bewilderment at Mego's costumed superdoers and the company's expanded line of *Planet of the Apes* figures.

In 1974, Mego introduced what may be the

Racing cars were still hot in 1970 when Topper Toys weighed in with these Johnny Lightning Jetpower Cars.

most beautifully done of all the *Wizard of Oz* toys. In addition to plastic figures of Dorothy, Toto, the Scarecrow, the Tin Woodman, the Cowardly Lion, the Wizard, the Wicked Witch, Glenda the Good Witch, Mayor Munchkin, a General, a Dancing Girl, and a Flower Girl, there were a fair number of accessories.

The action-figure bandwagon rolled along, and none other than Fisher-Price, that symbol of toyland goodness and gladness, hopped aboard in 1976. Naturally, Fisher-Price's Adventure People were wholesome types, designed "for kids 4 to 9." The first batch included Mountain Climbers, Scuba Divers, Wilderness Patrol, Rescue Team, Construction Workers, Air-Sea Rescue Copter, Super Speed Race, Sea Explorer, Wild Animal Safari, and Emergency Rescue Truck, each toy with figures and the requisite equipment, much of it elaborate.

Nineteen seventy-seven was a good year for the toy business. A record $3.1 billion was inked on manufacturers' ledger books. But in 1978 those cranks were at it again, protesting that TV advertising was having too big an influence on toy design. Items, it was claimed, were made primarily to look good during a thirty-second TV display; enjoyment and durability were secondary considerations. It wasn't just the customers who were complaining; retailers were getting grumpy, too.

The last year of the decade brought another first: Knickerbocker, at the top of the stuffed-toy heap, became the first manufacturer of soft dolls and plush toys to advertise on TV. But 1979 also saw twenty thousand Holly Hobbie toy telephone sets withdrawn from the market because their cords so closely resembled household electric cords and plugs, kids might try to force them into wall sockets.

It just never seemed to let up. On top of that there was the video game. Toy manufacturers reeled as those damned kids took their quarters and dollars and promptly waltzed off to a video arcade instead of installing themselves in their rightful place—in front of a toy counter. Some companies, like Coleco, fattened on the fad. But a lot of good it did them just a couple of years later, when the 1980s rolled in and Pac-Man and the rest of his kind rolled out. Suddenly the folks who had confined themselves to toy making looked a whole lot smarter.

G.I. Joe as a superhero. The original Bulletman had debuted in 1940 in Nickel Comics. This 1976 version from Hasbro resembled him somewhat. (Charles D. Richards, Pevely, Missouri)

10

THE CORPORATE EIGHTIES

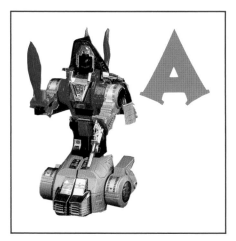

quick walk through a toy department in the 1980s was a disconcerting event for a jingoist. A glance at the fine print somewhere on the box or bubble pack of toys put out by American companies often revealed the actual manufacture took place in China, Malaysia, Taiwan, or Macao. Occasionally, manufacture in one of these countries would be overseen by a Japanese corporation somehow tied to the U.S. "manufacturer."

Some toys were still made in the United States. Most Tootsietoys were American-made, and Hasbro appears to have employed U.S. factories for at least some of its line. But too often American workers, factories, and land proved to be too expensive. If one wanted to survive, one had to seek help from the Third World.

Individuals whose names stood for their whole company were a part of the past, too. There were no more Iveses, Lionels, or Marxes. Instead, there were conglomerates. In 1983, Hasbro acquired some of the assets of the Knickerbocker Toy Company from Warner Communications, giving it two of the oldest continuing toys in American history: Raggedy Ann and Raggedy Andy (the latter had emerged as a doll in 1920). The same year, Hasbro bought Glenco Infant Items, which owned the Playskool Baby Line of infant care products. In 1984, Hasbro gobbled up the Milton Bradley Company —a rather large mouthful, as Bradley had earlier acquired (and Hasbro now got) the Playskool toy line, which as a result of mergers in 1943 and 1958 included Lincoln Logs and Holgate. In 1985, still conglomerating, Hasbro picked up some of the assets of Child Guidance, including Tinkertoys, and some of Ideal's games. In 1986 Child Guidance forked over rights to more toys, including its *Sesame Street* and Disney Poppin' Pals (not to be confused with the Pillsbury Poppin' Fresh character) playthings.

Hubley had been sold to Gabriel Industries in 1955. In 1967, Gabriel had bought the A. C. Gilbert line of toys, including Erector. In 1978 CBS, in turn, had scooped all of this up into its DBS Toys. This aggregation became yet another part of the Hasbro empire in 1986, but somehow Ideal now had Erector.

As a result of these and other acquisitions, Hasbro, which at this writing, is the largest toy company in the world, had further expanded a domain that in 1985 included seven thousand employees and generated $1.2 *billion* in revenue.

Hasbro's inventive Transformer toys from 1987. (Hasbro) OPPOSITE AND INSET

In 1968 Ohio Art had acquired Emenee (which had begun on March 15, 1960, taking its name from the initials of its founders, Herbert L. Merin and Jack Eisner), long known for its toy musical instruments, including a three-octave organ and Juke Box Jamboree. In 1972 Ohio Art had purchased the assets of Conway Valley Toy Company of North Wales, England, which made wooden dollhouses, castles, garages, and forts, and the same year Ohio Art bought the Fli-Back Company of High Point, North Carolina, which it subsequently sold to Eagle Rubber Company of Ashland, Ohio. (Fli-Back, manufac-turers and distributors of paddleballs and other wooden toys, batons, and rubber and vinyl balls, had been founded in 1931 in a High Point buggy shed by James E. Gibson and his wife, Rozena; their first product was a paddleball.) In 1982, Ohio Art reached an agreement with Byron International, of England, to distribute and manufacture certain of its toys, some of which had earlier been made by Western Stamping Company, of Jackson, Michigan.

Ertl had joined the conglomeration mania in 1975 by acquiring Structo and Carter Tru Scale, but by then it was a subsidiary itself, hav-

In 1987, Ertl was selling this No. 265EO 1/32-scale Case International FWDA Tractor. Die-cast metal with vinyl wheels. (Ertl)

A colorful set of Tootsietoys from the late 1980s. (Strombecker)

its Bubbl-Matic Gun (1947), Play-Doh (1955), Baby Alive (1973), Six Million Dollar Man (1975), and Strawberry Shortcake dolls (1980s), joined in 1985 with Parker Brothers (also part of General Mills at the time) to form Kenner Parker Toys, Inc., the country's fourth-largest toy company. So what happened? In 1988 Tonka acquired Kenner.

Another characteristic of the 1980s was the continuation—for a while—of that phenomenon begun by *Star Wars*: the blockbuster toy. The first to keep the trend going was a little number called *E.T.* As a movie it was as wildly successful as *Star Wars*. By September 1982, fifteen million effigies of the little Extra Terrestrial who had seized the hearts of half the world were sold—an impressive number, but made even more impressive when it is noted that those fifteen million were all sold since their initial release in *July* of the same year! Needless to say, E.T. was the toy hit of Christmas 1982.

In 1983, Hasbro introduced the Transformers, innovative and remarkable toys: colorful, eye-catching robots that could be transformed into equally arresting futuristic vehicles and vice-versa. The Transformers were one of a growing number of toys developed with an eye toward introducing them simultaneously at toy counters and on TV shows of their own. Between the very popular series and the even greater impact of the ingenious toys themselves, the Transformers (founded on the theme of "More Than Meets the Eye") became an overwhelming success. They came with their own story line: Decepticons, the villainous form of the Transformers, had arrived on earth to steal this planet's vital resources. The good-guy Transformers were called Autobots and could change into such mundane objects as vehicles, which enabled them to sneak up on the Decep-

ing become a division of the Victor Comptometer Corporation, which in turn was acquired (with its Ertl assets) by Walter Kidde & Company. Other Kidde Companies were Daisy Toys and Vanity Fair.

In 1961 Tootsietoy had picked up Strombecker, for some odd reason then changing its *own* name to Strombecker, though retaining the Tootsietoy trademark on its toys. Somewhere along the line, Esquire/Nichols' toy weapons became a part of Strombecker-Tootsietoy.

Tonka had acquired Vogue dolls in 1973. Meanwhile, in 1967, Kenner, which was formed in 1947 by Al, Phil, and Joe Steiner (all brothers) on Kenner Street in Cincinnati, Ohio, had been taken over by General Mills. Kenner, known for

ticons, at which time they would transform themselves back into Autobots. How many children bothered with the story is unknown; what is certain is that the kids emptied store shelves of Transformers.

The Transformers were *the* phenomenon of 1983, and by the end of 1984 sales had reached one hundred million dollars. That was only the beginning. As time went on, Hasbro (and others) made transforming toys that had more than

a second identity. Scorponok (1986), for instance, changed from a Decepticon Defense Base to a scorpion with pincerlike claws. The scorpion's head could then be changed into Lord Zarak, leader of the "dread Nebulon forces." The Decepticon Six-Shot went even further, changing into six different toys. It also came with "sealed instructions to test a child's Transformers ability."

Fortress Maximus, which retailed in the

Play-Doh was invented in 1955, and in 1988 age hadn't dimmed its luster. Here's that year's new Disney Duck Tales Play-Doh play set. (Kenner)

An impressive *Star Wars* toy, this one from *The Empire Strikes Back.* By Kenner, 1980.

4

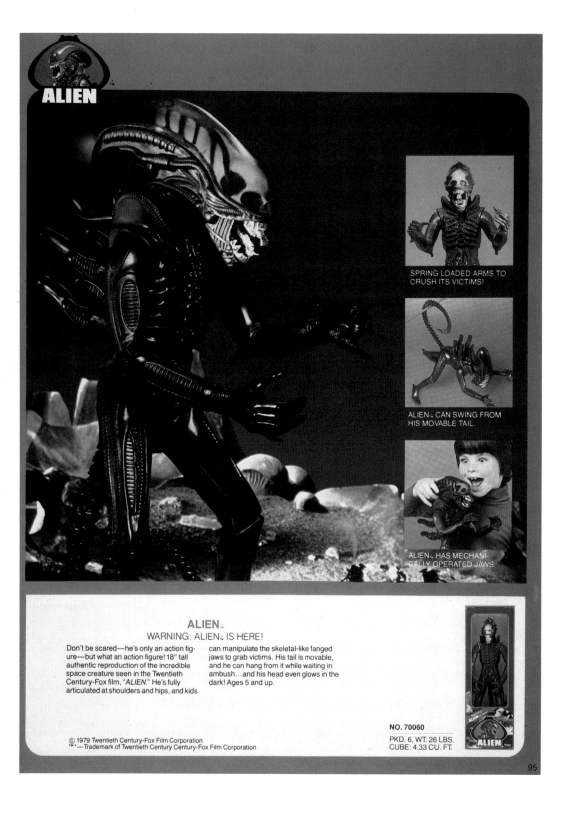

ALIEN

SPRING LOADED ARMS TO CRUSH ITS VICTIMS!

ALIEN™ CAN SWING FROM HIS MOVABLE TAIL.

ALIEN™ HAS MECHANI-CALLY OPERATED JAWS.

ALIEN™
WARNING: ALIEN™ IS HERE!

Don't be scared—he's only an action figure—but what an action figure! 18" tall authentic reproduction of the incredible space creature seen in the Twentieth Century-Fox film, "*ALIEN.*" He's fully articulated at shoulders and hips, and kids can manipulate the skeletal-like fanged jaws to grab victims. His tail is movable, and he can hang from it while waiting in ambush…and his head even glows in the dark! Ages 5 and up.

NO. 70060
PKD. 6, WT. 26 LBS.
CUBE: 4.33 CU. FT.

© 1979 Twentieth Century-Fox Film Corporation
™*—Trademark of Twentieth Century Century-Fox Film Corporation

95

2 2 0

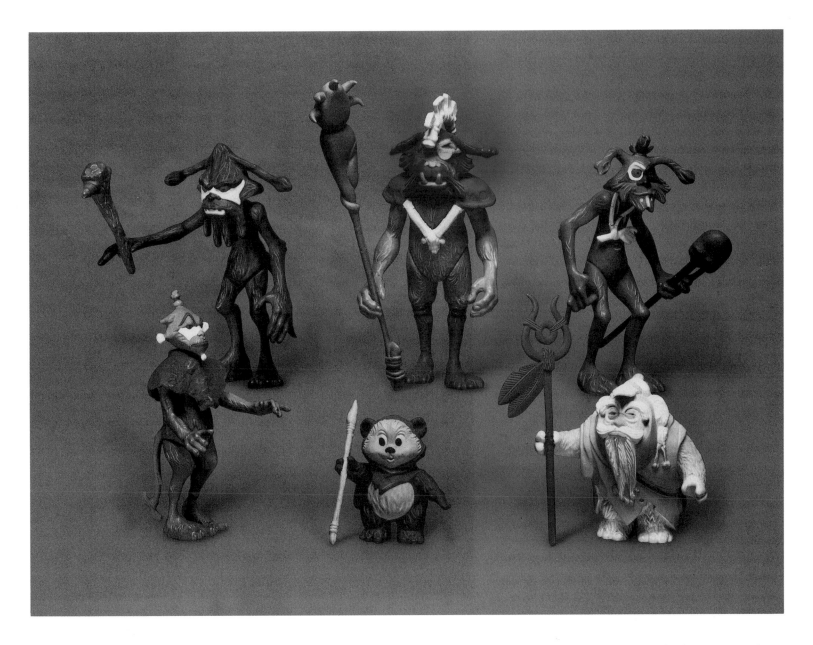

More *Star Wars* fall-out: Kenner's Ewok Action Figures of the 1980s. (Kenner)

ninety- to one-hundred-dollar range, transformed "from a city of great stature to a rolling battle station with immense fire power, and finally to a 2' tall robot." As a city, Fortress Maximus had a working elevator, three different launch ramps, a "detention center for enemy Headmasters" (presumably big with the private school crowd), two new vehicles, a repair bay, and "Spike, leader of the good guy Nebulon forces, who possesses supreme intelligence and compassion." *Compassion* was a key word, incidentally, since more and more toy companies had to protect themselves from vigilant parents' groups violently opposed to toys that encouraged violence. Hasbro, for instance, defended its revived G.I. Joes by describing them not as war toys, but as "defenders of the peace."

Naturally, a success as dazzling as that of the Transformers did not escape the notice of rival companies. Tonka, long known for its line of steel trucks—its seven millionth Mighty Dump was sold in 1982, the same year it introduced its first battery-powered toy, the Power Shift Mountain Master—came up with Go-Bots. Like the Transformers, these toys had their own cartoon series and a remarkably similar story line. Renegade Go-Bots had landed on earth for the purpose of enslaving it; Guardian Go-Bots were the good guys who tried to counter them. Go-Bots could practice their own form of deception; in addition to changing into vehicles, they could become weapons, including a pistol that looked very much like a German Luger. In 1985 at least, the competing Transformers and Go-Bots were both made in Japan by Bandai.

Ideal had its own robotic entry: Maxx Steele. Maxx (short, no doubt, for Maxximum), had a digital clock that could be set as an alarm; instead of buzzing or ringing, Maxx was able to tell its sleepy owner, "Hello, I'm Maxx Steele. Good morning. It's time to get up." Maxx had a vocabulary of 140 words or "word fragments" and played music as well as a form of paddleball. His hands could be lowered and made to grasp things, then pick them up and bring them wherever the robot was directed, all by remote control—and those were just some of his attributes.

But as huge a hit as the Transformers and their imitators were, they were as motes of dust compared to what has probably been the greatest success in the history of toys. The only transforming these babies did was to convert their inventor, Xavier Roberts, into a multimillionaire. The toys were dolls, though they weren't sup-

One of the more flamboyant action figures: Kenner's Quicksilver, with a Tally-Hawk "weapon bird." (Kenner)

posed to be referred to as such. They were more properly called the Cabbage Patch Kids, and each individual kid was given a first and middle name different from all of his/her brothers and sisters. Coleco introduced them to the mass market in February 1983, though they had been around for a while before that.

Born and raised in Cleveland, Georgia,

Roberts was a sculptor who, in 1977, began "sculpting" dolls out of stretch fabrics and polyester, having closely studied the proportions of babies. He was also doing pottery at the time and began taking both the dolls and the pots to art shows and flea markets. Roberts found that when people looked at the dolls, they immediately began investing them with lifelike characteristics—"she looks short-tempered," that kind of thing—and then, after further contemplation, buying them. Some customers would send letters to Roberts afterward to let him know how the kids were doing.

By the next year it was obvious something was happening, and Roberts and some college friends formed Original Appalachian Artworks, Inc., which began marketing at trade shows in major cities. The toys were sold in specialty shops, together with adoption forms (Roberts was always named as the father), which kids could fill out and send in to make the "adoption" official. Moreover, the Cabbage Patchers, which

Roberts continued to think of as art objects (selling them for an arty $125 each), were made in a former medical clinic in the sculptor's hometown. Roberts renamed it Babyland General Hospital, and personnel wore lab coats and nurse's uniforms.

When the deal was made with Coleco, reaction to the mass version was almost instantaneous. Soon, the Cabbage Patch Kids craze was on the way. Competition to buy the Cabbage Patchers was brutal. Christmas of 1983 saw parents acquiring scars not unlike those picked up by veterans of the world wars. Parents lined up for as long as eight hours (after having searched fruitlessly for two months or more) on rumors that a tiny shipment of Cabbage Patchers had reached a store. In Wilkes-Barre, Pennsylvania, a woman had her leg broken and four other shoppers were injured when a thousand people stampeded into the Zayre department store to buy the few Kids the store had to sell. One store manager armed himself with a baseball bat. In

Stuffed toys are perennial pleasers, and none could be much cuter than these 1980s entries from Kenner. (Kenner)

Charleston, West Virginia, 120 dolls were for sale and five thousand people waited outside Hills Department Store to buy them. When the doors were opened, according to one onlooker, "They knocked over tables, fighting with each other—there were people in mid-air. It got ugly."

The $25 suggested retail price was forgotten in a number of places: 50 or 60 simoleons became the accepted tab. And it wasn't a one-season craze. In 1984, $500 million worth of Cabbage Patch Kids were sold. The next year, $600 million was taken in. It seemed it would never end. In 1986, the funny-faced babies were sixth on the toy best-seller list. And in 1987? Though considerably cooled off, with prices

now below the $20 range for the mass-produced version, they were sixth again. Total sales since 1978 reached $50.5 million. But in 1988 Coleco unexpectedly went into bankruptcy, somewhat dimming the Kids' luster, though not enough to keep Hasbro from trying to acquire Coleco in 1989.

After E.T., the Transformers, and the Cabbage Patch Kids, came Teddy Ruxpin in 1985, manufactured by Worlds of Wonder, whose initials fittingly formed the word *wow*. The firm was founded in 1985 by Donald Kingsborough, a former marketing executive for Atari. Teddy was a Bear with a Difference. He could talk and sing (by means of a concealed tape recorder). Adding verisimilitude to the chatter and song were his

With *Star Wars* figures no longer in their line, Kenner turned to similar action figures, such as these Super Powers items, all nicely done. (Kenner)

mouth and eyes, which moved in synchronization with the words—maybe not Maxx Steele, but still pretty impressive. Actually, more impressive. The bear, which was licensed from its Southern California creators, Alchemy II, catapulted WOW to $93 million worth of sales in its first fiscal year.

In 1986, Worlds of Wonder scored again, with Lazer Tag, a modern version of the age-old game, which had participants trying to "tag" each other with infrared light beams. By the end of WOW's second fiscal year (which closed in March 1987), sales were $327 million, a growth record for a publicly held company. How much of that was profits? In fiscal year 1986–87, $18.6 million.

Of course, mega-sellers didn't blot out the rest of the market. The 1980s had a variety of toys. A number of them were still inspired by *Star Wars*, either directly or indirectly. It was understandable. As of 1987, *Star Wars* and its two sequels, *The Empire Strikes Back* (1980) and *Return of the Jedi* (1983), had sold an astonishing $1.2 billion worth of tickets. Perhaps even more mindboggling was the amount realized from toys and related items—$1.5 billion!

Nontransforming robots, particularly in the early 1980s, were still capturing the hearts of the younger generation. The robots continued to rumble in from the Far East, but American companies got in their innings, too, even if only the concepts and selling were originated here.

The short-lived TV space series, "Battleship Gallactica" sired Mattel's plush robot dog, Daggit. The somewhat more successful "Buck Rogers" series prompted a windup robot, Twiki, from Mego, and the two *Star Wars* sequels were responsible for a host of nicely crafted (and expensive) robot toys. "V," an alien-invasion TV show, first aired as a miniseries on May 1 and 2,

1983, and again on May 6, 7, and 8, 1984. The regular series began October 26, 1984, and lasted just nineteen episodes. Despite this decidedly mild success, there was a cult quality to the show, and just as the series neared the end of its run, a variety of "V" items hit the stores, among them action figures, a Sound Pistol with holster, a Sound Rifle, a target gun, and an Action Set (pistol, grenade, binoculars, compass).

Somewhat less popular were space toys that came closer to reality. Space shuttles were designed and sold, but the kids didn't respond as they did to the more fantastic space toys, like He-Man—who was one of those lucky fellows who probably wouldn't have come into existence if it had not been for the Lucas trilogy and the Federal Communications Commission. He-Man was the star of the "Masters of the Universe" TV cartoon series and a direct beneficiary of the FCC's reversal of a prior decision, the one that had prohibited children's shows that were more or less full-length toy commercials.

By 1987, fifty-eight shows were product-oriented, and Mattel, now second only to Hasbro as a toy maker, put out a large array of impressive-looking "Masters of the Universe" space beings and creatures, plus the usual accessories (including a juicily bizarre castle with a skull-shrouded entrance). Mattel, like Hasbro, was a leader—in part, at least—because its creations looked good and bespoke quality.

Perhaps the eyes of toy buyers who went back a generation or more saw nothing but garish-looking plastic, but the fact was that the toys of the top makers were generally well designed and nicely colored, whereas the products of the lower-priced competition often looked cheaper and badly designed. Many were downright ugly.

Ugly on purpose was a constant stream of wrestler action figures. Wrestling was big again, thanks to cable TV. So big, in fact, that even some of the wrestlers' managers—colorful types, most of them—became toyland stars. LJN offered not only WWF Stretch Wrestlers in the 1987 Christmas season, but WWF Managers as well, advertising these worthies as "The mischievous masterminds of the WWF" (World Wrestling Federation).

G.I. Joe, the action figure who had started it all, was revived in 1982. According to Hasbro, he had never been discontinued, but only "furloughed" in 1978. The official reason given was the lingering effects of the 1973 oil embargo, which set the prices of plastic soaring. No doubt the equally soaring sales of *Star Wars* toys contributed to the furlough, too.

When G.I. Joe came back, he was no longer a loner. He was now part of a whole team of fighting men *and* women. He had also licked the high price of plastics by shrinking in size, to about three-and-a-half inches, just the right height to fit into some well-crafted space vehicles Hasbro managed to come up with at the time of Joe's return to active duty.

By 1986, G.I. Joe teamed with the Transformers to form the number one and two punch of the industry's action and adventure toys. By 1987, the new G.I. Joe had been bought nearly one hundred million times. In 1983 a cartoon feature, *G.I. Joe: A Real American Hero*, had been released as a movie, and in 1987 *G.I. Joe—The Movie* was produced as a ninety-three-minute fea-

Masters of the Universe figures from Mattel, 1987. (Mattel Toys)

ture sold directly as a home video cassette (priced at a hefty $79.95). In early 1989, at the age of twenty-five, Joe was still a Hasbro mainstay.

Toy companies always seem to be giving what's known as "concerned parents" fits. Mattel came up with a dandy: Dissect-an-Alien in 1986–87. The Right Sort of Little Boy could happily spend rainy afternoons dissecting a five-inch-high alien figure. Using a plastic scalpel, a future president could extract twelve alien or-

gans, impressively dripping with "glow-in-the-dark Alien Blood." But concerned parents were obviously on the wrong track protesting here. With Dissect-an-Alien, Mattel, in its infinite wisdom had come up not with a sadistic fantasy, but with yet another toy aimed at teaching dexterity. For there was only one way those alien organs would fit together, according to Mattel's preachment. It was, the toy company said, "the slimiest puzzle on earth!"

All that dissecting seems to have caused

SNOOPY Copter

Pull Toy

ROMPER ROOM

17

822 SNOOPY Copter   Ages: 1 to 4

A unique sound and action pull toy features SNOOPY and his pal WOODSTOCK.
- SNOOPY's soft ears spin round 'n round like a helicopter.
- Funny boing – boing sound.

6¼ x 5½ x 7¾"
WT.: 14 lbs.
PACK: 12 pcs.
CU.FT.: 1.8

PEANUTS Characters ©1958, 1965, 1966, 1972 United Feature Syndicate, Inc.

SNOOPY Jack-in-the-Box

820 SNOOPY Jack-in-the-Box   Ages: 2 to 6

The **only** jack-in-the-box with **Double Popping** action! SNOOPY and WOODSTOCK means double the fun and surprise.
- Turn the crank and play "Pop Goes the Beagle."
- SURPRISE! WOODSTOCK pops up from his nest.
- SURPRISE! SNOOPY pops through the front door.

7 x 6 x 5¾"   PACK: 12 pcs.
WT.: 12 lbs.   CU.FT.: 1.7

PEANUTS Characters: ©1958, 1965 United Feature Syndicate, Inc.

U.S. Pat. Pending

Two of the zillions of Snoopy toys from the highly popular "Peanuts" comic strip. These are by Hasbro in 1980.

A toy that never goes out of style: Playskool's classic Cobbler's Bench. (Hasbro)

Tinkertoys of the 1980s, now more plastic than wood. (Hasbro)

concerned parents less concern than something called the "interactive toy." During the 1980s the FCC, taking its cue from the incumbent in the White House, consistently made things easier for businessmen who wanted to hawk their wares on television. So it was no surprise when they gave an official thumbs-up to television shows coding in signals on their soundtracks, which could be picked up by various electronic toys, activating them, and, in a sense, making them a part of the show's story Thus, "Captain Power and the Soldiers of Fortune" was both a Mattel-sponsored series and a host of figures, "battle vehicles," and weapons that could be triggered by the TV show Another toy along the same lines was Axlon's Tech Force and the Moto Monsters. According to the manufacturers, kids without the toys would have just as good a time watching the shows, a theory that at least may have made the *manufacturers* feel better.

In another area, Hasbro's My Little Pony, which went into production in 1983, was a big seller for the company, remaining consistently among the top ten toys. My Little Pony, with his dozens of pony friends, was not a doll, but did feature two long-important aspects of doll appeal: hair care and fashion. Pony's "hair" was a silky mane that could be twisted, braided, and styled. A matching ribbon and comb came with the horse.

Some old-timers enjoyed success, too. On December 16, 1987, Macy's took out nearly a full-page ad spotlighting a batch of old favorites. The headline read, "Put A Little Christmas Past Into Your Kids' Christmas Present." Back—along with a 1935 commemorative edition of Monopoly—were Tinkertoys, Mr. Machine, Etch A Sketch, forty-inch-high Mickey and Minnie Mouse dolls, a Lionel train set (The Gold Rush Special at $275), a plush pull toy, and that favorite 1950s walker-down-the-stairs, Slinky.

Slinky at that time was forty-two years old, having reached the market in 1945. Richard James, a mechanical engineer and naval architect, had thought of the idea in 1943 while on a ship, watching a torsion spring fall from a table and bounce. After two years of experimentation with various types of steel, Mr. and Mrs. James demonstrated the toy at the end of a counter at Gimbel's in Philadelphia. Four hundred of the metal coils were sold in an hour and a half at a dollar apiece.

Mrs. ("Big Betty") James took over control of the Hollidaysburg, Pennsylvania, company in 1960 when her husband "lost interest and left the family to join . . . a religious cult in Bolivia." Today, 120 people are employed to turn out Slinkies by the millions.

Superman was another revitalized old-timer. His fiftieth anniversary was in 1988, but ever-enterprising licensors (and toy makers) decided they could also talk up 1987, since it was his fiftieth year in business. In 1987, new Superman toys included a Superman watch (an Armour hot dogs premium), and, from Imperial, such goodies as Superman Fun Putty (similar to Silly Putty), a paddleball, a water rocket with pump, a bubbletoy water gun, and foot-high and six-

As a comic strip it was long gone, but it was still healthy as an air rifle. In 1988 Daisy proudly promoted the Fiftieth anniversary of "Red Ryder" and the introduction of "the most popular BB gun in American history." (Daisy Manufacturing Company, Inc.)

Lincoln Logs, still in business in the 1980s, now owned by Hasbro. (Hasbro)

foot-high inflatable Supermen. From Kenner came Superman and Clark Kent action figures. These were in addition to the regular line of Superman toys, which had been continually pumped out beginning in 1978 with the series of generally well-received and successful *Superman* (and *Supergirl*) feature films, and their subsequent TV and videocassette incarnations.

Hot Wheels celebrated its twentieth anniversary in 1988, and, hey, what about Mr. Potato Head? The old boy was still kicking, even if he was a settled married man now, with Mrs. Potato Head about as much of a looker as one might expect. The Potato Head Kids? A natural issue. And just as natural, this being the toy world, the whole bunch now came with vehicles and playhouses.

Etch A Sketch was not only still around, it

A handsome man looks good in anything he throws on. Mr. Potato Head, still a dazzler in his mid-thirties. The pipe disappeared at the end of 1987, due to anti-tobacco protests. (Hasbro)

came in both its original form and in an advanced state that animated whatever drawings were made. Alphabet blocks were as present as ever, only now there was a version that could go into the dishwasher.

Another longtimer that had kind of sneaked up on people was the toy department store. By 1987, Toys-'R'-Us had become the country's largest seller of toys, with 313 stores across the United States. In 1986 it owned 17 percent of the market; by 1987, that figure was up to 20 percent. Wall Street expected sales in 1987 to jump to about $2.24 billion.

The Toys-'R'-Us stores were—and are—enormous. One in Valley Stream, Long Island, covers forty-six thousand square feet. Electronic scanning cash registers reduce the time spent on the checkout line and keep track of what is being sold.

But as these final pages were written, odd things were happening in the toys field. Annual sales of dolls dropped from $758 million to $365 million. Action figures were off by about 30 percent, perhaps, some in the industry speculated, because of a glut of such toys. There may have been another reason, as well: the cartoon shows

Uncle Sam's Bank, originally brought out in 1907 by New York's Durable Toy & Novelty Company, still in business in 1987, under the aegis of Ohio Art. (Ohio Art)

NEW

SESAME STREET®
ARTICULATED FIGURES

Kids will want to collect them all! Hail, hail—that Sesame Street gang's all here. What child could resist these four articulated TV superstars? Big Bird, Cookie Monster, Ernie and Bert have realistic, highly articulated bodies. Their soft, colorful fun outfits are specially designed so that even preschoolers can dress and undress them. Accurately scaled to each other, figures range in size from 5½" to 6½". Big Bird wears red vest, Ernie and Bert have on their customary shirt and pants, and Cookie's all decked out in apron and chef's hat. Appeals to both boys and girls. Window-boxed. **Box size:** 4-1/16"x2-13/16"x8¼" **Pack:** 18 pcs. 6 Cookie, 6 Ernie, 4 Bird, 2 Bert **Asst. No.** 9334

79

Classic "Sesame Street" characters in an articulated version by Knickerbocker, 1981.

**2
3
4**

that were created to sell toys had lost more than a third of their audience. In 1987, publicly held toy companies lost $120 million.

The toy business has always been a tough one. It was still a tough one in 1987. Remember Worlds of Wonder? Suddenly, Teddy Ruxpin wasn't selling as he had before—not with all those competing dolls and animals he had inspired. And Lazer Tag, superhot in 1986, was in a tailspin, as kids went back to squirting each other with water pistols. ("Gotcha!" Entertech's Splatmaster Enforcer Gun Set, shot a washable colored liquid that certified every hit.)

And Worlds of Wonder did not come up with a toy to equal its former winners. There were problems with its deliveries, too, and some concern about the quality of its toys. On December 21, 1987, Worlds of Wonder, a true wonder of the toy industry, filed for bankruptcy under Chapter Eleven.

In 1988 industry profits were estimated at $120 million, but people in the industry continued to worry; sales continued flat, and there were no new hot toys on the horizon.

But there was another side to the coin. Some things endure forever. One toy that may possibly fit into that category was twenty-eight years old in 1987 and already was reaching legendary status. After all, how many twenty-eight-year-olds are accorded their very own biography? *Barbie: Her Life & Times* was published by Crown with a cover price of twenty-five dollars. And guess what the number one toy of 1987 and 1988 was?

Good guess.

The trend in recent years has been obvious. More and more toy manufacturing has left the country, and more and more companies have been swallowed up by faceless conglomerates.

But there is something else going on as well.

All over the United States, cottage industries are merrily turning out toys. Their chief customer is the toy collector.

Toy collectors go back as far as the heyday of mechanical banks. Train collectors were making themselves known before World War II began. But those were isolated phenomena. It has only been since the early 1970s that the field of toy collecting, which had been quietly going on for some years, has enlarged. A major reason is *Antique Toy World* magazine, which began in 1970 and has served as a rallying point for collectors, a forum in which ideas are exchanged, passions reinforced, and ads, many ads, can be placed and answered. More and more of these ads have been announcing toy shows. In 1988 alone, more than one hundred U.S. shows were listed, and there were others that did not make the listings. Prestigious auction houses have plunged into the toys area, too, with spectacular results, generating publicity in the form of media attention, attracting more and more collectors.

The result has been a demand that can't be satisfied by the old toys still in existence. It has also created a need for new parts to restore old, incomplete toys. Manufacturers—most, perhaps all of them, from the ranks of the toy collectors—have sprung up to fill these needs.

The three areas that have especially burgeoned are trains, soldiers, and vehicles. Some manufacturers make only new "old" toys, reproductions. Some make only new toys. Some make both. Others have located molds abandoned by the original manufacturers and are turning out the same toys first seen decades ago.

For trains people in 1988 and 1989 there were such outfits as T-Reproductions of Johnson City, Tennessee, which offered a 17½-inch flat car (ca. 1926–31), a wrecking crane, 35-inches long (ca. 1927–30), and a 34-inch-long locomotive dredge (ca. 1927–30); Chris Rossbach's Restoration Trains Parts of Gloversville, New York, which offered newly reproduced parts for certain American Flyers; Harry A Hennig, Jr., of Lansdale, Pennsylvania, who offered Lionel reproduction parts; Steve Latta's Nostalgia Train Works of Escondido, California, which offered "expert restoration, custom painting,

Bugler, Old Guard Band. See page 239.

reproductions and . . . short-run limited-edition custom-decorated items in minimum quantities"; and Harry Osisek of Roswell, Georgia, which advertised "Ives Replicas for the Ives collector," including the Ives Railway Circus. Some offerings were even more esoteric. Robert Scott of Portland, Oregon, sold "Lumber repro loads" for various prewar Lionel cars in O gauge. Ted Moncky of Abbotsford, British Columbia, manufactured "Coal loads of styrofoam for any size of rail car." Then there was the luckless entrepreneur who produced beautiful tinplate facsimiles of items—buildings, a bridge, stations, and a roundhouse—that Lionel hadn't made for decades. He was told, in 1987, by the latest in what was becoming a very long line of Lionel Corporation owners, to cease and desist.

In toy soldiers, a score or more manufacturers turned out originals and copies. Eccles Brothers of Burlington, Iowa, had caught up with sixteen of Barclay's pre–World War II soldier molds and two postwar molds, sixteen of Man-

oil's prewar molds and twenty-nine postwar, plus a number of other slush molds from various companies, including those for vehicles, planes, and trains. In addition, as collectors' requests have increased, Eccles has found itself offering more than one hundred parts for toy soldiers and vehicles—everything from tin helmets, rifle tips, and arms, to horses' tails, typewriters, pianos, propellors, tables, benches, tires, and wheels.

Bill Lango's Vintage Castings of North Bergen, New Jersey, is another company with a similar idea, having secured a couple of dozen pre–World War II Barclay toy soldier molds and a number of molds for winter figures and vehicles. In addition, Vintage Castings has produced its own molds of original figures and rare dimestore soldiers. It has also issued versions of soldiers Barclay had modeled in plaster but never produced.

Most companies making original soldiers are issuing them in the 54-millimeter format generally favored by connoisseurs. But Holt's Hob-

Using wax, Ron Wall of Ron Wall Miniatures sculpts nude figures. After making a pewter casting from the model, he adds wax clothes to it. The next casting produces the master figure, from which the final mold is made. The warriors shown here are from Wall's Sioux Indian War 1876 series. (Ron Wall)

"Antique Toys," still being produced by John Wright of Wrightsville, Pennsylvania. Molds or patterns are made from original toys and then cast in iron. (John Wright)

bies of Miami, Florida, features original versions of dimestore-sized (3¼-inch) soldiers, both U.S. and German. Hampstead, New Hampshire's Wayne and Mary Hill are even more specialized, having grown up with Barclay's postwar podfoot soldiers (so-called by collectors because of the podlike individual stands attached to each foot). Wayne Hill has begun producing beautifully crafted figures similar to these, diverging from the originals only in their greater variety of postures and in that they somehow look better than the originals.

Among the 54-millimeter producers are DJ's Miniatures of Wheat Ridge, Colorado (owned by Don and Jean Porter), which specializes in World War I American toy soldiers, and Ron Wall Miniatures of Frohna, Missouri. Wall fell in love with toy soldiers at the age of three and has yet to fall out. He produces mainly American figures, both modern and of the Civil War period, plus a twenty-piece version of the Battle of the Little Big Horn. Wall employs two full-time painters and several part-time workers.

Martin Ritchie of Staten Island, New York,

sculpts and molds American military figures exclusively, supporting himself and five part-time workers; he also farms out some of the casting work.

In the area of toy vehicles, New Era Quality Toys of Lambertville, New Jersey, owned by Marv Silverstein, has been in business since about 1974. New Era seems to have been the first company to issue pressed-steel truck restorations. The firm provides a full-time living for both Silverstein and his son, restores and customizes, using as much as 90 percent new parts, which it buys from others in the field. Julian Thomas of Fenton, Michigan, provides pressed-steel reproductions and lead and stamped-steel parts. Dick Trickle, of Berwyn, Pennsylvania, supplies lead copies of cast-iron parts, and Brian Cowdry, of Long Prairie, Minnesota, helps out with other parts. He has also produced a wholly new toy version of the Model T Ford, much admired by collectors.

New Era begins by first totally disassembling the original truck, or what is left of it. It straightens out bent metal and blasts away the old finish. Everything—old and new—is primed and sanded twice, and then lacquer is applied. A week of drying, and then it's all hand rubbed, after which the finishing touches—decals or hand painting—are added. The price for each customization runs into the thousands of dollars.

Joe Freeman's Tin Toy Works in Allentown, Pennsylvania (in the heart of toy-collecting country), employs six full-time workers, plus a single part-timer. According to Freeman, "our purpose is to provide a customer with a single part or a complete restoration. We manufacture thousands of individual parts for boats, autos, go-rounds, animated tin, etc. We make tin and composition replacement figures. We also repair mechanisms. We can make any missing part;

however, to make a part there has to be a need for more customers or it would not be feasible to make. Therefore, before we make a part we usually have many requests or an individual willing to pay for the tooling himself.

"Tin Toy Works begins with flat tin stock material and finishes with an exact duplication of the missing part—painted, aged, and weathered to match the rest of the toy." Toys restored by Tin Toy Works appear in many collections and museums throughout the world.

The firm also makes toys from scratch, among them a 28½-inch tinplate ocean liner with a live-steam motor. A limited edition of twenty-five was planned, all of which were spoken for before the first was ready for delivery. As to parts for original toys, the company now has thousands of tin parts for toys from the 1860s through the 1960s.

All of this carries an echo of the earliest

Marv Silverstein's New Era toys took a beat-up 1925 Buddy "L" fire engine and used it as the basis for this customized moving van. Liberty Warehouse is famous in New York for its 155-foot-high replica of the Statue of Liberty. (Marv Silverstein)

days of the American toy industry and suggests that a rebirth may be in the works. In the comic-book field, the sudden surge of collector interest in the 1960s resulted in massive industry changes. A whole generation of artists and writers, starting off as collectors, has been spawned by the movement, important new publishing companies have been started by former collectors, and shops devoted to comics and comics-related materials have sprung up in virtually every town in the country. Even a new method of distribution was developed by a collector turned entrepreneur.

The toy-collecting movement got into gear a decade later. This suggests, as *The Story of American Toys* goes to press, that these cottage-industry stirrings may be evolving into something greater, a new approach to toys, and one that may be far more oriented to the adult than to the child.

Meanwhile, everyone seems to be having fun, which, after all, is what toys are all about.

This impressive original-concept mechanical bank was produced by Reynolds Toys of Falls Church, Virginia, in 1987 in a very limited edition for the Mechanical Bank Convention in Detroit. Charles V. Reynolds has been turning out limited-edition cast-aluminum toys in his spare time since the 1960s. In addition to banks, he designs and produces original animated cap pistols. The toys generally sell out within three months of manufacture. (Reynolds Toys)

S O U R C E S

BOOKS

Arcade Toys Catalog Number 33 (reprint ed.). Mundelein, Illinois: Noble House, 1988.

Barenholtz, Bernard, and Inez McClintock. *American Antique Toys.* New York: Harry N. Abrams, Inc., 1980.

Barenholtz, Edith F. *The George Brown Toy Sketchbook.* Princeton, N.J.: The Pyne Press, 1971.

Bartholomew, Charles. *Mechanical Toys.* New York: Chartwell Books, Inc., 1979.

Best, Charles W. *Cast Iron Toy Pistols.* Englewood, Col.: Rocky Mountain Arms & Antiques, 1973.

Billy Boy. *Barbie: Her Life and Times.* New York: Crown, 1987.

Cadbury, Betty. *Playthings Past.* New York: Praeger Publishers, 1976.

Fraser, Antonia. *A History of Toys.* New York: Delacorte Press, 1966.

Freeman, Ruth and Larry. *Cavalcade of Toys.* New York: Century House, 1942.

Fritz, Peter, and John Mautner. *The Big Toy Box at Sears.* Auburn, Mass.: Toytown Classics, 1987.

Garratt, John G. *The World Encyclopaedia of Model Soldiers.* London: Frederick Muller Ltd., 1981.

Gottschalk, Lillian. *American Toy Cars & Trucks.* New York: Abbeville Press, 1985.

Grober, Karl. *Children's Toys of Bygone Days.* London: B. T. Batsford, Ltd., 1928.

Harmon, Jim. *Jim Harmon's Nostalgia Catalogue.* Los Angeles: J. P. Tarcher, 1973.

——. *Radio Drama and Comedy—And Its Adaptations to Film, TV and Other Media.* Charleston: McFarland & Co., 1990.

Hertz, Louis. *The Complete Book of Building and Collecting Model Automobiles.* New York: Crown Publishers, 1970.

——. *The Complete Book of Model Aircraft, Spacecraft and Rockets.* Crown Publishers, 1967.

——. *The Handbook of Old American Toys.* Wethersfield, Conn.: Mark Haber & Co., 1947.

——. *Messrs. Ives of Bridgeport.* Wethersfield, Conn.: Mark Haber & Co., 1950.

——. *The Toy Collector.* New York: Funk & Wagnalls, 1969.

Hill, William Richard. *Gibbs Toys.* Canton, Ohio: Privately printed, 1986.

Hillier, Mary. *Pageant of Toys.* New York: Taplinger Publishing Co., Inc., 1966.

Hollander, Ron. *All Aboard!* (Lionel trains). New York: Workman Publishing, 1981.

Holme, C. Geoffrey. *Children's Toys of Yesterday.* New York: The Studio Publications Inc., 1932.

Hough, Cass S. *It's A Daisy!* Rogers, Arkansas: Privately printed, 1976.

Johnson, Doris McNeely. *Children's Toys & Books.* New York: Charles Scribner's Sons, 1982.

Kelley, Dale. *Collecting The Tin Toy Car 1950–1970.* Exton, Pennsylvania: Schiffer Publishing Ltd., 1984.

King, Constance Eileen. *The Encyclopedia of Toys.* New York: Crown, n.d.

Lackmann, Ron. *Remember Television.* New York: G. P. Putnam's Sons, 1971.

Lesser, Robert. *A Celebration of Comic Art and Memorabilia.* New York: Hawthorne Books, 1971.

Long, Earnest and Ida. *Dictionary of Toys Sold in America,* vols. 1 and 2. Privately printed: Mokelumne Hills, California, 1971 and 1978.

McClintock, Marshall and Inez. *Toys in America.* Washington, D.C.: Public Affairs Press, 1961.

McClinton, Katharine Morrison. *Antiques of American Childhood.* New York: Bramhall House, 1970.

MacKay, James. *Childhood Antiques.* New York: Taplinger Publishing, 1976.

Maltin, Leonard. *The Disney Films.* New York: Crown Publishers, 1973.

Manchester, William. *The Glory and the Dream.* New York: Bantam Books, 1974.

Milet, Jacques, and Robert Forbes. *Toy Boats.* New York: Charles Scribner's Sons, 1979.

Munsey, Cecil. *Disneyana.* New York: Hawthorne Books, 1974.

Murray, John, and Bruce Fox. *Fisher-Price 1931–1963.* Florence, Alabama: Books Americana, 1988.

O'Brien, Richard. *American Premium Guide To Electric Trains* (2nd Edition). Florence, Alabama: Books Americana, 1986.

——. *The Barclay Catalog Book.* Port Murray, New Jersey: Privately printed, 1986.

——. *Collecting Toy Soldiers.* Florence, Alabama: Books Americana, 1988.

——. *Collecting Toys* (5th Edition).

Florence, Alabama: Books Americana, 1990.

Pressland, David. *The Art of the Tin Toy.* London: New Cavendish Books, 1976.

Robinson, Jerry. *The Comics.* New York: G. P. Putnam's Sons, 1974.

Schroeder, Joseph J., Jr. *1908 Sears Roebuck Catalogue* (reprint ed.). Chicago: Gun Digest Company, 1969.

———. *The Wonderful World of Toys, Games, and Dolls.* Northfield, Illinois: Digest Books, Inc., 1971.

Shea, James J., as told to Charles Mercer. *It's All in the Game* (story of Milton Bradley). New York: G. P. Putnam's, 1960.

Tippett, James S. *Toys and Toy Makers.* New York: Harper & Brothers, 1931.

White, Gwen. *Antique Toys and Their Background.* New York: Arco Publishing Company, Inc., 1971 and 1972.

Whitton, Blair. *American Clockwork Toys 1862–1900.* Schiffer Publishing, Ltd., 1981.

———. *Bliss Toys and Dollhouses.* New York: Dover Publications, 1979.

———. *Toys.* New York: Alfred A Knopf, 1984.

Wieland, James, and Edward Force. *Tootsietoys—World's First Diecast Models.* Osceola, Wisconsin: Motorbooks International, 1980.

The World Almanac and Book of Facts. New York: Newspaper Enterprise Association, Inc., 1967.

ARTICLES

Blood, Judith. "American Tin Toys at the Abby Aldrich Rockefeller Folk Art Collection." *Antiques,* December 1976.

Hersey, John. "My Summer Job with Sinclair Lewis." *New York Times Book Review,* May 10, 1987.

"The Prancing and Pawing of Each Little Hoof," *New Yorker,* December 7, 1987.

PERIODICALS

Antique Toy World, P.O. Box 34509, Chicago, Illinois, 60634

Collectors' Showcase, 1018 Rosecrans St., San Diego, Calif. 92106

The Comic Buyer's Guide, 700 E. State St., Iola, Wisconsin, 54990

Marx Toy Collector Newsletter, 9 Old Farm Road, Auburn, Massachusetts (publication suspended)

Old Toy Soldier Newsletter, 209 North Lombard, Oak Park, Illinois 60302

Playthings, 51 Madison Avenue, New York, N.Y.

Toys & Novelties (later, *Toys & Bicycles*) (defunct).

Toy Collector News, P.O. Box 451, River Forest, Illinois, 60305 (publication suspended)

Toy Soldier Review, 127-74th St., North Bergen, N.J. 07047

MUSEUMS

Auburn–Cord–Duesenberg Museum
(Mostly real cars, with some
Auburn Rubber toys)
Auburn, Indiana 46706

Lawrence Scripps Wilkinson Collection
(available only for traveling exhibitions)
c/o Detroit Antique Toy Museum
6325 West Jefferson
Detroit, Michigan 48209

Margaret Woodbury Strong Museum
One Manhattan Square
Rochester, New York 14607

Museum of Childhood
8 Broad Street
Greensport, New York

Museum of the City of New York
5th Avenue and 103rd Street
New York, New York 10029

Perelman Antique Toy Museum
270 South Second Street
Philadelphia, Pennsylvania 19106

Smithsonian Institution
900 Jefferson Drive
Washington, D.C. 20560

The Sterling Collection (soldiers)
Stone Castle
804 North Third Street
Bardstown, Kentucky

Toys and Soldiers
1100 Cherry Street
Vicksburg, Mississippi, 39180

Toy Train Museum
Paradise Lane
Strasburg, Pennsylvania, 17579

Washington Doll's House & Toy Museum
5236 44th St., NW
Washington, D.C. 20015

INDEX

Italic page numbers refer to illustrations

A

Acme Company, 57
Acme Electric Lamp Company, 68
Acrobats, 26–27
acrobat toy, scrimshaw, *14, 15*
Action Boy, 192
action figures, 185, *190,* 190–93, *192,* 195,
    204, 206, 207, 210, 212–13, *219, 220,
    221, 222, 224,* 225–27, *227,* 231, 233
Action Jackson, 210
Adams, Peter, 44
Adams diesel road grader, 165
"Adirondack" steamboat, *85*
Adventure People, 213
Aero Miniature Flying Machine, *55,* 94
Aeroplane Flyer, 95–96
Airacuda, *117,* 136
Air Blaster, 198
airplanes, 55, 78, 94–96, *94, 95, 96, 97,* 100,
    113, *117, 134, 135, 136, 137, 139, 142,
    143,* 150, 152, *153,* 154, 162, *162,* 181,
    183, 200, *201, 202, 203,* 208
Airport Gasoline Tanker, 100
Airport set, Ford Trimotor, *142*
air rifles, 54–55, 145, 150, 230
Ajax Company, 168
Alabama Coon Jigger windup toy, 82
Albright and Lightcap, 61
Alchemy II, 225
Alien action figure, 220
All Metal Products Company. *See* Wyandotte
All-Nu, 125; soldiers, 156, *158*
alphabet blocks, 28, *28, 61,* 233
Althof, Bergmann, 47–48, *49*
aluminum toys, 100, 166
Amberg, Louis, 92
American Agriculturist (magazine), 26
American Flyer, 56, 90, 92, 96, 133, 137, 138,
    169–70, 201, 236
American Logs, 152, 182
American Model Toys, 182
American Railroad Express truck, *130*

American Soldier Company, 53, 62–63
American Songster whistling bird, 38
American Toy Company, 47
American Toy Watch Company, 35
America trimotor airplane, *95*
Amloid Company, 142
"Amos 'n' Andy" toys, *144,* 144–45
Andy Gump car, *93*
Antique Toy World (magazine), 236
Arcade Company, 87, 88, 92, 93, 96, 97, 152,
    167, 172
Arnold Print Works, 79
Artillery Bank, 66
Auburn Rubber, 122–23, 125, *155, 156,* 172,
    182
Aurora Plastics, 181, 189, 193, 196, 203
Autobots, 217–18
Autogyro Plane, *135*
automobiles. *See* cars
automotive kits, 103–4
Autoperipatetikos, 35
Axlon Company, 229

B

Baber Toy Aeroplane Mfg. Co., 95
Baby Alive doll, 217
baby carriages, 19–20
Baby Snooks doll, *144*
Bachman Brothers, 182
Bad Accident mechanical bank, *42,* 44
Baetz, Walter, 124
Bailey, Charles A., 43
Bain, B. F., 113
Bakelite Corporation, 152–53
Baker, Lynn F., 168
Balky Mule and Cart, *177*
Ball Turret Gunner, 188
Baltimore Bargain House, 53, *54*
Bandai Company, 222
banks, 41–45, *42, 43, 44, 45, 66, 76,* 100,
    151, *233, 241*
Banner Company, 168
Barbera, Joe, 197, 211
Barber-Greene bucket loader, 165

Barbie doll, *184,* 184–85, 209, 235, *235*
Barbie: Her Life and Times (Billy Boy), 184, 235
Barclay Mfg. Co., 96, 97, 120–22, 124, 125,
    159, 161, 172, 179, 191, 205, 237, 239
Barenholtz, Bernard, 172
Barney Google toys, 90
Barnum, P. T., 26
Barton, William, 39, 40
baseball player figures, *122, 123*
Batman action figures, 191, 212
battery operated toys, 54, 68–69, 179–80, 182,
    184, 188, 200, 204
"Battleship Gallactica," 225
bazooka, 145
beach toys, 47, 113. *See also* sand toys
Beany and Cecil toys, *197*
bears, clockwork, 37, *38. See also* teddy bears;
    Teddy Ruxpin; Yogi Bear
beaver, friction-powered, 82
Beggs, Eugene, 46, 47, 68
Beiser, C. W., 62–63
Bell and Hammer Game, *19*
Bell Telephone Truck, 128
bell toys, 39, 39–40, 48, *54, 56,* 93, 182
Ben Hur Playset, 185
Benny, Jack, 181
Bergen Toy & Novelty Co. *See* Beton
Bergmann Brothers, 48
Berle, Milton, 173; car, *172*
Berryman, Clifford, 78
Beton (Bergen Toy & Novelty Co.), 125, 152,
    153, 160, 184
bicycles, 59, 156. *See also* Kiddie Kar
Big Boy Company, 102
Big Caesar sea toy, 188–89
Big Loo robot toy, 194
Big Parade windup toy, 105
Big 6 train set, 48
"Billy and Ruth" catalog, *157*
Billy Boy, 184
birds, mechanical, 37, 38
Bixler, L. S., 77
blacks, toys caricaturing, 44
Blakeslee, Cornelius, 35
Bliss, Rufus, 34

Bliss, R., Manufacturing Company, 34, 35, 72, 73
blocks, 22, 25–26, *26*, 27, *27*–28, *28*, 29–30, 35, *61*, 182
Blondie toys, 147, 149
Bloomingdale's, 114
boats, 8, *9*, 36, *46*, 49, 72, 84, 85, 100, 115, 197. *See also* ships
"Bonanza," 193, 198
Borgfeldt, George, 48–50, 91, 139–40
Bowen, James H., 43, 44, 45
Boycraft Company, 96, 97
Boyd, S., 108
Boyd, William, 173
Boyer, Edith and Israel, 57
Boy on Velocipede clockwork toy, 35
Boy Robbing Bird's Nest mechanical bank, *66*
Bradley, Milton. *See* Milton Bradley Company
brakes, cast-iron, 67
"Bringing Up Father," 90
Britains Company, 63, 126
Brown, George W., 18–19, 34, 35, 47, 49
Brownies: Their Book (Cox), 79
Bubbl-Matic Gun, 217
Buck Jones air rifles, 150
Buckman, A. and E., Manufacturing Co., 46
Buck Rogers toys, 143, 144, 145, 147, *149*, 168, *169*, 192, 225
Buddy "L" toys, 87–89, 102, 103, 139, 160, 182, 210–11
Buffalo Toy Works, 51
building blocks, 25–26, *26*, 27, 152, 182
buildings, 73. *See also* villages
Built-Rite Company, 155, 157, 159
Bulletman, *213*
bull-roarer, 13
Burdette-Murray dump truck, 102
Burlington Zephyr train, *138*
Burns, Bob, 145
Burp Gun, 182, 208, 209
buses, 34, 87, 103, 107, *112*, 130, *133*, 152, 160, *167*
Bush, C., 41
Bushnell, E. W., 17
Buster Brown toys, 60
Busy Bridge windup toy, 105
Butler, Benjamin Franklin, 36
Butler Brothers, 53, 83
Buttercup and Spare Ribs pull toy, *86*
Butting Match cap pistol, 65
Buzz Barton air rifles, 150
Byron International, 216

C

Cabbage Patch Kids, 222–24
Cabin Cruiser, 114, *115*
cabriolet, *50*

Calamity Bank, 45
Camel, Circus Chariot, Clown, 77
Campbell Kids dolls, 208
cannon, 65, *120*; marble-shooting, 31
cap bombs, 60, 66
Caplan, Frank, 172
cap pistols, 23, *65*, 65–66, 99, 100, 150, 152, 155, *163*, 203. *See also* Burp Gun
Captain Action, 191–93
Captain America, 192
Captain Kidd's Castle, *26*
Captain Lazer, 194
"Captain Midnight," 143
"Captain Power and the Soldiers of Fortune," 229
"Captain Video," 176
cardboard toys, 61, 157, 163
Carlisle & Finch, 54, 69
carousel toy, 48, *49*
Carpenter, Francis W., 50
cars, 55–59, *57*, *59*, 71, 76, 78, 87, 88–89, *88*, *89*, *93*, 98, 99, 101, 103, 104, 113, *116*, 123, 124, *124*, 125, 132, 134, *134*, *139*, *143*, *153*, 160, *166*, *168*, *170*, *171*, *172*, *176*, *177*, 180–81, *196*, 196–97, 198, 200, 205, 210, *212*, *231*, 240. *See also* pedal cars; racers; taxicabs
Carter, C. E., 83
Carter Tru Scale, 216
cartoon character toys, 91–92, 211–12. *See also* comic-strip toys; Disney toys; television cartoon toys
Case International FWDA Tractor, *216*
cast-iron toys, 21, 38, 39–40, 42, 65–68, 76, 87, 97–101, 120, 129, 152, 155
catalogs, 53
CBS Toys, 215
celluloid, 35; baby rattles, 142
cement mixers, *103*, *128*
Champion Company, 129
Chandler, John Greene, 22
"Chandu the Magician," 143
Charleston Trio windup toy, 104
Charlie Chaplin toys, 83, 92, 103, 211
Charlie McCarthy toys, *116*, 144, *144*, 176
Charlotte, Queen, 14
Checkered Game of Life, The, 32, 34
Chein, J., & Company, 53, 75–76, 98, 142, 146, 147, 182
Chevrolet Coupe, 88
Chicago Cutlery, 163
Chicago World's Fairs, 57, 71, 76, 162
Child Guidance, 210, 215
Children's Foundation, 203
Child World, 204
China Clipper airplane, 134

Chinese, toys caricaturing, 43, 65–66
Chinese Must Go cap pistol, *65*, 65–66
Chris Craft boat, 100
Christmas, 14, 54
Chromatrope, 41
Chrysler Air Flow car, *139*
circus toys, 45, 74, 75, *75*, 97–98, *98*, 99, 160, 178
Civil War toys and games, 31, 32–33, 36, 239
Clampett, Bob, 197
Clark, D. P., 57, 58
Climbing Monkeys windup toy, 104
Clock Movement toy, 68
clockwork toys, 18, 19, 34, 35, 35–38, *37*, 38, 48, 49, 65, 66–68, *68*, 71, 114
Cloninger, Margaret Ruth, 125, 126
Cobbler's Bench, 229
Cob House Blocks, 27
Coca-Cola truck, 160
Cohn, T., 182
Coleco, 213, 222, 223, 224
College Boy cars, 104
Colorforms, 207
Columbia bank, 76
Columbian Wheel, 74
Columbia Protektosite, 152
Comet Metal Products, 126, 155
comic-book toys, 149–50, 191, 211, *213*
comic-strip toys, 59–61, *60*, 74, 76, 86, 90–91, *93*, 145–49, *175*, 198. *See also* cartoon character toys
Connecticut, early toy makers in, 15–16, 18–19, 21, 39
Connell, Stan, 108, 109
construction equipment, 102, 165. *See also* Tonka Toys
construction sets. *See* Erector Set; Lincoln Logs; Tinkertoy(s)
Consumer Products Safety Commission, 204
Consumers Union, 203
Contraband Gymnast, 33
Controlophone, 71
Converse, Morton G., and Company, 56, 57, 68, 129
Conway Valley Toy Company, 216
Coogan, Jackie, 92
Coon Jiggers windup toy, 104
Cooperative Manufacturing Company, 30
Copmobile, Dick Tracy, 200
Cord cars, 123, *124*, 125, *134*
Cosmo Ornament Co. Inc. (Cosmo Novelty), 120
cowboy guns, 145, 150, 173, 182, 198
Cowboys and Indians, toy, 123, 125
Cowdry, Brian, 240
Cowen, Joshua Lionel, 68–69, 90, 127, 200

Cox, Gideon, 17
Cox, Palmer, 79
Crandall, Asa, 17
Crandall, Benjamin, Jr., 19, 30
Crandall, Benjamin Potter, 19
Crandall, Charles M., 17, 25–29, 30, 46, 87
Crandall, Charles T., Jr., 30
Crandall, Charles Thompson, 19, 30
Crandall, Fred W., 30
Crandall, Jesse Armour, 19–20, 23, 29–30
Crandall, William Edwin, 19, 30
Creative Playthings, 172
Crounse, Avery F., 168
Crown Toy Mfg., 142
Curtain Wall Builder Set, 199
Cushman & Denison Mfg. Co., 81

D

Dagger Derringer, 180
Daggit, 225
Dagwood's Solo Flight windup toy, 149
Daisy Manufacturing Company (Daisy Toys), 55, 145, 147, 150, 178, 180, 217, 230
dangerous toys, 45–46, 73, 203–4, 213
Darktown Battery bank, 44–45
"Dart" locomotive, 69, 70
Davy Crockett toys, 178–79, 182
Dayton(-Schieble) Friction Works, 57, 68, 129
Decepticons, 217–18
Deiser, John, & Sons, 73
Dent (Hardware Co.), 68, 85, 96, 97, 99–100, 101, 137
department stores, 51, 54, 81, 125, 224, 230, 233
Depression era, 109, 117–53
Destroyer, clockwork, 71
"Dexters," 47
Diabolo, 12
Dick Tracy toys, 143, 147–49, 175, 200
Dillon-Beck Mfg. Co., 152
dirigibles, 96–97
Dirks, Rudolph, 60
Disneyland, 189
"Disneyland" (TV show), 178
Disney toys, 92, 140, 140–42, 174, 178–79, 182, 189, 211, 215, 218. See also Mickey Mouse toys
Dissect-an-Alien, 227
District School, 28, 29
DJ's Miniatures, 239
Dr. Evil action figure, 192
Dr. No (film), 193
Doepke, Charles and Frederick, 165
Doepke's Model Toys, 165–66, 168, 179, 182
doll carriage, wooden spindle, 30
doll furniture, 71–72; injection-molded, 208

dollhouses, 13, 34
dollhouse furnishings, 17, 18, 34, 48
dolls, 10, 11, 19, 21, 21, 23, 30, 35, 48, 61, 66, 79–80, 92, 93, 140, 141, 142, 144, 144, 150, 152, 162, 182, 184, 184–85, 203, 208, 209, 217, 222–24, 229, 233, 235, 235
Donald Duck toys, 140, 151, 174, 182, 189
"Don Winslow," 143
Donze, Leon, 125
Dorfan Company, 90, 129
Doughboy Tank, 132
Dowst, Samuel, 71
Dowst Manufacturing Company, 71–72, 96
Dracula monsters, 189
"Dragnet," 198
Drum Major windup toy, 84
drums, 13–14, 17, 22, 57, 163
Dunbee-Combex-Marx, 210
Dyke, Samuel C., Company, 61

E

Eagle Air Scout Plane, 96
Eagle Rubber Company, 216
East Hampton, Connecticut, 39, 40
Eccles Brothers, 237
educational toys, 93–94, 151–52, 172, 210. See also kindergarten toys
Eisner, Jack, 216
Eldorado-Klondike wagon, 57
electrical toys, 54, 204. See also battery-operated toys; trains
Electric Express, 68–69
Elevated Railway, 68
"Elgin, The," Street Sweeper, 126
Ellis, Joel, 30–31, 80
Elm Toys, 198
Emenee musical toys, 182, 216
Empire Pencil Company, 190
England, 14; toys from, 11, 12, 19, 80, 216
English Trap pull toy, 76
Entertech, 235
Erector Set, 80, 81, 182, 215
Erie Toy Plant, 83, 108
Ertl, Fred, Sr., 166–68, 198, 209, 216–217
Esquire/Nichols, 217
Etch A Sketch, 186, 187, 229, 231–33
E.T. toy, 217
Eureka American Soldiers, 62
Evel Knievel action figures, 204
Exposition Doll Co., The, 79
Expression blocks, 27–28

F

Fallows, James, 17, 40
Fallows, James, & Company, 37, 40, 49, 56, 57

Famous Funnies (comic book), 149
Famous Monsters (magazine), 189
Fanny Gray (book), 22
Far East (Third World), toys made in, 42, 179, 204, 209, 215, 225
farm equipment toys, 78, 87, 166–68, 172, 198. See also tractors
farm sets, 74, 182
Federal Communications Commission (FCC), 197, 225, 229
Feix, William, 63
Felix the Cat, 91
Ferdinand the Bull (film), 141
Ferguson Novelty Co., 92
Ferriot, Joe, 178
ferris wheels, 74, 98, 182
ferry, windup, 115
Fighting Lady battleship, 188
Fink, Manuel, 94
fire toys, 19, 59, 65, 73, 77, 78, 79, 89, 102, 103, 104
Fisher, Herman, 151
Fisher-Price, 81, 141, 150, 151, 155, 161, 182, 213
Flash Gordon toys, 147, 168, 175, 191
Flasho windup toy, 113
Fleeson, Plunkett, 13
Fleischer, Max, 91, 142
Fli-Back Company, 216
"Flintstones, The," 197; vitamins, 211
Focke-Wolfe airplane, 154
Food and Drug Administration (FDA), 203–4
Forcheimer, Julius and Milton, 90
Ford cars, 71, 87, 89, 104, 197, 210, 240
Ford Tri-Motor airplane, 100; airport, 142
Fort Apache playset, 178
Fortress Maximus, 218–21
forts, 142, 157, 158, 159
Fox, Fontaine, 90
Fox, George L., 45
Foxy Grandpa roly-poly, 60
Francis, Field & Francis, 16–17, 40
Francis, Field & Francis, 16–17, 40
Frankenstein's Monster, 189
Franklin, Benjamin, 11–12
Freeman, Joe, 240
Fresh Air Taxi, 145
friction toys, 57, 59, 68, 82, 103, 177
Frisbie, R., 47
Frisbies, 185
Froebel, Friedrich, 34
frog pull toy, 40
Frontierland Logs, 182
Fuchs, F. E., 95
Fulton, Robert, 14
Funny Face windup toy, 92

G

Gabriel Industries, 193, 215
games, *12*, *13*, *19*, 20, 25, 28–29, 32, 34, *137*, 225, 229
garage, *168*
Garloo, 189
Garton, E. Bassingdale, 48
gas station, *132*
Gee Whiz horse race, 113
Gene Autry toys, 150, 173
General Mills, 201, 217
"General" Shovel Truck, *128*
Georgene Novelty Co., 79
Gerbst, Herbert S., 204
Germany, 14, 96; toys, 11, 53, 66, 73, 82
Gibbs, Lewis, 72–73
Gibbs Manufacturing Company, 53, 72–73
Gibson, James E., and Rozena, 216
G.I. Joe action figures, *190*, 190–91, 194, *213*, 222, 226, 227
G.I. Joe and His Jouncing Jeep, *165*
G.I. Joe—The Movie, 226–27
Gilbert, Alfred Carlton, 80
Gilbert, A. C., Company, 53, 58, 80, 102, 104, *137*, 169, 193, 201, 215
Gimbel's, Philadelphia, 230
Girard Model Works, 93, 108–13
Give-A-Show Projector, *198*
glass toys, 14
Gleason, Jackie, 197
Glenco Infant Items, 215
Gobble, the Gobbling Goose, 113
Go-Bots, 222
Godey's Lady's Book (magazine), 22
Godzilla (film), 189
Gong Bell Company, 39–40, 57, 93
Goodrich, Chauncey, 18
Goodyear, Charles, 21
Grandjean, Arthur, 187
Grant, Ulysses S., clockwork figure of, *37*
Grant, W. T., Co., 117
Grantco Import Services, 208
Green Hornet action figure, 192
Greenwood, Asa, 22
Greenwood, G. S., 22
Grey Iron, 60, 68, 100, 119, 120, 123, 155
Grey Klip toy soldiers, 119
grocery store, *112*
Gropper Toys, 147
Gruelle, Johnny, 79
guillotine kits, 203
Gulliver's Travels toys, 142
Gumps toys, 90, *93*
guns, toy, 23, 25, 33–34, 142, 150, 157, 163, *163*, 169, *171*, 173, *175*, 176, 180, 182,
184, 198, 208, 209, 217, 222, 225. *See also* air rifles; cap pistols
"Gunsmoke," 185
Gyroplane, *136*

H

Hafner, W. F., Company, 56
Hall, John, 42, 45
Hall's Excelsior Bank, 42
Halsam's American Logs, 152
Ham and Sam windup toy, 82, 83, *111*
Hamilton, Charles J., 54
Handler, Ruth and Elliot, 208–9
Hanna, Bill, 197, 211
Happy Hooligan toys, 60, 76
Hasbro Toys, 165, 190–91, 209, 213, 215, 217–18, 222, 224, 225, 226–27, 228, 229, 230
Hassenfeld Brothers, 190
"Have Gun Will Travel" toys, 185, 198
Hawes Mfg. Co., 22
Heiliner earth scraper, 165
He-Man space toy, 225
Hemenway, Luther, 22
Hennig, Harry A., Jr., 236
Hermann-Vaughan Mfg. Co., 59
Herriman, George, 91
Hersey, John, 155
Heywood Brothers, 22
Higginson, John, 12
Hill, N. N., Brass Company, 40, 141, 182
Hill, S. L., 22, 28
Hill, Wayne and Mary, 239
Hill Climber toys, 57, 68
Hills Department Store, 224
hobby horses, 17, 23, 182
Hoge, 138, 146
Hohner harmonicas, 53
Holgate, Cornelius, 151–52
Holgate Co., 152, 209, 215
Holly Hobbie telephone sets, 213
Holt's Hobbies, 237–39
Hometown Battery bank, 45
Honeymoon Express, 104–5
hoops and hoop toys, *10*, 47, 48, 185
Hopalong Cassidy toys, 173
horse-drawn toys, *16*, *34*, 39, 47, 50, 51, *64*, 65, 67, 68, 76, 77, 78, 97, *103*
horse pull toys, 18, 37, 47, 73
horse toys, walking, 36, 64, 65
hot-air toys, 35, 38
Hotchkiss, Arthur, 36
Hot Wheels, *196*, 196–97, 210, *213*
"Howdy Doody," 173; toys, 176
Hubley, John E., 97
Hubley Company, 67, 68, 74, 93, 95, 96, 97–
99, 100, 117, 126, 127, 128, 129, 146, 150, 152, 155, 163, 179, 180, 181, 182, 183, 198, 200, 201, 203, 208, 215
"Huckleberry Hound" toys, 197
Hula Hoop, 185
Hull and Stafford, 51
Humpty Dumpty toys, *45*, 74, *75*
Hurley, Edward N., 114
hypodermic needles, toy, 203

I

Ideal (Novelty &) Toy Co., 53, 119–20, 142, 144, 150, 152, 180, 181, 182, 187, 191, 192, 193, 200, 204, 215, 222
Imperial, 230
Incredible Hulk, 211
Ingersoll Mickey Mouse watches, 142
International Harvester, 166–68, 209
Irish immigrants, 43
iron, malleable, 50. *See also* cast-iron toys
Iron Bandwagon, *64*
Irwin Toy Co., 92, 166
Italian-Ethiopian War, 121
Ives, Edward, 35, 38, 64, 65
Ives, Harry, 57, 64, 65, 66, 69, 71, 114–15, 131
Ives, Riley, 35, 64
Ives (& Company), 35–38, 39, 40, 46–47, 56, 57, 60, 64–68, 69–71, 83, 91, 114–15, 135, 210, 237

J

Jack Armstrong toys, 143, 144, *154*
Jackee the Horn Pipe Dancer, 82
jack-in-the-boxes, 23, *197*, 228
Jacob, Joseph, 18
"Jaeger" Cement Mixer, *128*
James, Mr. and Mrs. Richard, 230
James Bond toys, *192*, 193, 198
Jantzen Beach Patrol and Surf Girl, 99
Japan, toys made in, 179–80, 184, 189, 193, 194, 195, 197, 209, 222. *See also* Far East
Jazzbo Jim windup toy, 82, 83, *111*
jeeps, 146; toy, *161*, *165*
Jenny the Balky Mule, 83
Jerry Mahoney ventriloquist dummy, 182
"Jetsons, The," 197
"Jimmie Allen," 143
Joe Penner "Wanna Buy A Duck?" toy, *145*
John Bunny dolls, 92
John Deere toys, 166–68, 209
John Gilpin wood toy, 29
Johnny Express, 200
Johnny Lightning Jetpower Cars, 210, *212*
Johnny West and Jane West figures, 193
Jonah and the Whale bank, 45

Jones, J. Edward, 125; toy soldiers, 118
Joseph Lumber Company, 94
Joy Line windup trains, 105–8
Jumping Jack Clown, 22
jumping jacks, 47, 184
Jump Rope Tinker, 93
Just Out cap pistol, 66

K

Kaleidoscope, 41
Katzeman, John, 109
"Katzenjammer Kids" toys, 45, 60–61
Kelmet Company, 102–3
Ken doll, 185, 191, 235
Kenner Company, 198, 206–7, 210, 211, 217–24, 231
Kenner Parker Toys, Inc., 217
Kenton Toys (Kenton Hardware Company), 50, 59–60, 68, 76–77, 97, 99, 102, 103, 128, 150–51
Keuls, Henry, 81
Keystone Company, 96, 102, 103, 104, 151, 157, 168
Kidde, Walter, & Company, 217
Kiddie Kampers, 113
Kiddie Kar, 83
Kilgore Company, 100, 142, 150, 152
kindergarten toys, 34
King, Lucille, 93
King Racer, 131
Kingsborough, Donald, 224
Kingsbury, Harry T., 77–78
Kingsbury Company, 42, 77–78, 79, 96, 102, 103, 105
kitchen, toy, 48
kites, 31
Knapp Electric Company, 69
Knickerbocker Toy Company, 79–80, 210, 213, 215, 234
Knights in Shining Armor, 193
Koerber, John C., 90
Koko the Clown, 91–92
Kooken, Olive, 122, 124, 125
Korean War, 179
Kraft and Huffington, 46
Krazy Kar windup toy, 83
Krazy Kat toys, 90–91
Kresge's, 83
Krupp, Frank, 121–22, 124, 125, 158
Krypto-Ray Gun, 150
Kyser and Rex, 39, 42, 45

L

Lango, Bill, 237
Latta, Steve, 236
Lauth-Juergens Co., 57

"Lawman," 185
Lazer Tag, 225, 235
lead toys, 62–64, 71, 120, 121, 155, 172, 203
Leakin' Lena boats, 197
Lee, Benjamin F., 21
Lee Toy Aeroplane, 95
Levy, Michael, 125
Lewis, Sinclair, 155
Liberty bell toy, 39
Liberty Warehouse moving van, 240
Lido Company, 168
Li'l Abner Band, 83, 170–72
Lincoln Logs, 31, 80, 152, 215, 230
Lincoln sedan, 103
Lindbergh, Charles, 96
Lindstrom Tool & Toy Company, 113, 119
Linemar Company, 175, 197
Linotype, 71
Lionel Manufacturing Company (Lionel Corp.), 68–69, 83, 89–90, 126–27, 133, 135–37, 140, 141, 161, 163, 169–70, 196, 200–201, 204, 229, 236, 237
Lion Hunter mechanical bank, 66
lithography, 32, 34, 76
"Little Nemo in Slumberland" dolls, 61
"Little Orphan Annie," 143
LJN Company, 226
Lloyd, Harold, 92
Lockheed Sirius airplane, 139
locomotives, toy, 24, 38, 38, 46, 48, 54, 64–65, 69, 70, 80, 89, 137, 151
logs, toy, 31, 152, 182, 215, 230
Lone Ranger toys, 143, 150, 173, 192
Long, William, 14
"Lost in Space" robot toy, 193–94
Lowe Company, 157
Lucas, George, 206, 207, 225
Lucky Boy airplane, 96
Lundahl, Fred, 87–88

M

McCallum, David, 193
McCay, Winsor, 61
machine guns, toy, 33–34, 171, 184
McKinley, William, 72–73
Mack trucks, toy, 87, 88
McLoughlin Brothers, 22, 27, 61, 62, 63–64
McNair, James, 47
Macy's, 51, 81, 229
magazines, toy industry, 53
magic kits, 80
magic lantern, 41
Magic Screen, 187
magnetic toys, 35
Mailplane, 113

Main Street windup toy, 105
Major Matt Mason, 194
Malleable Iron Works, 50
man doll, 21
"Man From U.N.C.L.E." toys, 193
Manoil, Jack and Maurice, 123–24
Manoil Mfg. Co., 122, 123–24, 125, 155–56, 172, 179, 237
Mansion of Happiness, The, 20
marbles, 13, 61; shot from cannon, 31
Marcak, Charles, 184
Marching Majorettes, 125
Marcus, Archie, 111
Markham Air Rifle Company, 54
Marks Brothers Company, 142
Martin and Runyan, 35
Marvelous Mike, 182
Marx, Dave, 104
Marx, Louis (Marx Toy Company), 13, 83, 92, 96, 97, 104–13, 116, 129–31, 132, 133, 141, 145, 146, 147, 149, 150, 155, 169, 172, 173, 174, 175, 176, 177, 179, 180, 184, 189, 191, 193, 194–95, 197, 198, 201, 209–10
Mary and Lamb pull toy, 40
Mary Had a Little Lamb, 74; doll, 162
Mary Hartline Super Circus playset, 178
Masquerade blocks, 27
Massachusetts, early toy makers in, 17, 22
"Masters of the Universe" toys, 225, 226
Matt Dillon action figures, 185
Mattel Toys, 176–77, 182, 194, 196, 197, 198, 204, 208–9, 225, 226, 227, 229, 231
Mattson, Harold, 208
"Maverick," 198
Max and Moritz figures, 74
Maxx Steele, 222, 225
Maynard Tape Primer, 23
Meccano construction toys, 80
mechanical banks. See banks
Mechanical Bear, 37
Mechanical Grinder, 113
Mego Company, 210, 212–13, 225
Megow Company, 162
Menagerie, 27
Merin, Herbert L., 216
Merriam Manufacturing Company, 19, 47
Merrill Company, 157
Merry Juggler windup toy, 83
Messmer, Otto, 91
Metal Cast Company, 125
Metalcraft Company, 129
Metal Ware Corporation, 142
Meythaler, Robert, 94
"Mickey Mouse Club, The," 209
Mickey Mouse toys, 136, 137–40, 140, 141,

142, 161, *174*, 182, 211, 229
microscopes, toy, 41
Mighty Matilda aircraft carrier, 189
Miller, J. H., Company, 179
Milton Berle Car, *172*
Milton Bradley Company, 31–34, 61, 63, 94, 151, 215
Minnie Mouse toys, 136, 140, 161, 229
Mishler, M. B., 61
Mr. Machine, *187*, 229
Mr. Potato Head, *164*, 190, 209, 231, *232*
Mitchtom, Morris, 78
model airplane kits, *162*, 162–63, 181
model cars, plastic, 180–81
Molded Products, 161, 162
Moline Pressed Steel Company, 88
Mollye's Doll Outfitters, 79
Moncky, Ted, 237
"Monitor" pull toy, *49*
Monogram, 181
Monopoly, 229
Monsanto, 152
monster toys, 189, 203
Montgomery Ward, 51
Moon, William "Bert," 129
moon rockets. *See* space toys
Morrison, Enoch Rice, 35, 37
Mortimer Snerd, *116*, 144, *144*
motorcycles, 99, *100*, *126*, *127*
Mound Metalcraft, Inc., 168
movie projectors, toy, 103
movies, 92, 180, 189, 193, 198, 206–7, 217, 225, 226–27, 231; cartoon, 140–42
movie stars, 92, 103, 142, 150
MPC Company, 207
Mulford, Clarence E., 173
Multiple Toy Products, 189
Munn, E. H., 87
Murray, A. L., 123
musical instruments, 73, 141, 146, 163, 176–77, 182, 208, 216. *See also* drums
My Little Pony, 229
Myrioptician, 33
Mysto Manufacturing Company, 80

N

Nabisco, 203
National Toy Company, 47
Navarre Glass Marble Company, 61
Neff, J. C., 129
Nerf Ball, 203
New England, 13, 18, 31, 34, 46
New Era Quality Toys, 240
New Haven Clock Co., 36
New York City, 19, 81
New York Rubber Co., 21, 35

New York *Sunday World*, 59
New York Toy Fair, 80, 81, 168, 184, 208
"Niagara" pull toy, *49*
Nice, H. J., Co., 94
Noah's Arks, *17*, 47, 57
Noble & Cooley, 22, 141
Nostalgia Train Works, 236
Novelty Electric Company, 54, 69
Novelty Iron Works, 87
nursery-rhyme figures, 125, 210
Nylint Company, 168, 179, 182, 198

O

Obelisk Alphabet Blocks, 28
Oddjob action figure, *192*, 193
Ohio Art Company, 83, 187, 216, 233
Ohio marble industry, 61
Old Dutch Cleanser woman, 99
Old Guard Band, 239; Bugler, 236
Oldsmobile, curved-dash, 57, 59
Old Toy Soldier Newsletter, 61
Old Woman in Shoe, *66*, 210
optical toys, 41
organ-grinder banks, 45
Original Appalachian Artworks, Inc., 223
Orkin, Samuel, 84, 114
Osisek, Harry, 237
Oswald the Rabbit, 92
Ott, Joe, 162
Outcault, Richard Felton, 59, 60
Outer Space Men, The, 207
Owens-Illinois, Inc., 211

P

packaging of toys, 203; in plastic, 204
Packard cars and trucks, 98, 103
Pac-Man, 213
paddleballs, 216
Paddy and the Pig bank, *43*, 43–44
Paint-A-Toy kits, 120
Pajeau, Charles, 80–81
Palace Guard figures, 123
Panama Canal toy set, 180
"Panama" Shovel Truck, *128*
pandas, 206
paper dolls, 22, 142, 157, 209
paper soldiers, 22, 61–62
papier-mâché, 40
Parcel Express truck, cast-iron, *101*
Paris Exposition Universelle, 25
Parker Brothers, 61–62, 203, 217
Parrish, Maxfield, 62
patents, 23, 25, 30, 42–43
Patterson, Edward, 15–16
Payne, W. L., 100

Peabody, Elizabeth, 34
"Peanuts" toys, 198, 211, 228
Pearlytoys, 120
Pecking Goose, Witch, and Cat, *145*
pedal cars, 48, 59, 182
Penn, William, 11
Penner, Joe, 145
Pennsylvania toy makers, 14, 17, 22, 47
pewter toys, 23
Phantom of the Opera monsters, 189
Philadelphia Centennial Exhibition, 30, 38
Philadelphia Tin Toy Manufactory, 16
philosophic toys, 40–41, 45
Phoenix Hose Reel, *65*
Pia, Peter F., 22–23
pianos, toy, 73, 182
Picture Gallery Bank, *43*
Pierce, J. A., 47
Pigs in Clover, 25, 28–29
Pillsbury Corporation, 207–8
Pinocchio toys, 141
Pirate Pistol, 152
pistols. *See* cap pistols; guns
Planet of the Apes figures, 212
plastic toys, 125, 152–53, 157–60, 168, 169, 170, 177–78, 179, 182, 187, 204, 226
Plasticville buildings, 182
playballs, 182
Play-Doh, 217, *218*
Playsets, 177–79, *178*, 189, 194–95, *195*, 197
Playskool, 80, 93–94, 151–52, 182, 209, 215, 229
Playthings (magazine), 53, 127–29, 131, 204, 208; advertisements, *55*, 59, 63, 74, 75, 81, 94, 161
Playwood Plastics, 161–62
Plymouth Iron Windmill Company, 55
"Pogo" toys, 198
Polar Ice wagon, cast-iron, *39*
pole vaulting, 80
police toys, 52, 76, *175*
Polk's Hobbies, 163
Polyopticon, 41
Pontiac Catalina, *176*
Popeye toys, 93, 145–46, *146*, 147, *148*, *175*, 198
Poppin' Fresh doll, 208
Poppin' Pals, 215
Porter, Don and Jean, 239
Potato Head. *See* Mr. Potato Head
Pratt & Letchworth, 51, 67
Praxinoscope, 41
Preacher at the Pulpit, 37
Presley, Elvis, 185
Pretty Village, 62
Price, Irving, 151

Price, Margaret Evans, 151
Prince, William, 12
Product Miniature, 182
Pullman, George Mortimer, 135
pull toys, 18, 37, 40, 47, 49, 65, 72, 73, 73, 76, 81, 86, 87, 93, 97, 141, 228
Punch and Judy toys, 42, 45, 66
puppet, Ojibwa Indian, 14, 15
puppet show, Beany and Cecil, 197
"Puritan" riverboat pull toy, 49
push-and-pull toys, 73, 93, 141–42. See also pull toys
putty blower, 47
Pyro, 181

Q

Quaker Oats Company, 209
Questor, 210
Quicksilver action figure, 222

R

racers, 53, 78, 105, 120, 122, 131, 142, 196, 210, 212
radio shows, 142–45
Raggedy Ann and Raggedy Andy, 79–80, 215
Ramar of the Jungle figures, 182
rattles, 142, 203
Rayco, 161
"Rebel, The," 198
Reclining Chinaman mechanical bank, 43
Record Cars, 105
"Red Devil" toy autos, 76
Red Ryder air rifles, 145, 230
Reed, W. S., Toy Company, 34–35, 72, 85
Remco, 188–89, 203, 204
Renwal, 180
reproductions, 210–11, 236–40, 238
Republic Company, 129
Restoration Trains Parts, 236
Revell, Inc., 181
Rex Mars Tank, 169
Reynolds Toys, 241
Rich Toys, 114, 142, 158
rifles, 182, 225. See also air rifles
rings, from premiums, 143, 144, 176
Ritchie, Martin, 239–40
Roberts, Xavier, 222–23
Robert the Robot, 180, 181, 182
Robot Commando, 193
robots, 180, 181, 182, 193–94, 195, 217, 222, 225
rocket toys. See space toys
rocking horses, 11, 14, 18, 23, 30
Rockwell, Jerry, 152, 209
Rockwell, Norman, 152

Rodeo Joe Whoopee Car, 171
Rodeorope, 52, 92
roly-polys, 60, 142, 182
Roney, Benjamin T., 17
Ron Wall Miniatures, 237, 239
Roosevelt, Franklin D., bank, 151
Roosevelt, Theodore, 45, 74, 78
Rosenberg, S., 120
Rossbach, Chris, 236
rowing toy, mechanical, 36
Royal Bus, 130
Royal Circus, 97–98, 98, 99
Roy Rogers toys, 163, 173, 178, 185
rubber tires, black, 165
rubber toys, 21, 35, 123, 141, 155, 156, 160
Rum-Tum drum, 163

S

Saalfield, 142
sad irons, 101
safety. See dangerous toys
Sand Toy Company, 84
sand toys, 30, 83, 84–85, 113
Santa Claus at the Chimney mechanical bank, 45
Santee Clause windup toy, 109
Savoye Company, 125
"Say It with Flowers" motorcycle cart, 127
Scarab car, 139
Scheider, Joseph, Inc., 141
Schieble, William (Dayton-Schieble), 57, 68
Schlesinger, Leo, Company, 47
Schoenhut, Albert, 73–74
Schoenhut Co., 53, 60, 73–75, 90, 91, 92, 129, 182
Schroeder, John, Lumber Company, 93–94
Scientific American (magazine), 54
scientific toys, 41
Scorponok transforming toy, 218
Scott, Robert, 237
Sears (Roebuck and Co.), 51, 83, 178, 182–84, 185, 188, 194
sea toys, motorized, 188–89. See also ships
Secor, Jerome B., 37–38
Segar, E. C., 145
Seiberling Latex Products Company, 141
Selchow & Righter, 63
service station, 132
"Sesame Street" toys, 34, 210, 211, 215, 234
Seversky P-35 airplanes, 183
"Shadow, The," 143
Shepard, Charles G., 42, 43, 44, 45
ships, toy, 15, 18, 34, 71, 72, 83–84, 84, 114, 152, 188, 188–89
Shirley Temple dolls, 142
shovel trucks, toy, 128

Showboat toy, 92
Shure, Inc., 163
Silver Arrow Flying Plane, 78
Silverstein, Marv, 240
Single Oarsman, No. 2, 36
Sioux Indian War miniatures, 237
Six Million Dollar Man, 217
sleds, 18, 21, 30, 48, 156
Sleeping Beauty figure, 185
Slik-Toy Company, 179
Slinky, 230
Smith-Miller (Smitty Toys), 166, 168, 179
Snoopy toys, 198, 228
Snow, Leonard, 22
Snow White and the Seven Dwarfs (film), 141
soap bubble toy, 32
soldiers, 61–64, 61, 62, 63, 75, 100, 117–26, 118, 120, 121, 122, 123, 153, 155, 156, 157, 158, 159, 160, 161, 161–62, 170, 172, 178, 179, 191, 236, 237–40, 239
Soljertoys, 120
Sound Rifle, "V," 225
space toys, 134, 176, 184, 193–94, 194, 207, 225. See also Buck Rogers toys; Star Wars toys
Spang Industries, 113
Speaking Dog Mechanical bank, 42
Spelling Blocks, Hill's, 28
Spic and Span windup toy, 104, 111
Spiderman toys, 192, 211
Spirit of St. Louis airplanes, 96
Spitfire airplane, 154
Splatmaster Enforcer Gun Set, 235
Sputnik, 184
"Star Trek" toys, 207
Star Wars toys, 206, 206–7, 217, 219, 221, 225, 226
steamboats, 46, 85
Steamboat Willie (film), 137, 140
steam-operated toys, 45–47, 46, 70, 85; engines, 38, 45, 46, 47, 68
Steelcraft Company, 96–97, 102, 139
steel toys, 21, 40, 57, 78, 80, 88–89, 102–3, 113, 155, 165, 168, 179, 198, 222
Steiff Company, 53
Steinau, Leslie S., 161
Steiner, Al, Phil, and Joe, 217
Stevens, J. & E., Company, 21, 23, 40, 42, 43, 44, 45, 47, 48, 57, 66, 68, 100
Stiegel, Henry William, 14
Stokes, Lee, Industries, 170
Stony action figure, 191
Story Book Dolls, 162
stoves, 48, 76, 142
Strasburg, Pfeiffer & Co., 48

Strauss, Ferdinand, 75, 82–83, 96, 97, 104, 107, 108, 109, 111, 132
Strawberry Shortcake dolls, 217
streamlined toys, 132–34; trains, 135
streetcars, 54, 68. *See also* trolleys
Streeter, L. E., Company, 168
Strobel & Wilken Co., 61
Strombecker Company, 162–63, 217
Structo, 102, 103–4, 182, 198, 216
stuffed toys, 78, 162, 204, 206, 210, 213, *223*
Stump Speaker, 44
Sturditoy Company, 129
Stutz cars, *53*, 100, 104
submarine, 84–85
Sullivan, Pat, 91
Sunny Andy Fun Fair, 113
Sunnyside Service Station, *132*
Sun Rubber Company, 141, 182
Super Circus playset, 178
Super Heroes Action Figures, 212
Superman toys, 143, 149–50, *150*, *175*, 191, 211, 212, 230–31
Super Powers action figures, *224*
Super Sleuth, 211

T

Tammany mechanical bank, 42, 45
Tank and Cannon mechanical bank, 45
tanks, *132*, *156*, *169*, *175*
"Tarzan," 143
taxicabs, 87, *109*, *128*, *129*, 145, 160, *182*
Taylor, Zachary, 16–17
tea sets, 83, 152
Tech Force and the Moto Monsters, 229
teddy bears, 78, 79. *See also* Teddy Ruxpin
Teddy Ruxpin, 224–25, 235
Teddy's Adventures in Africa, 74
telephone, 25; toy sets, 34, 93, 141, 213
television cartoon toys, 197, 211, 225, 233–35
television shows, 173–76, 178, 182, 185, 191, 193–95, 198, 207, 212, 225, 229; advertising and, 190, 197, 204, 208–9, 213, 229
"Tennessee Jed," 143
"Terry and the Pirates," 143
Tesch, Alvin F., 168
Texan revolver, 152
"Thimble Theatre" toys, 145, *146*
Thomas, Julian, 240
Thomas Toys, 168
Thorncraft, Inc., 94
Three Little Pigs toys, 141
Tinkertoy(s), 80–81, 93, 182, *199*, 215, *229*, tin toys, 15–19, 35, 38, 40, 47, 51, 76, 82–85, 131, 240. *See also* windup toys
Tin Toy Works, 240

Tip Top the Walking Porter, *107*
Tobor the Great, 180
Toledo Metal Wheel, 53, 59
Tom Corbett playset, 178
Tom Mix toys, 92, 103, 143, 144
Tommy Toy, 124, 125
Tonka Toys, 168, 179, 182, 198, 207, 210, 217, 222
Toonerville Trolley, 90
"Toots and Casper" toy, 86
Tootsietoy(s), 72, 96, 142, 143, 147, 163, 215, 217
Topper Toys, 210, 212
tops, spring-operated, 72–73
Tornado pull toy, 72
Tory Royal Gazette (newspaper), 61
Tower, William, 17–18
Tower Guild, 18
Toy Auto Company, 56
toy collectors, 236–41
Toy Fair. *See* New York Toy Fair
toy industry, growth of, 14, 51, 53–54, 85, 113–14
Toy Kraft Company, 141
Toy Manufacturers Association, 82, 83
Toy Manufacturing Company, 47, 184
Toys and Bicycles (magazine), 53
Toys and Novelties (magazine), 17, 53
Toys-'R'-Us, 204, 233
toy stores, 11–12, 19, 118, 204
Toy Yearbook, The, 182
tractors, 87, 113, 123, 155, 166, 172, 182, 209, *216*
trains, 19, 30, 47, 48, 50, *51*, 54, 56, 66–68, 68, 69–71, 79, 89–90, *89*, *90*, *91*, 92, 104–8, 111, *133*, 135, *138*, *141*, 163, 168–170, *171*, 200–201, *205*, 229, 236–37. *See also* locomotives
Train To Build, 90
Transformer toys, *214*, *215*, 217–22, 226
Transogram Company, 161
T-Reproductions, 236
Trick Dog mechanical bank, 45
Trickle, Dick, 240
Trick Pony bell toy, *39*, 56
Tricky Taxi, *129*
trolleys, 68, 78, 90, *131*. *See also* streetcars
trucks, 52, 58, 87, 88, 88–89, 100, *101*, 102–3, *108*, *110*, *119*, *128*, 130, 132, 134, *143*, 155, 160, *160*, 165, 166, *167*, 168, 182, 198, 200, 210–11, 222, 240
Trumodel, 102
Tru-Smok toys, 203
Turner, John C., Company, 102, 103
Turnover Tank, 197
Twiki, 225

U

Uncle Sam roly-poly, 60
Uncle Sam's Bank, 233
Union Manufacturing Company, 18, 46, 51
Union Pacific railroad, 135
Unique Art Manufacturing Company, 83, 145, 165, 170–72
Universal Pictures, 189
"Untouchables" Playset, 194–95, *195*

V

"V" toys, 225
Vanity Fair Company, 217
velocipede toys, 17, 19, 30, 35–36
Vermont Novelty Works, 30
Victor Comptometer Corporation, 217
video games, 213
Vietnam War, 204
villages, 62, 63, 182
Vintage Castings, 237
Vogue dolls, 217
Volland, P. F., Co., 79
Voltamp, 69

W

wagons, 18, 57, 132, 134, 156
"Wagon Train," 198
wagon trains, 16
Walbert Mfg. Co., 84, 114
Walking Doll (Autoperipatetikos), *35*
"Walking Zouave," 37
Wall, Ron, Miniatures, 237, 239
"Waltons, The," 212
Wanamaker, John, department store, 81
"Wanna Buy a Duck?" toy, *145*
Wannatoys, 152
"Wanted Dead or Alive," 198
Warner Communications, 215
Warren, John, 126
war toys, 204, 222
Wason Car-Manufacturing Company, 31
watches, 35, 142, 230
watercolors, for children, 34
Waterman Pen Company, 84
water pistols, 235
Watrous Manufacturing Co., 40
Waverly Toy Works, 29
Weeden, William N., 46, 69, 70
"Wells Fargo," 185
Western Stamping Company, 216
Wham-O, 185, 198
White, H. C., Company, 83
White, John, 11
White Horse Game, *19*
White trucks, 102–3

Whitman Company, 157
Whitney Reed Chair Company, 35
Wiebe, Edward, 34
Wilkins-Kingsbury fire toys, 79
Wilkins Toy Company, 77–78
Williams, A. C., 100–101
William Tell mechanical bank, *42, 45*
windmills, 35, 83
windup toys, 56, *57, 58, 75, 76,* 82–85, 92,
    94, 95, 96, 98, 104–8, *107, 108, 109,*
    110, 111, 113, *115, 116,* 129, 130, *131,*
    132, 136, *139,* 141, 144–45, *144, 145,*
    147, 147, 148, 149, 150, 155, *177, 177,*
    187
Winzeler, H. S., 83
Wise Little Hen, The (film), 140
Wizard of Oz toys, 213
Wolf, Louis, 83
Wolfman monster model kit, 189
Wolverine Company, 84, 112, 113
Wonder Woman, 212
Wood, C. G. and Frank G., 108
Woodcock, W. L., 22
wooden toys, 17–18, 22, 26–30, 34–35, 54,
    57, 68, 73–75, 80–81, 93–94, 139, 142,
    151–52, 156–57, 160, 163, 172
Wood's Mechanical Toys, 108; *Airplane, 94*
Woolworth, F. W., Co., 25, 83, 181–82
World's Fair Bus, 152
Worlds of Wonder (WOW), 224, 225, 235

World War I, 33, 81–82, 84, 119
World War II, 153, 155–63, 170, 179
Wrather, Jack, 201
wrestler action figures, 225–26
Wright, Frank Lloyd, 80
Wright, John, Company, 42, 238
Wright, John Lloyd, 80
Wright, Wilbur and Orville, 94
wringers, miniature, 78
Wyandotte, 56, 132–34, 135, 136, 155, 165,
    179, 182

X

xylophones, toy, 163

Y

Yell-O-Taxi, toy, *109*
Yellow Cab, toy, 87, *128*
Yellow Kid toys, 59–60
Yogi Bear, 197
Young America engines, 46
Youth's Companion (magazine), 46, 70
yo-yo, 105

Z

zamac toys, 172
Zayre department store, 223
zeppelins, toy, 96–97, *97,* 132
Ziesenheim, Fred, 108, 109

Zig-Zag Chap, 92
zinc alloy, 152
Zoetrope, 33, 41
Zorro action figures, 185

PHOTOGRAPHER CREDITS

Mike Adams: pp. 145 (left), 165; Ron
Chojnacki: pp. 98, 112, 149, 175 (top), 181
(top), 181 (bottom); John Courville: pp. 24, 42,
144; Burt Davis, Jr.: p. 28; Richard L. MacNary:
pp. 90, 106, 133, 150 (bottom), 154, 156 (left),
156 (bottom), 160 (top), 161 (top), 162 (top),
169 (top), 171 (top, left), 176; Gordon Monro:
p. 143 (top, right); Steven Mark Needham: pp.
116, 119, 149 (bottom), 174 (right), 174
(bottom, left); David Stubbs: pp. 52, 53, 58
(top), 58 (bottom), 62, 75 (bottom), 81, 86, 89,
96, 105, 107 (top), 107 (bottom), 108, 109, 110
(top), 110 (bottom), 114, 115 (top), 115
(bottom), 130 (top), 130 (bottom), 131 (top),
131 (bottom), 133 (top), 133 (bottom), 134,
135 (top), 138 (top), 139 (top), 142 (top), 142
(bottom), 143 (bottom), 148, 151, 152, 166,
167 (both), 175 (right and middle), 182;
Thomas Vinetz: pp. 26 (top), 26 (bottom), 27,
28 (top), 62 (top), 81, 199.

DATE